THE SCHOOL QUESTION

A Bibliography
on Church-State Relationships
in American Education

1940-1960

Compiled by
BROTHER EDMOND G. DROUIN, F.I.C., M.S.L.S.
Librarian at Walsh College
Canton, Ohio

1963
THE CATHOLIC UNIVERSITY OF AMERICA PRESS
Washington 17, D. C.

Imprimi potest:

Brother Patrick J. Ménard, F.I.C.
Provincial Superior
Alfred, Maine

Nihil obstat:

Reverend Harry A. Echle
Censor Librorum

Imprimatur:

Patrick A. O'Boyle, D.D.
Archbishop of Washington
October 2, 1962

Library of Congress Catalog Card Number: 62-21859

TO

Brother Patrick J. Ménard, F.I.C.

CONTENTS

INTRODUCTION

In his *Civil Liberties in the United States,* Robert E. Cushman notes that "the controversy over religion in the public schools has produced a literature of its own, much of it strongly argumentative."[1] He could have written the same about the literature on the entire 'school question.' The abundance of printed material about it stands as a constant reminder of the attention which it commands.

This bibliography was compiled as an attempt to provide a classified approach to the literature written about the education phase of Church-State relationships in the United States, especially from 1940 to 1960. In more than 1,300 entries it includes books, pamphlets, periodical articles, book reviews, unpublished dissertations (over 140) and court decisions (over 70), organized in twelve units.

The compilation represents all significant positions—religious, secular, 'liberal,' nondenominational, and denominational, and, in the spirit of the open forum, interrelates contributions from the various professional groups. Material was drawn from general sources as well as from the fields of religion, education and law. Though coverage spans the years 1940 through 1960, more recent material which could still be entered while editing progressed was not left aside.

A classified arrangement was decided upon to provide analysis of content and group sources for better use. Because there is so much overlapping of subject matter in literature of this type, classification may not always prove an unmixed blessing. It should be kept in mind that material listed in the general units (I, II, III and VIII) should be checked along with the contents of the lists on more specific subjects. Unit I, an introductory unit, supports all others. Unit II should be used with

---

[1] Robert Eugene Cushman. *Civil Liberties in the United States, A Guide to Current Problems and Experience.* Ithaca, N.Y.: Cornell University Press, 1956. P.107.

III to XII, unit III with IV to VII, unit VIII with VI and IX to XI. The subject approach is supplemented with an *Index* listing authors, editors, book titles, state material (by state) and court decisions. Entries were numbered consecutively to facilitate references from the *Index*. A separate list of cases was added for convenience.

The link between original text and continuing material was preserved by integrating over one thousand additional entries with the list as sub-entries relating critiques, book reviews, reviews of court decisions, discussions, replies, etc. . . . with relevant sources. Notes and entries which could not easily be worked into the main sequence were grouped in appendices and related to the proper units with cross-references.

Entries in each unit were categorized as A. BACKGROUND MATERIAL B. BOOKS AND PAMPHLETS C. PERIODICAL ARTICLES D. UNPUBLISHED DISSERTATIONS E. CASE MATERIAL (U. S. Supreme Court) F. STATE MATERIAL (With cases). An introductory *Note* opens each unit to help clarify the relation between lists and determine the scope of each. The *Background Material* following these notes is meant to introduce the field with bibliographies, summary material, earlier studies, charts and tables, legal background, and, in some units, with suggested readings in very closely related fields.

The standard indexes were searched systematically for material issued since 1940. It would have been impossible to interrelate entries to books, periodicals, review articles and case material from the varied sources represented in this list without the use of the following services.

American Theological Library Association Index to Religious Periodical Literature (ATLA Index)
Bibliographic Index
Book Review Digest
Catholic Periodical Index
Cumulative Book Index
Education Index
Essay and General Literature Index
Guide to Catholic Literature
Index to Legal Periodicals
Readers' Guide to Periodical Literature

Titles of unpublished dissertations were largely drawn from

Doctoral Dissertations Accepted by American Universities

(Compiled for the Association of Research Libraries).
New York: H. W. Wilson Co., 1934-1955. (Annual volumes)

*Dissertation Abstracts; Abstracts of Dissertations and Mono-
graphs on Microfilm.* Ann Arbor, Michigan: University
Microfilms, 1950- . (Formerly *Microfilm Abstracts*)

Lyda, Mary Louise, and Brown, Stanley B. *Research Studies in
Education, A Subject Index of Doctoral Dissertations, Reports and Field Studies, 1941-1951.* Boulder, Colorado:
Beta Delta Chapter, Phi Delta Kappa, 1953. 121pp. (Xerox
process). (Also: Supplement for 1951-52).

Brown, Stanley B., Lyda, Mary Louise, and Good, Carter V.
Research Studies in Education. A Subject Index. Bloomington, Indiana: Phi Delta Kappa, Inc. (Annual volumes covering material from 1953).

Master's Theses in Education. Cedar Falls, Iowa: Research
Publications, Bureau of Research, Iowa State Teachers College, 1951- . (Annual volumes).

Entries for dissertations are as complete as the finding lists
and auxiliary research tools made it possible. Abstracts, when
found, were listed with dissertations. When microfilming was
known to have been done, mention of it was made and the
source of the film was given.

Footnotes, library card catalogs and oblique references led
to numerous entries not listed in guides and indexes. Search
for local material (such as articles in local newspapers) was
generally considered beyond the scope of this project.

Because index and other references are frequently not
specific enough for purposes of classification, the inclusion of
entries was determined after direct recourse to the text. The
collections at the

Boston Public Library
Canton Public Library (Canton, Ohio)
Catholic University of America Library
Cleveland Public Library
Georgetown University Library
Harvard University Libraries (Andover-Harvard Theolo-
gical Library, Law School Library, education library,
Widener Library)
Library of Congress (general collection and Law Division)
U. S. Department of Health, Education and Welfare Library
(education collection)

Walsh College Library (Canton, Ohio)

were used to search and verify materials. Incidental use was made of the library facilities at

Boston College Law School
District of Columbia Public Library (central branch)
Enoch Pratt Free Library (Baltimore)
Stark County Bar Association Library (Canton, Ohio)
Teachers College (Columbia University)
Trinity College (Washington, D. C.)
Union Theological Seminary (New York)
U. S. Supreme Court
Wesley Theological Seminary (Washington, D. C.)

Without access to the book collections of numerous libraries, and without the dedicated assistance of the staffs which service them, this project would have been difficult to complete.

The list is not completely annotated in the strict sense, but many descriptive notes are entered and background information was added to a number of entries. Where needed, content notes were incorporated. Over two hundred individual articles, all keyed to authors' names in the *Index*, are listed in them. The classification scheme remains the major subject approach.

Court decisions are included in most units. Cases which fall in the same section are entered chronologically and material related to a case is entered under it. Decisions are briefly described, without attempt to achieve the thorough coverage which persons interested in law will find without difficulty in the text of reports and in the notes provided with many of them. For the benefit of persons unaccustomed to interpret citations, a table (with notes) was provided before unit I and introductory material in law literature is suggested in Appendix E. Because the volumes of the "National Reporter System" are more generally available, persons without training in legal bibliography would save time by learning to recognize references to them in parallel citations.

There are related purposes which this list was not meant to serve directly. The theory of Church-State relationships, from the viewpoints of sociology, philosophy and theology, as such, the development, organization and administration of Church-related schools, the philosophy of education in its relation to religion, the methodology of religious education, and Church-State problems in higher education are all special areas which were not considered in the preparation of this bibliography on the school in American Church-State relationships.

* * *

THE 'SCHOOL QUESTION': The Church-State problem in American education flows from the nature of God and man, of Church and State. It arises from the specific functions of both Church and State and from the kinship of some of these functions with respect to the dual nature of man. The issues involved are woven into the very fabric of our society, and, as is the case with so many social problems, their intricacy should not be lightly dismissed. In a society composed of groups which disagree on the nature of both God and man, consensus about the relationship which should exist between Church and State is bound to be difficult to achieve, especially in those areas of social action where both project their influence.

Church and State are societies distinct in purpose and organization, but not alien to each other, because so many of their subjects hold membership in both, and loyalty to each is rooted in the same individuals. Since both so often rule the same lives, both must meet in the individual as well as in the civic body which individuals compose. True, their objectives and functions differ, but, by the unity of life activities, by the interaction of the spiritual and the temporal, Church and State may not, can not, ignore each other if they are to help man attain his end. That purpose is certainly not served when both collide.

Church and State do meet on the American scene, and in few areas are their encounters more frequent than in the field of education. Unfortunately, their meeting here is not always a happy one.

The American 'school question' dates from the first concerted efforts to expand and reorganize the public school system. There were no difficulties at first. Early American schools were religious schools where the question of religion in education was not a problem. God "belonged."

The nineteenth century ushered in a new order. The structure of American society changed. Our somewhat uniform population became ethnically and religiously pluralistic. Free

xi

public education was organized. The problem of religion in education became the problem of which religion for whom and educators found it progressively difficult to deal with the issue. Much against the intent of most of them, the conditions which eventually prevailed favored anything but religion. In the words of Nicholas Murray Butler, "so far as the tax-supported schools are concerned, an odd situation has been permitted to arise. The separation of Church and State is fundamental in our American political order, but so far as religious instruction is concerned, this principle has been so far departed from as to put the whole force and influence of the tax-supported school on the side of one element of the population, namely, the side which is pagan and believes in no religion whatever. Even the formal prayer which opens each session of the United States Senate and each session of the House of Representatives, and which accompanies the inauguration of each President of the United States would not be permitted in a tax-supported school."[2] The consequences could not escape notice. While the claim that religion was the province of the Church and the home echoed as a slogan from some quarters, other groups raised their own questions. If learning was by doing, if the child made the man, would not the next generation ignore what the school ignored in an age when the school had progressively become the child's other home? Some would not countenance the risk of seeing the next generation grow in an educational atmosphere where religion seemed relegated to the condition of a peripheral hazard, and chose to educate their children as citizens of two worlds in Church-related schools. Several denominations had set up such schools. More were established and the Catholic Church organized its parochial school system. This sequence of changes raised two sets of questions.

a) Could the Church-related school be financed from public funds? Could it be helped? Could it be controlled? Should it be encouraged, 'allowed' or suppressed?

b) What should be the place of religion in public education? The public school could not be denominational. Could it be neutral? Was it to be drastically secular, vaguely religious, 'ethical,' simply tolerant or 'democratic'?

The Church-related school was respected in being allowed to exist without excessive control. Comparatively short-lived

---

[2] Nicholas Murray Butler. "Report of the President of Columbia University for the Year Ending June 30, 1934," *Columbia University Bulletin of Information*, 35th series, No. 36 (June 8, 1935). Pp.22-23.

attempts were made to finance it completely or help it substantially, but, in the end, it was left to finance itself. Partisans
of this solution advance 'democratic' ideals, the separation of
Church and State, the fear that entanglements between religion
and government will work against the interests of both, the
will of the majority and the "inviolability' of the public treas-
ury in support. A free society allows dissent, however. While
the majority rules, many ask why part of their own compulsory
deposit in the education fund could not be used to help them
educate their offspring, as the law commands, in a way which
they have chosen by the dictate or preference of conscience,
as the law allows. When other governments have found a way
to compromise, they wonder why a democracy conceived to
reflect the will of the governed could not achieve enough flexi-
bility in the distribution of education revenues to avoid sub-
jecting taxpayers of one conviction to the rule of taxpayers of
another in matters where conscience is a major determinant.
They feel that somewhere in the balance of rights and duties,
some of their liberties are partly sacrificed when controlling
groups concede a "constitutional liberty" but "exact a price"
for its exercise.[3]

Religion in public education still remains a problem. Against
a place for religion in the tax-supported school, some voices
argue freedom of religion, the fear of sectarian conflict, the
presumed inability of religion to meet the challenge of what
is termed 'modern science,' and, again, the separation of
Church and State. Here F. Ernest Johnson reminds us
that "there is also secularist indoctrination,"[4] and his warning
against the "enthronement of an authoritarian secular philosophy which is in effect a sectarian religion, and the defense of
it as a child of modern science"[5] is far from irrelevant. Such
is not the object of the majority of our educators. Have they
not been dragged to court often enough for trying to recognize
the importance of religion in so many ways? By their efforts to
emphasize moral and spiritual values they have proven their
resentment for godlessness, but conflicting religious beliefs,
official policies and objecting groups have countered their
initiatives in this direction.

---

[3] Wilber G. Katz, "Freedom to Believe," *Atlantic Monthly*, 182:66-69
(Oct., 1953). P.69.

[4] *Christian Century*, 65:515 (May 16, 1948)

[5] F. Ernest Johnson, "Religion in Public Education; A Major Force in
History and Contemporary Life," *Vital Speeches*, 16:311-314 (March 1,
1950). P.313.

Attempting a return to religion which would respect the sensibilities of confessions and convictions, both religious and non-religious, is not a simple venture. Religious leaders who observe the movement toward reemphasized 'moral and spiritual values' in public education hope that these values will remain religious. They cannot always conceal the fear to witness an acceptable terminology become a glorified misnomer while purely human and clearly material values are ingloriously ushered into the empty chair of religion. The course between Charybdis and Scylla is not easily charted but dedicated navigators are bending over the chart and plotting.

Both the Church-related school deprived of subsidy and the tax-supported public school deprived of religion still present unsolved problems. Bus rides, anti-garb bills, Bible reading and released time have been argued for decades with a number of related problems. Whatever the immediate issues, whatever the elements of each problem, the one question which still begs for an answer remains. How shall we, as a nation, recognize the role of religion in education, without allowing the economics of the education function overburden citizens of any one persuasion, with due respect for the rights of those professing divergent convictions? This remains our 'school question.'

The question and its implications will have to be faced repeatedly and its elements will not be solved without good will, understanding and leadership. As Dr. Louis Evans expresses it, "one thing I know we will have to do; we will have to bring religious leaders, educators and parents together around a table and decide what can be done."[6] The Presbyterian minister from Hollywood was speaking about released time, but all points of the 'school question' will have to be examined with many participants "around the table." In this forum, intemperate statements should be dismissed as irrelevancies. The effort to maintain that calm reflection, that judicial attitude which alone can give us decisions that will protect and balance all our liberties is essential, for the "right decision in concrete and complex cases will lie in a fine balance of principles and a harmony of all the factors involved. . . . All parties to the discussion, Protestants, Catholics, Secularists and the rest, all have their bigots, but these must not guide our decisions" if we are to achieve equitable adjustments and a legal status

---

[6] Louis Evans, "Religious Stewardship for To-day's Children," *American Association of School Administrators, Official Report*, 1952. P.35.

so ordered "that neither is the conscience of the citizen violated or impeded, nor is the state turned into a church."[7]

In the attempt to reach whatever consensus is possible, Arthur S. Adams, President of the American Council on Education, expresses his confidence "in the democratic process of discussing difficult issues and reaching general consensus," not in the foolish expectancy to see all become of one mind on any particular issue, but with the hope that "through a realistic and friendly exchange of views, we can find and enlarge the area of common agreement." In the process may we, as he reminds us that we should, "keep uppermost in our minds the best interests of the pupil and his education,"[8] and remember that "the basic trend of our society is to accommodate divergent views, not to suppress them,"[9] and that the separation (of Church and State) required by the Constitution is the separation which is compatible with religious liberty."[10]

Brother Edmond G. Drouin, F.I.C.

---

[7] R. J. Henle, S.J., "American Principles and Religious Schools," *Saint Louis University Law Journal*, 3:237-251 (Spring, 1955). Pp.237-241.

[8] Arthur S. Adams, "Introduction," in *The Study of Religion in the Public Schools, An Appraisal*. Washington, D.C.: American Council on Education, 1958. P.4.

[9] Robert E. Rodes, Jr., "Religious Education and the Historical Method of Constitutional Interpretation, A Review Article," *Rutgers Law Review*, 9:682-695 (Summer, 1955). P.690.

[10] Wilber G. Katz, *op. cit.*, p.67.

ACKNOWLEDGMENT

The initial project from which this compilation developed was submitted as a master's thesis to the faculty of the School of Arts and Sciences of the Catholic University of America in 1958. For guidance and encouragement, I wish to thank my teachers in the Department of Library Science of the University. I am particularly grateful to Dom Bernard Theall, Assistant Professor of Library Science, who directed the thesis, to the Rev. James J. Kortendick, Head of the Department of Library Science, who approved it as reader, and to Mr. George E. Reed, Lecturer in the Department of Education at the University and Associate Director of the Legal Department at the National Catholic Welfare Conference, who assisted with advice and suggestions.

The initial bibliography covered the period 1940-1957. It has since been substantially enlarged, sections have been recast and numerous entries have been reedited. Without the financial support made available by the Brothers of Christian Instruction, and without the time during which I was generously released from my functions by Brother Thomas S. Farrell, F.I.C., President of Walsh College, where I serve as Librarian, this work would have been impossible.

When I decided to prepare the bibliography for publication, Dr. Vaclav Mostecky, previously on the teaching staff of the Department of Library Science at the Catholic University of America, actually Assistant Librarian for Reference at the Harvard University Law School Library, was kind enough to assist me with the solution of a number of technical problems. I appreciate his help in a very special way.

If I had to thank individually all the teachers, librarians, students and friends who helped and encouraged while this compilation was in progress, I would have to compile a new list which my memory could not complete. I do thank all of them and I only wish there were a way to contact them all.

Since so much of the work of compilation was done at the Library at the Catholic University of America, the Library of Congress and the education library at the U. S. Department of Health, Education and Welfare, I am particularly indebted to the librarians who administer these collections and to the staffs which service them. This bibliography would have been arrested in its development without the materials made available at these and at all the other libraries where I was able to work.

Brother Edmond G. Drouin, F.I.C.

Periodical References

The volume and page references of the periodical articles in this bibliography were entered according to the style used in the standard indexes issued by the H. W. Wilson Co.

(Example)

LAFARGE, OLIVER. "We Need the Private Schools," *Atlantic Monthly*, 193:53-56 (Feb., 1954)

The numerical key entered here should be read as volume 193, pages 53 to 56.

Court Cases

Case citations are very similar to periodical references.

(Example)

CITATION:

Meyer v. State of Nebraska, 262 U.S. 390; 43 S.Ct.625 (1923)

INTERPRETATION:

Name of case:	*Meyer v. State of Nebraska*
Volume number:	262
Title of report:	*United States Reports*
First page of decision:	390
Year of decision:	1923

Cases are made available in volumes of bound 'reports,' and are located very much the way periodical articles are traced in volumes of bound periodicals. Citations sometimes list more than one source for the same case. Such parallel citations make it possible to locate the same text in more than one report. The entry given above cites the text of the decision in the (official) *United States Reports* and in the (unofficial) *Supreme Court Reporter.*

Official sources are cited first in law literature. The various sections of the "American Reporter System" are more generally available, however.

Essential abbreviations are included on the following page. Persons unaccustomed to work with law literature should consult some of the materials suggested in Appendix E.

Court Cases: Abbreviations

a) REPORTERS in the "NATIONAL REPORTER SYSTEM"

A.	*Atlantic Reporter*
F.	*Federal Reporter*
F. Supp.	*Federal Supplement*
N. E.	*North Eastern Reporter*
N. W.	*North Western Reporter*
N. Y. S.	*New York Supplement*
P.	*Pacific Reporter*
S. Ct.	*Supreme Court Reporter*
S. E.	*South Eastern Reporter*
S. W.	*South Western Reporter*
So.	*Southern Reporter*

b) COMMON ABBREVIATIONS FOUND IN CITATIONS

U. S.: *United States Reports* (official).
et al. (et alii) : and others.
ex rel. (ex relatione) : by the relation of,
    at the information of.
v. or vs. (versus) : against

Abbreviated state names in citations
stand for official state court reports.

I

Church-State Relationships

in the United States

(An Introduction)

Note. The education phase of government relations with religion is inseparable from the broader problem of Church-State relationships. That problem is beyond the scope of this bibliography. The following list is not a guide to it but serves as an introductory unit which includes representative materials selected mainly because they incorporate discussions of the educational aspects of the problem or bear some relationship with topics recurrent in the literature devoted to it.

Discussion of religious liberty and the relation between government and religion was stimulated by the United States Supreme Court decisions in the Gobitis (1940), Barnette (1943), Everson (1947), McCollum (1948) and Zorach (1952) cases. The materials listed with these decisions in units V, VII and IX should be consulted along with the following list.

It should be remembered that, in this bibliography, classification was resorted to primarily to provide some analysis of the content of entries. There is constant overlapping of subject matter in the literature grouped in the various units, and the interrelationships between topics are so varied and often so closely-knit that no unit should be used alone. Units I and II supplement all others. The link between the writings of an author was often broken in the process of classification. That link has been reestablished in the Index.

1

A. BACKGROUND MATERIAL

1. BIBLIOGRAPHIES:

1 BARRETT, (Mother) PATRICIA, R.S.C.J. *Church and Society; A Bibliography: July, 1956 - January, 1958* (Continuing a service begun in the ISO Political Science News Letter). Saint Louis, Mo.: Institute of Social Order, Saint Louis University, 1958. 30pp. (Offset)

> Previous bibliographies appeared in the *Service Letter* (Institute of Social Order, Political Science News Letter) for September, 1953; September, 1954; September, 1955; September, 1956. This mimeographed service has been discontinued. A selection of materials from these bibliographies was printed in the *Theology Digest*, 4:97-99 (Spring, 1956).
>
> New series in progress: "Church and State; A Bibliography," *Theology Digest*, 7:185-190 (Autumn, 1959), 8:59-63 (Winter, 1960).

2 BURR, NELSON R. "Religion and the Law," in James Ward Smith and A. Leland Jamison, eds. *A Critical Bibliography of Religion in America* (Religion in American Life, Vol. 4). Princeton, N.J.: Princeton University Press, 1961. Pp.582-600.

> The following should also be checked. "From State Churches to Disestablishment," pp.87-110. "The Battle for Disestablishment," pp.111-116.

3 STOKES, ANSON PHELPS. "Critical and Classified Bibliography," in *Church and State in the United States*. New York: Harper, 1950. Vol. III, pp.769-836.

> An abundance of additional material is listed in the notes at the end of each volume.

2. LEGAL BACKGROUND:

3a KATZ, WILBER G. "Religion and Law in America," in James Ward Smith and A. Leland Jamison, eds., *Religious Perspectives in American Culture* (Religion in American Life, Vol. 2). Princeton, N.J.: Princeton University Press, 1961. Pp.53-80.

4 ZOLLMAN, CARL FREDERICK GUSTAV. *American Church*

Law. Saint Paul, Minn.: West Publishing Co., 1933. 675pp.

B. BOOKS AND PAMPHLETS

5 BETH, LOREN PETER. *American Theory of Church and State.* Gainesville, Fla.: University of Florida Press, 1958. 183pp.

REVIEW:
Social Order, 9:387-388 (October, 1959) Patricia Barrett, R.S.C.J.

6 BILLINGTON, RAY ALLEN. *The Protestant Crusade, 1800-1860; A Study of the Origins of American Nativism.* New York: Rinehart, 1952. 514pp. Bibliography: pp.445-504.

Originally issued by Macmillan (1938).

For a follow-up study, see John Higham, *Strangers in the Land; Patterns of American Nativism, 1860-1925.* New Brunswick, N.J.: Rutgers University Press, 1955. 431pp.

REVIEWS:
America, 61:93 (May 6, 1939) W. J. Benn
American Catholic Sociological Review, 14:108 (June, 1953) T. Neill
American Historical Review, 44:930 (July, 1939) G. M. Stephenson
American Political Science Review, 33:336 (April, 1939) R. W. McCulloch
American Sociological Review, 4:437 (June, 1939) R. K. Merton
Best Sellers, 13:11-12 (April 1, 1953) F. Brown
Books on Trial, 11:242-243 (April, 1953) Sister M. Augustina, B.V.M.
Boston Transcript, p.2 (Jan. 7, 1939) Donald Born
Catholic World, 148:629 (Feb., 1939)
Christian Century, 56:516 (April 19, 1939)
Churchman, 153:17 (Feb. 15, 1939) L. L. Riley
Menorah Journal, 31:18-33 (Jan., 1943) Sylvia Kopald Selekman

New England Quarterly, 12:136 (March, 1939) Carl Witke
New Republic, 98:56 (Feb. 15, 1939), 99:315 (July 19, 1939)
   Rebecca Pitts
New York Herald Tribune Books, p.11 (Jan. 22, 1939) H. S.
   Commager
Springfield Republican, p.7 (Jan. 1, 1939)
Wisconsin Library Bulletin, 35:60 (April, 1939)

BLANSHARD, PAUL. See *Appendix A* and *Appendix B.*

7   BLAU, JOSEPH LEON. *Cornerstones of Religious Freedom
   in America.* Boston: Beacon Press, 1949. 247pp.
   Notes: pp.240-245, "Sources": pp.246-247.

   REVIEWS:

   Churchman, 163:15 (Dec. 1, 1949)
   Crozer Quarterly, 27:83 (Jan., 1950) C. H. Moelman
   Bulletin from Virginia Kirkus' Book Shop Service, 17:539
      (Oct. 1, 1949)
   Library Journal, 74:1315 (Sept. 15, 1949) O. G. Lawson
   New York Times Book Review, p.13 (Dec. 25, 1949) J. A. Pike
   School and Society, 71:277 (May 6, 1950) W. W. Brickman

8   BROWN, ROBERT MCAFEE, AND WEIGEL, GUSTAVE, S.J.
   An American Dialogue. Garden City, New York:
   Doubleday, 1960. 216pp.

   Comment. "Church and State," *Time,* 76:27 (Oct. 10, 1960).
   — Reinhold Niebuhr, "Catholics and the State," *New Republic,* 143:13-15 (Oct. 17, 1960). — Gustave Weigel, S.J.,
   "A Theology of Church and State," (Address) *Catholic Mind,*
   59:100-110 (March-April, 1961). Excerpts. *Commonweal,* 73:
   68-70 (Oct. 14, 1960).

9   COGLEY, JOHN (ed.) *Religion in America: Original Essays on Religion in a Free Society.* New York: Meridian Books, 1958. 288pp.

   Essays based on papers delivered at a Seminar on Religion
   in a Free Society sponsored by the Fund for the Republic,
   Inc. The seminar was held at the World Affairs Center in
   New York, from May 5 to May 9, 1958.
   Contents. "America's Four Conspiracies," John Courtney
   Murray, S.J., 12-41. "A Note on Pluralism," Reinhold Niebuhr,
   42-50. "The Case For Separation," Leo Pfeffer, 52-94. "The
   Case For Religious Liberty," Wilber G. Katz, 95-115. "Re-
   ligion, Democracy and Public Education," Will Herberg, 118-
   147. "Religion and Education in a Free Society," James
   Hastings Nichols, 148-167. "The Religious-Secular Dialogue,"
   Walter J. Ong, 170-207. "Censorship in a Dialectical Repub-
   lic," Stringfellow Barr, 208-222. "The Present Embarrass-
   ment of the Church," Gustave Weigel, 224-243. "The Religious
   Message," Abraham Joshua Heschel, 244-271. "Freedom and

the Ultimate Concern," Paul Tillich, 272-286. "Notes on Contributors," 287-288.

10 COWAN, WAYNE H. (ed.) *Facing Protestant-Roman Catholic Tensions; How to Think Clearly about them as Suggested by Leading Roman Catholics and Protestants.* New York: The Association Press, 1960. 128pp. Bibliography: pp.121-125.

Includes articles by John C. Bennett, Paul Blanshard, Daniel J. Callahan, William Clancy, Robert McAfee Brown, Bernard Dauenhauer, Wayne H. Cowan, Msgr. Francis J. Lally, C. Stanley Lowell, F. Ernest Johnson, Thomas F. O'Dea, Robert L. Schlager, Henry P. Van Dusen, Gustave Weigel, S.J.

10a CUNNINGGIM, MERRIMON. *Freedom's Holy Light.* New York: Harper, 1955. 192pp. "Notes," pp.165-82. Bibliography: pp.183-88.

11 CUSHMAN, ROBERT EUGENE. "Freedom of Religion: Separation of Church and State," in *Civil Liberties in the United States; A Guide to Current Problems and Experience.* Ithaca, N.Y.: Cornell University Press, 1956. Pp.92-108. Includes bibliographies.

REVIEWS:
American Academy of Political and Social Science. Annals, 308:191 (Nov., 1956)
Georgetown Law Journal, 45:327 (Winter, 1956-1957) L. A. Huard
Miami Law Quarterly, 11:319 (Winter, 1956)
New York Herald Tribune Book Review, p.9 (July 29, 1956)
State Bar Journal of California, 31:484 (Sept.-Oct., 1956) E. L. Barrett

12 DOUGLAS, WILLIAM ORVILLE. *A Living Bill of Rights.* Garden City, N.Y.: Doubleday, 1961. 72pp.

13 DRINKER, HENRY SANDWITH. *Some Observations on the Four Freedoms of the First Amendment: Freedom of Speech, Freedom of the Press, Freedom of Assembly and Petition, Freedom of Religion* (Boston University. The Gaspar G. Bacon Lectures on the Constitution of the United States). Boston: Boston University Press, 1957. 69pp. Reprinted from *Boston University Law Review,* 37:1-69 (Winter, 1957).

See: "The 'Establishment of Religion' and the Preference Between Religions in the Public Schools," pp.49-69. Includes remarks on "The State and Religious Education," 49-61, and "The McCollum and Zorach Cases," 61-69.

REVIEW:
Social Order, 9:86-89 (Feb., 1959) William J. Kenealy, S.J.

14   FELLMAN, DAVID (ed.) *The Supreme Court and Education (Classics in Education, No. 4).* New York: Bureau of Publications, Teachers College, Columbia University, 1960. 120pp.

See: "Education and Religion," pp.1-66.
Statements from decisions of the United States Supreme Court.

15   FUND FOR THE REPUBLIC. *Religion and the Free Society (Fund for the Republic Pamphlets),* by William Lee Miller, and others. New York: Fund for the Republic, 1958. 107pp.

"A contribution to the discussion of the free society." Discussions by William Lee Miller, William Clancy, Arthur Cohen, Mark de Wolfe Howe, Maximilian W. Kemper.

16   GREENE, EVARTS B. *Religion and the State; The Making and Testing of an American Tradition.* New York: New York University Press, 1941. 172pp. Bibliographical notes: pp.147-162.

REVIEWS:
American Journal of Sociology, 48:276 (Sept., 1942) W. W. Sweet
American Political Science Review, 36:549-50 (June, 1942) T. I. Cook
Canadian Historical Review, 23:88 (March, 1942) H. F. Langford
Christian Century, 59:49 (Jan. 14, 1942)
Churchman, 156:14 (Nov. 15, 1942) W. F. Thompson
Library Journal, 66:1093 (Dec. 15, 1941) A. H. Campbell
New England Quarterly, 15:390 (June, 1942) E. S. Morgan
Review of Politics, 4:515-16 (Oct., 1942)

17   HARDON, JOHN AUGUSTINE, S.J. *Christianity in Conflict; A Catholic View of Protestantism.* Westminster, Md.: Newman Press, 1959. 300pp. Notes: pp.281-89.

See: "Church and State Relations," 107-137. "Religious Education," 139-157.

18   HERBERG, WILL. *Protestant-Catholic-Jew; An Essay in American Religious Sociology.* Garden City, N.Y.: Doubleday, 1955. 320pp. Bibliography: pp.299-313.

REVIEWS:

American Catholic Sociological Review, 16:66 (March, 1956)
American Journal of Sociology, 61:646 (May, 1956) Lee
  Braude
American Sociological Review, 21:237 (April, 1956) Y. M.
  Yinger
Best Sellers, 15:159 (Oct. 1, 1955) J. Cronin, S.S.
Books on Trial, 14:117 (Nov., 1955) R. Coffey, C.P.
Catholic Historical Review, 42:214 (July, 1956) C. Nuesse
Catholic World, 182:234 (Dec., 1955) J. B. Code
Chicago Sunday Tribune, p.9 (Nov. 13, 1955) Clarence Side-
  spinner
Commonweal, 63:383 (Jan. 13, 1956) Alban Baer
Cross Currents, 6:87 (Winter, 1955)
Integrity, 10:39 (Jan., 1956) J. Kane
Jubilee, 3:51 (Nov., 1955)
Library Journal, 80:1828 (Sept. 1, 1955) R. P. Tubby
Manchester Guardian, p.4 (Jan. 6, 1956) D. W. Brogan
Nation, 181:581 (Dec., 31, 1955) M. L. Barron
New Republic, 133:18 (Nov. 14, 1955) Nathan Glazer
New Statesman and Nation, 51:189 (March 3, 1956) H. L.
  Short
New York Times Book Review, p.6 (Sept. 25, 1955) Reinhold
  Niebuhr
Review of Politics, 18:103 (Jan., 1956) T. McAvoy
Saturday Review, 39:39 (March 3, 1956) Siegfried Mandell
Social Order, 6:188 (Apr., 1956) J. Blewett
Theological Studies, 16:651 (Dec., 1955) G. Weigel
Thought, 30:595-600 (Winter, 1955) J. Fitzpatrick
Today, 11:28 (March, 1956) M. Schweitzer

19   HOWE, MARK DE WOLFE. *Cases on Church and State in
      the United States.* Cambridge, Mass.: Harvard Uni-
      versity Press, 1952. 393pp. (A preliminary edition.)

   See: "Education," 316-393.

   REVIEWS:

   Catholic Historical Review, 39:58-60 (Apr., 1953) Sister M. C.
     Klinkhamer
   Georgetown Law Journal, 41:126-28 (Nov., 1952) R. F.
     Drinan
   Journal of Legal Education, 6:145-48 (1953) C. W. Summers
   Modern Law Review, 16:390-91 (July, 1953) R. H. Pear

20   JOHNSON, ALVIN WALTER, and YOST, FRANK H. *Separa-
      tion of Church and State in the United States.* Min-
      neapolis, Minn.: University of Minnesota Press, 1948.
      279pp.

   A complete revision with additions of *The Legal Status of
   Church-State Relationships in the United States, with Special
   Reference to the Public Schools,* by Alvin W. Johnson, Uni-
   versity of Minnesota Press, 1934.

REVIEWS (1934 edition):
American Journal of Sociology, 41:554 (Jan., 1936) E. C.
    Hughes
American Political Science Review, 29:526 (June, 1935) B. L.
    Pierce
American Academy of Political and Social Science. Annals,
    181:225 (Sept., 1935) J. H. Barnett
Christian Century, 52:732 (May 29, 1935)
Current History, 43:xv (October, 1935)
Elementary School Journal, 36:230 (Nov., 1935) H. Holton
Georgetown Law Journal, 23:617-19 (March, 1935) C. Zollman
Harvard Law Review, 48:1466-67 (June, 1935)
Iowa Law Review, 21:165-66 (Nov., 1935) E. C. Carlson
Marquette Law Review, 19:268 (June, 1935) C. Zollman
Minnesota Law Review, 19:723 (May, 1935)

REVIEWS (1948 edition):
America, 80:548 (Feb. 19, 1949) J. M. O'Neill
American Academy of Political and Social Science. Annals,
    263:257 (May, 1949) Theodore Brameld
American Catholic Sociological Review, 10:137 (June, 1949)
    R. C. Hartnett
American Political Science Review, 43:376-77 (April, 1949)
    M. R. Konvitz
American Sociological Review, 14:437 (June, 1949) O. C. Cox
Catholic Educational Review, 47:284-85 (April, 1949) M. J.
    McKeough
Catholic Historical Review, 35:309-10 (Oct., 1949) R. J.
    Purcell
Christian Century, 65:1367 (Dec. 15, 1948) W. E. Garrison
Commonweal, 49:596 (March 25, 1949) Anne Fremantle
Journal of Higher Education, 20:386-87 (Oct., 1949) C.
    Frankel
Law and Contemporary Problems, 14:164-67 (Winter, 1949)
    P. R. Chandler
Minnesota Law Review, 33:328-29 (Feb., 1949)
Nation, 169:285 (Sept. 17, 1949) Paul Blanshard
New York University Law Quarterly Review, 24:470 (April,
    1949)
Oregon Law Review, 28:289-90 (April, 1949) P. B. Means
Progressive Education, 26:125-26 (Feb., 1949) A. S. Clayton
Religious Education, 44:314 (Sept., 1949) J. C. Bennett
School and Society, 68:400 (Dec. 4, 1948); 71:278-79 (May
    6, 1950) W. W. Brickman
School Review, 57:181 (March, 1949) G. W. Brown
Thomist, 12:384-85 (July, 1949) J. C. Murray
University of Pittsburgh Law Quarterly Review, 10:440-42
    (March, 1949) T. L. Anderson

21   KERWIN, JEROME G. *Catholic Viewpoint on Church and
      State*. Garden City, N.Y.: Hanover House, 1960.
      192pp.

      Excerpts. *Commonweal*, 72:342-44 (July 8, 1960).

22 KONVITZ, MILTON RIDVAS. *Fundamental Liberties of a Free People; Religion, Speech, Press, Assembly* (Cornell University. Cornell Studies in Civil Liberties). Ithaca, N.Y.: Cornell University Press, 1957. 420pp. Notes: pp.363-406.

See: "Freedom of Religion," 3-106.

23 METHODIST CHURCH. NEW YORK EAST METHODIST CONFERENCE. *First Church and State Assembly: Research Consultation on Church and State.* Reports. (Processed.)

Assembly held at the Methodist Training Center, Shelter Island, N.Y., June 12 to 14, 1958.
(Copyright, Board of Social and Economic Relations of the Methodist Church, 740 Rush St., Chicago, Ill.)
Contents. "Merry Christmas: A Case Study in Community Conflict," Dean M. Kelly. "The American Heritage of Religious Freedom," Claud D. Nelson. "The Nature and Function of the Church," Colin Williams. "A Perspective on Religious Freedom in America," William H. Bernhardt. "Church and State: The Cooperative View," Allyn P. Robinson (Text published in the *Catholic Mind*, 56:485-95 [Nov.-Dec., 1958]). "Church and State: The Militant View," G. Barrett Rich III. —Discussion of the papers: Excerpts and summaries. Some findings of the task teams: 1) When the Conflict Comes, 2) Preventing Conflict, 3) Issues of Concern for Further Research. Bibliography for Further Study. Common approaches to Church-State problems that have proved of limited fruitfulness. Outline of Church-State relations in America. Index. (Papers are individually paginated.)

24 MOEHLMAN, CONRAD HENRY. *The Wall of Separation Between Church and State; An Historical Study of Recent Criticism of the Religious Clause of the First Amendment* (*Beacon Press Studies in Freedom and Power*). Boston: Beacon Press, 1951. 239pp. Bibliography: pp.222-31.

REVIEWS:
Christian Century, 68:740 (June 20, 1951) W. E. Garrison
Commonweal, 54:269-70 (June 22, 1951) H. H. Ashley, Jr.
Crozer Quarterly, 29:64-65 (Jan., 1952) H. M. Gehr
Bulletin from Virginia Kirkus' Book Shop Service, 19:51 (Feb. 1, 1951)
Library Journal, 76:864 (May 15, 1951) F. E. Hirsch
Nation, 172:590 (June 23, 1951) Norman Thomas
School and Society, 74:272 (Oct. 27, 1951); 85:122 (Apr. 13, 1957) W. W. Brickman
Social Forces, 30:243 (Dec., 1951) M. J. William
Theology Today, 9:271-272 (July, 1952) F. E. Johnson

25 MORRISSON, CHARLES CLAYTON. *The Separation of Church and State in America.* Indianapolis, Indiana: International Convention of the Disciples of Christ (516-519, K. of P. Building), 1947. 14pp.

> Address delivered at the International Convention of the Disciples of Christ, Buffalo, N.Y., July 30, 1941.

26 MURRAY, JOHN COURTNEY, S.J. *We Hold These Truths; Catholic Reflections on the American Proposition.* New York: Sheed and Ward, 1960. 336pp.

> Excerpts. *Commonweal,* 73:433-35 (Jan. 20, 1961).
> Comment. "City of God and Man," *Time,* 76:13, 64-70 (Dec. 12, 1960) and cover feature.

27 NELSON, CLAUD D. *Church and State, a Guide to Study and Discussion. The American Pattern of Interaction Between the Forces of Religion and of Government.* New York: National Council of the Churches of Christ in the U. S. A., 1953. 39pp.

28 O'BRIEN, F. WILLIAM, S.J. *Justice Reed and the First Amendment: The Religion Clauses.* Washington: Georgetown University Press, 1958. 264pp. Bibliography: pp.243-56.

> REVIEWS:
> *America,* 99:416 (July 12, 1958) E. Corwin
> *American Bar Association Journal,* 44:876 (Sept., 1958) H. D. Crotty
> *Catholic University Law Review,* 7:117 (May, 1958) T. F. Butler
> *Notre Dame Lawyer,* 33:510-13 (May, 1958) R. E. Rodes
> *Sign,* 37:59 (June, 1958) F. Gallagher
> *Virginia Law Review,* 44:677 (May, 1958) W. Bern

29 ONG, WALTER JACKSON, S.J. "Religious-Secular Dialogue in a Pluralistic Society," in *American Catholic Crossroads; Religious-Secular Encounters in the Modern World.* New York: Macmillan, 1959. pp.16-45.

30 PARSONS, WILFRID, S.J. *The First Freedom, Considerations on Church and State in the United States.* New York: D. X. McMullen, 1948. 178pp.

> REVIEWS:
> *America,* 79:312-13 (July 3, 1948) W. E. McManus
> *American Ecclesiastical Review,* 120:153-54 (Feb., 1949) J. A. Magner

Ave Maria, 68:538 (Oct. 23, 1948) J. F. Menez
Books on Trial, 7:43 (July, 1948) H. Graham
Catholic Educational Review, 46:546 (Oct., 1948) J. T. Farrell
Catholic Educator, 19:287-88 (Jan., 1949) J. L. O'Brien
Catholic Historical Review, 35:306-09 (Oct., 1949) J. J.
   Wright
Catholic World, 167:377 (July, 1948) J. McSorley
Christian Century, 65:853 (Aug. 25, 1948) W. E. Garrison
Christian Science Monitor, p.16 (Nov. 12, 1948) Tully Nettle-
   ton
Dominicana, 33:245-46 (Sept., 1948)
Homiletic and Pastoral Review, 49:908 (Aug., 1949) C. Bruehl
Law and Contemporary Problems, 14:44-60 (Winter, 1949)
   M. R. Konvitz
Lutheran Quarterly, 1:107-08 (Feb., 1949) R. Iversen
Mid-America, 31:121-22 (Apr., 1949) C. C. Chapman
New Scholasticism, 23:344-45 (July, 1949) J. G. Kerwin
Notre Dame Lawyer, 24:134-40 (Fall, 1948) D. E. O'Brien
Orate Fratres, 22:429 (July 25, 1948)
Progressive Education, 26:158-60 (March, 1949) A. S. Clayton
School and Society, 71:280 (May 6, 1950) W. W. Brickman
Sign, 27:56 (July, 1948) A. P. Hennessey
Thought, 23:589-91 (Dec., 1948) R. C. Hartnett

31 PFEFFER, LEO. *Church, State and Freedom*. Boston:
   Beacon Press, 1953. 675pp. Bibliography: pp.650-54,
   Notes: pp.607-49.

DISCUSSION:

Paul G. Kauper. "Church, State and Freedom: A Review,"
   Michigan Law Review, 52:829-49 (Apr., 1954).
Leo Pfeffer. "Released Time and Religious Liberty: A Reply,"
   Michigan Law Review, 53:91-98 (Nov., 1954).
Paul G. Kauper. "Released Time and Religious Liberty: A
   Further Reply," *Michigan Law Review*, 53:233-35 (Dec.,
   1954).

REVIEWS:

American Academy of Political and Social Science, Annals,
   291:188 (Jan., 1954) W. L. Sperry
American Historical Review, 59:386 (Jan., 1954) L. W. Levy
American Political Science Review, 48:556 (June, 1954) M. Q.
   Sibley
Christian Century, 70:1024 (Sept. 9, 1953) W. E. Garrison
Christian Science Monitor, p.11 (Jan. 21, 1954) Kent Bush
Columbia Law Review, 54:1168-72 (Nov., 1954) Shad Polier
Foreign Affairs, 32:675 (July, 1954)
Harvard Law Review, 67:536-38 (Jan., 1954) C. S. Desmond
Hibbert Journal, 52:198 (Jan., 1954) R. V. Holt
Interpretation, 8:362 (July, 1954) E. T. Thompson
Nation, 177:236 (Sept. 19, 1953)
New York Times Book Review, p.37 (Sept. 13, 1953)
New York University Law Review, 29:536-38 (Feb., 1954)
   O. K. Fraenkel
Political Science Quarterly, 69:127 (March, 1954) M. D. Howe

Saturday Review, 36:27 (Nov. 7, 1953) W. L. Sperry
School and Society, 78:15 (July 11, 1953); 85:124 (Apr. 13, 1957) W. W. Brickman
University of Chicago Law Review, 21:507-509 (Spring, 1954) M. R. Konvitz
U. S. Quarterly Book Review, 9:439 (Dec., 1953)
Utah Law Review, 4:149-52 (Spring, 1954) R. D. Poll
Vanderbilt Law Review, 7:437-39 (April, 1954) S. E. Stumpf
Yale Law Journal, 63:437-39 (Jan., 1954) F. Krinsky

32   —————. *Creeds in Competition; A Creative Force in American Culture.* New York: Harper, 1958. 176pp.

See: "God and the Schools," 57-74. "Private Schools and Public Purse," 75-92.

33   POWERS, FRANCIS JOSEPH. *Religious Liberty and the Police Power of the State; A study of the jurisprudential concepts underlying the problem of religious freedom and its relationship to the police power in the United States with special reference to recent decisions of the United States Supreme Court on the subject.* Washington, D.C.: Catholic University of America Press, 1948. 184pp. (Doctoral dissertation) Bibliography: pp.164-82.

REVIEWS:
Notre Dame Lawyer, 24:270-72 (Winter, 1949) R. W. Mulligan
Progressive Education, 26:158-60 (March, 1949) A. S. Clayton (This review lists the title incorrectly.)

34   REED, GEORGE E. "The First Amendment—Historical Background," *The National Catholic Almanac, 1960.* Paterson, N.J.: Saint Anthony's Guild. pp.652-58.

35   RUTLAND, ROBERT ALLEN. *The Birth of the Bill of Rights: 1776-1791.* Chapel Hill, N.C.: University of North Carolina Press, 1955. 243pp.

36   SCHARPER, PHILIP (ed.) *American Catholics; A Protestant-Jewish View.* New York: Sheed and Ward, 1959. 235pp.

Includes articles by Stringfellow Barr, Robert McAfee Brown, Arthur Cohen, Arthur Gilbert, Martin Marty, Allyn Robinson, Gustave Weigel, S.J.

37   STOKES, ANSON PHELPS. *Church and State in the United*

States. New York: Harper, 1950. 3 Vols. Bibliography: Vol. III, pp.769-836. Notes by chapter at the end of each volume.

Education is given special treatment in Vol. I, Chapter 12, pp.769-836; Vol. II, Chapter 19, pp.642-758.

REVIEWS:
American Academy of Political and Social Science. Annals, 271:222 (Sept., 1950) W. W. Sweet
American Bar Association Journal, 37:49-51 (Jan., 1951) J. S. Savage
Catholic Historical Review, 38:285-316 (Oct., 1952) John Tracy Ellis
Chicago Sun-Times, p.5 (July 9, 1950) J. O. Supple
Chicago Sunday Tribune, p.5 (July 16, 1950) John Evans
Christian Century, 67:589 (May 10, 1950) W. E. Garrison
Christianity and Crisis, 11:9-10 (Feb. 19, 1951) Edward L. Parsons
Commonweal, 56:41-45 (April 18, 1952) W. E. McManus
Crozer Quarterly, 27:343 (Oct., 1950) C. H. Moehlman
Georgetown Law Journal, 39:173-78 (Nov., 1950) R. F. Drinan
Harvard Law Review, 64:170-75 (Nov., 1950) M. D. Howe
Historical Bulletin, 30:244-46 (May, 1952) T. L. McDonnell
Homilectic and Pastoral Review, 51:503-507 (March, 1951) R. F. Drinan
Bulletin from Virginia Kirkus' Book Shop Service, 17:648 (Dec. 1, 1949)
Minnesota Law Review, 35:622-23 (May, 1951)
New York Herald Tribune Book Review, p.1 (July 9, 1950) H. S. Commager
New York Times Book Review, p.3 (May 28, 1950) J. A. Pike
Newsweek, 35:80 (May 15, 1950)
Religion in Life, 20, No. 1:36-46
Review of Politics, 13:261-62 (April, 1951) T. T. McAvoy
Saturday Review of Literature, 33:16 (July 1, 1950) W. L. Sperry
School and Society, 85:124 (April 13, 1957) W. W. Brickman
Time, 55:80 (May 22, 1950)
Yale Review (new series) 40:174 (Autumn, 1950) Liston Pope

38 SWEET, WILLIAM WARREN. "Protestantism in American History," in William K. Anderson (ed.), *Protestantism, A Symposium.* Nashville, Tenn.: Commission on Courses of Study, the Methodist Church, 1944. Pp.99-109.

39 TORPEY, WILLIAM GEORGE. *Judicial Doctrines of Religious Rights in America.* Chapel Hill, N.C.: University of North Carolina Press, 1948. 376pp. Bibliography: pp.333-71.

See: "Educational Practices Involving the Right of Religious Freedom," pp.233-276.

REVIEWS:

Catholic Historical Review, 35:453 (Jan., 1950) W. Parsons
Catholic World, 168-256 (Dec., 1948)
Christian Century, 65:1175 (Nov. 3, 1948)
Columbia Law Review, 48:1273 (Dec., 1948)
Cornell Law Quarterly, 34:696-97 (Summer, 1949) A. E. Sutherland
Iowa Law Review, 34:734-36 (May, 1949) O. H. Thormodsgard
Law and Contemporary Problems, 14:160-64 (Winter, 1949) Clyde W. Summers
Law Quarterly Review, 65:263-64 (April, 1949) H. Slesser
Lawyers' Guild Review, 8:509-11 (Nov.-Dec., 1948) J. M. Dawson
Lutheran Quarterly, 1:343-44 (Aug., 1949) R. Bruce
Miami Law Quarterly, 3:69-71 (Dec., 1948) B. Roth
Michigan Law Review, 47:444 (Jan., 1949)
North Carolina Law Review, 27:168-70 (Dec., 1948) H. G. Ruark
South Carolina Law Quarterly, 1:437-38 (June, 1949) R. D. Ochs
Stanford Law Review, 1:377-80 (Jan., 1949) C. C. Means
Texas Law Review, 28:128-33 (Nov., 1949) H. A. Calkins

39a TUSSMAN, JOSEPH, (ed.). *The Supreme Court on Church & State.* New York: Oxford University Press, 1962. 305pp.

40 VILLANOVA UNIVERSITY. *Institute of Church and State, Conference Proceedings, Volume I.* Villanova, Pa.: Villanova University Press, 1958. 114pp. (Offset)

"First Conference Held at Villanova University School of Law, Feb. 22 and 23, 1957."

Contents. "The Juridical Status of Churches," 6-55, Address by Mark De Wolfe Howe, Comments by Msgr. Joseph A. Brady and Harold F. Hartman, Discussion. "Religion in Adoption and Custody Cases," 56-114, Address of Rev. Joseph M. Snee, S.J., Comments by Leo Pfeffer, Discussion.

41 ————. *Institute of Church and State, Conference Proceedings, Volume II.* "Sectarian Freedom in a Democratic Society," Thomas J. O'Toole (ed.). Villanova, Pa.: Villanova University Press, 1959. 115pp.

Contents. "The Private Trust and Public Law," 1-61, Thesis: Elias Clark, Comments: John J. Stephenson III, William J. Coleman, Jr., Discussion. "The Private School and Public Law," 62-112, Thesis: William J. Kenealy, S.J., Comments:

Thomas M. Cooley II, Fritz Nova, Robert B. Kent, William B. Ball, Discussion. Table of Cases. Participants.

42 WALSH, GERALD GROVELAND, S.J. *Church and State in the U. S.* New York: Paulist Press, 1948. 32pp.

43 WELCH, ROBERT J. "Catholic Church in American Democracy," in Dan Herr and Clement Lane (eds.), *Realities; Significant Writings from the Catholic Press.* Milwaukee: Bruce, 1958. Pp.208-226.

44 WOOD, VIRGINIA. "Separation of Church and State," in *Due Process of Law: 1932-1949; The Supreme Court's Use of a Constitutional Tool.* Baton Rouge: Louisiana State University Press, 1951. Pp.81-90.

C. PERIODICAL ARTICLES

45 ASHLEY, HARMON H. and RIORDAN, JAMES Q. "Historical Note on the First Amendment," *Christianity and Crisis,* 9:29-30 (March 21, 1949).

Memorandum on the historical background of the First Amendment written at Columbia University School of Law.

46 BARRETT, (Mother) PATRICIA, R.C.S.J. "Church and State: Dialogue Continued," *Social Order,* 9:169-76 (April, 1959).

47 BILLINGTON, RAY ALLEN. "American Catholicism and the Church-State Issue," *Christendom,* 5:355-66 (Summer, 1940).

48 CANAVAN, FRANCIS P., S.J. "Politics and Catholicism: Conflicts and Challenges in a Pluralistic Society," *Social Order,* 9:458-563 (Dec., 1959).

49 CATHOLIC CENTRAL UNION OF AMERICA (Formerly Catholic Central Verein). "Separation of Church and State: Declaration of Principles Adopted by the 102nd Convention of the Catholic Central Union of America, Conducted at Allentown, Pa., August 24-28, 1957," *Social Justice Review,* 50:321-22 (Jan., 1958).

50 "Catholics in America; A Symposium on Catholic Aims," *The New Republic,* 142:11-15 (March 21, 1960).

   Answers to five questions by John C. Bennett, Arthur Schlesinger, Jr., and Jaroslav Pelikan.

51 "The Church in a Free Society," *Catholic Mind,* 59:100-191 (March-April, 1961).

   Contents. "A Theology of Church and State," Gustave Weigel, S.J., 100-110 (Address delivered at the Shrine of the Most Blessed Sacrament, Washington, D.C., Sept. 27, 1960). "Cultural Pluralism: The Religious Dimension," John C. Bennett, 111-124 (Address delivered upon receipt of the Morgenstern Award presented annually by the National Council of Christians and Jews). "American Catholics: History of a Minority," Thomas T. McAvoy, C.S.C., 125-134 (From *Thought,* Winter, 1960). "American Catholics Today," John Tracy Ellis, 135-152 (From the *American Benedictine Review,* Summer, 1960). "Church and State in the American Environment," Edward Duff, S.J., 153-171 (From *Social Order,* November, 1960). "Freedom and Authority in Roman Catholicism," Daniel J. Callahan, 172-178 (From *Christianity and Crisis,* Oct. 3, 1960). "The Laity Speaks," 179-191 (Statement on religious freedom, and press conference held at the Willard Hotel, Washington, D.C., Oct. 5, 1960).

52 "Church-State; Religious Institutions and Values: A Legal Survey, 1955-1957," *Notre Dame Lawyer,* 33:416-462 (May, 1958).

   Prepared by William D. Bailey, Jr., Richard C. Clark and Patrick F. McCartan, Jr.

   For a subsequent survey see 35:405-439 (May, 1960), prepared by William J. Gerardo, William R. Kennedy and Paul J. Schierl.

53 COGLEY, JOHN. "An Article of Peace," *Commonweal,* 68:372 (July 11, 1958).

54 ————. "God and Caesar," *Commonweal,* 66:563 (Sept. 6, 1957).

   Comment on the success of the First Amendment.

55 COUR, RAYMOND F., C.S.C. "Recent Teaching of the Supreme Court on the Subject of Church and State," *American Catholic Historical Society of Philadelphia, Records*, 68:96-105 (Dec., 1957).

Paper delivered at the American Civilization Seminar of the University of Notre Dame, Notre Dame, Indiana, March 15, 1957.

56 DRINAN, ROBERT F., S.J., "The Dilemma of the ACLU," *America*, 102:271-272, 274 (Nov. 28, 1959).

57 ————. "Religion and the ACLU," *America*, 99: 663-665 (Sept. 27, 1958).

Remarks about the American Civil Liberties Union.

58 DRUCKER, PETER F. "Organized Religion and the American Creed," *Review of Politics*, 18:296-304 (July, 1956).

Excerpt. *Commonweal*, 64:469-71 (August 10, 1956).

59 DUESENBERG, RICHARD W. "Jurisdiction of Civil Courts Over Religious Issues," *Ohio State Law Journal*, 20: 508-548 (Summer, 1959).

60 DUFF, EDWARD, S.J. "Church-State in the American Environment: An Historical and Legal Survey," *Social Order*, 10:385-402 (Nov., 1960). Same. *Catholic Mind*, 50:153-71 (March-April, 1961).

61 EBY, KERMIT. "God Requireth Not a Uniformity of Religion," *Brethren Life and Thought*, 3:34-38 (Winter, 1958).

62 ELLIS, JOHN TRACY. "Church and State: An American Catholic Tradition," *Harper's Magazine*, 207:63-67 (Nov., 1953). Same. *Catholic Mind*, 52:209-216 (April, 1954).

63 FIERMAN, FLOYD S. "The Jews and the Problem of Church and State in America Prior to 1881," *Educational Forum*, 15:335-41 (March, 1951).

64 GORDIS, RORERT. "Church, State and the Will of God; A Critical Analysis of the Nature of the Relation

between Religion and Democracy," *Christian Century*, 75:1504-1507 (Dec. 31, 1958).

65 GRAHAM, JOHN JOSEPH. "The Development of the Separation of Church and State in the United States of America," *American Catholic Historical Society of Philadelphia, Records*, 50:81-87 (Dec., 1939), 51:1-64 (March), 85-148 (June), 149-172 (Sept.-Dec., 1940).

66 GRAHAM, ROBERT ANDREW. "Our Constitution and the Church," *America*, 97:981-983 (July 6, 1957).

67 HARDING, ARTHUR L. "Religious Liberty: the Source of Freedom?" *Southwestern Law Journal*, 11:169-183 (Spring, 1957).

68 HARDON, JOHN AUGUSTINE, S.J. "Cooperation of Church and State: I) In American Legislation, II) In the Supreme Court, III) In American Education," *Homiletic and Pastoral Review*, 57:309-319 (Jan.), 419-427 (Feb.), 523-531 (March, 1957).

69 HENRY, CARL FERDINAND HOWARD. "Can We Salvage the Republic?" *Christianity Today*, 2:3-7 (March 3, 1958).

70 HERBERG, WILL. "Religious Communities in Present-day America," *Review of Politics*, 16:155-174 (April, 1954).

71 ——————. "The Sectarian Conflict over Church and State; A Divisive Threat to our Democracy?" *Commentary*, 14:450-462 (Nov., 1952). Considerably abridged reprint. *Christianity and Crisis*, 13:3-7 (Feb. 2, 1953). Discussion, same, p.2.

72 HUDSPETH, C. M. "Separation of Church and State in America," *Texas Law Review*, 33:1035-1056 (Oct., 1955).

73 "Issues Between Catholics and Protestants at Midcentury," *Religion in Life*, 23:163-205 (Spring, 1954).

Symposium. George H. Williams, Waldo Beach, H. Richard Niebuhr.

74   JACOBSON, PHILIP. "Should the Ayes Always Have It?
      —A Lawyer Argues that Majority Rule Cannot De-
      cide Questions of Religion," *Christian Century*, 75:
      1206-1208 (Oct. 22, 1958). (Was reprinted by the
      American Jewish Committee.)

75   JAFFE, LOUIS L. "The Judicial Universe of Mr. Justice
      Frankfurter," *Harvard Law Review*, 62:357-412
      (Jan., 1949).

      Includes a section on "Civil Liberties" (396-407) and re-
      marks about the Gobitis, Barnette, Everson and McCollum
      decisions.

76   JOHNSON, WILLARD. "Whose Country is This? Notes on
      Protestant-Roman Catholic Relationships," *Christen-
      dom*, 12:507-514 (Autumn, 1947).

77   LAKE, I. BEVERLY. "Freedom to Worship Curiously,"
      University of Florida Law Review, 1:203-241 (Sum-
      mer, 1948).

78   LARDNER, LYNFORD A. "How Far Does the Constitution
      Separate Church and State?" *American Political
      Science Review*, 45:110-132 (March, 1951).

      The theme is further developed in Frank J. Sorauf, "Zorach
      v. Clauson: The Impact of a Supreme Court Decision,"
      American Political Science Review, 53:777-791 (Sept., 1959).

79   "Limiting State Action by the Fourteenth Amendment:
      Consequence of Abandoning the Theory of First
      Amendment Incorporation," *Harvard Law Review*,
      67:1016-30 (Apr., 1954).

80   LIPNICK, STANLEY M. "A New Trend in Civil Rights
      Litigation? Sunday Laws, Released Time, and Bible
      Reading in the Public Schools as Affected by the
      First Amendment" (student note), *George Washing-
      ton Law Review*, 28:579-615 (March, 1960).

81   LOWRY, CHARLES WESLEY. "Catholic-Protestant Rela-
      tions; A Churchman Looks at Both," *Vital Speeches
      of the Day*, 27:130-134 (Dec. 15, 1960).

      Address delivered at the Mount Olivet Methodist Church,
      Arlington, Va., Oct. 16, 1960, the third in a series entitled
      "A Look at Roman Catholicism and Protestantism."

82 MACKINNON, VICTOR S. "Freedom?—or Toleration? The Problem of Church and State in the United States," *Public Law,* 1959:374-395 (Winter, 1959).

83 MARQUEZ, ANTONIO. "Catholic Controversy on Church and State," *Theology Today,* 15:531-541 (Jan., 1959).

84 MEYER, CARL STAMM. "Friction Points in Church-State Relations in the United States," *Concordia Theological Monthly,* 28:481-503 (July, 1957).

85 MORRISON, CHARLES CLAYTON. "Church, State and the Constitution," *Christian Century,* 65:875-78 (Sept. 1, 1948). Discussion. Paul G. Perkins, "The Logic Spelled Out," 65:113-114 (Oct. 20, 1948).

86 ——————. "Meaning of Separation," *Christian Century,* 64:1447-1448 (Nov. 26, 1947), "Getting Down to Cases," *Christian Century,* 64:1512-1514 (Dec. 10, 1947).

Reply. John Courtney Murray, S.J., "Dr. Morrison and the First Amendment," *America,* 78:627-29 (March 6), 683-86 (March 20, 1948).

87 MURRAY, JOHN COURTNEY, S.J. "A Church-State Anthology, the Work of Father Murray," edited by Victor R. Yanitelli. *Thought,* 27:6-42 (Spring, 1952). Comment. John J. McLaughlin, 569-71 (Winter, 1952-53).

88 ——————. "The Problem of Pluralism in America," *Thought,* 29:165-208 (Summer, 1954).

89 ——————. "Reflections on the Religiously Pluralistic Society," *Catholic Mind,* 57:196-288 (May-June, 1959).

Special issue containing an anthology of articles written by John Courtney Murray, S.J.

Contents. "Challenge Confronting the American Catholic," 196-200 (from *Life,* Dec. 26, 1955). "Church, State and Religious Liberty," 201-215 (from *Thought,* Summer, 1954). "Church, State and Political Freedom," 216-229 (from *Modern Age,* Fall, 1957). "America's Four Conspiracies," 230-241 (from John Cogley, ed., *Religion in America,* New York: Medidian Books, Inc., 1959). "The State University in a Pluralistic Society," 242-252 (from Erich A. Walter, *Religion and the State University*, Ann Arbor, Michigan: University of Michigan Press, 1958). "The Catholic University in a Pluralistic Society," 253-260 (Address delivered during the observance of Founder's Day, Saint Louis University, Saint Louis, Mo., Nov. 15-16, 1955). "The Confusion of U. S. Foreign Policy," 261-273 (from the Fund for the Republic, *Foreign Policy and the Free Society*, New York: the Fund, 1958). "God, Man and Nuclear War," 274-288 (from *Theological Studies*, March, 1959).

90 ————. "Separation of Church and State," *America*, 76:261-63 (Dec., 7, 1946).

91 ————. "Separation of Church and State: True and False Concepts," *America*, 76:541-45 (Feb. 15, 1947). Comment. L. J. Guzzardo, 76:616 (March 1, 1947).

92 NICHOLS, JAMES HASTINGS. "Protestantism and the Constitutional Problem," *Princeton Seminary Bulletin*, 53:30-36 (Oct., 1959).

93 ————. "What Disturbs Protestants About Catholics?" *Look*, 18:42-   (May 18, 1954). Discussion. John Courtney Murray, *America*, 91:218-19 (May 22, 1954). Reply. John Cogley, "Must Protestants Disturb Catholicism?" *Look*, 18:34-   (June 1, 1954). Comment. *Look*, 18:21 (June 29, 1954).

J. H. Nichols is the author of *Democracy and the Churches*, Philadelphia, Pa.: Westminster Press, 1951. 298pp.

94 "Nineteenth Century Judicial Thought Concerning Church-State Relations," *Minnesota Law Review*, 40:672-80 (May, 1956).

95 O'BRIEN, F. WILLIAM, S.J. "Has Government an Interest in Religion?" *Villanova Law Review*, 5:335-374 (Spring, 1960).

96 O'BRIEN, WILLIAM. "Religion and the State Governments," *University of Detroit Law Journal*, 38:34-44 (Oct., 1960).

97 O'GARA, JAMES. "Catholics and the Dialogue," *Commonweal*, 68:372 (July 11, 1958).

98 OXNAM, GARFIELD BROMLEY. "Our Protestant Heritage,"

Christian Century, 62:1267-68 (Nov. 14, 1945). Comment. G. E. Powers, same, p.1259.

Summary of an address delivered at Saint Louis, Mo., Oct. 30, 1945.

99 PFEFFER, LEO. "Church and State," *Princeton Seminary Bulletin,* 53:35-48 (Oct., 1959).

100 "Protestant-Roman Catholic Dialogue," *Christianity and Crisis,* 19:77-87 (June 8, 1959); 19:115-118 (August 3, 1959).

Contents. "Protestant-Roman Catholic Dialogue," John C. Bennett, 77-78. "Inside American Roman Catholicism," Gustave Weigel, S.J., 79-81. "The Ideologists and the Missing Dialogue," Thomas F. O'Dea, 81-84. "A Roman Catholic View of American Protestantism," William Clancy, 85-87. "American Catholicism: Grounds for Misgivings," Henry P. Van Dusen, 115-117. "The Dialogue Continued," Claud Nelson, 117-118.

PROTESTANTS AND OTHER AMERICANS UNITED FOR THE SEPARATION OF CHURCH AND STATE (POAU). See *Appendix C.*

101 REED, GEORGE E. "Separation of Church and State: Its Real Meaning," *Catholic Action,* 31:9-11 (March, 1949).

102 RUTHLAND, WALTER B. "Church-State Relations in America: Status and Trends," *Social Forces,* 28:83-86 (Oct., 1949).

103 SCHICKEL, RICHARD. "Catholic, Protestant, Jew; The Conflicts that Divide Us," *Look,* 22:102-106 (Sept. 30, 1958).

Reply. "Straw-man Issues; The Church in Caricature," by William Lawrence, *Social Justice Review,* 52:3-6 (April, 1959).

104 SELEKMAN, SYLVIA KOPALD. "A Wave of the Past; Lessons of the Anti-Catholic Movement in the United States," *Menorah Journal,* 31:18-33 (Jan., 1943).

105 "Separation of Church and State," I) "The Historical Background," by James Hastings Nichols, *Christian Century,* 65:265-68 (March 3, 1948), II) "Free Am-

erican Education," by John L. Childs, *Christian Century*, 65:378-80 (April 28, 1948).

> Discussion. "There is Also Secularist Indoctrination," F. Ernest Johnson, *Christian Century*, 65:515 (May 26, 1948). In this relation see "Is the Wall of Separation an Iron Curtain?" *America*, 83:75 (April 22, 1950).

106   SCHUSTER, GEORGE NAUMAN. "The Catholic Controversy," *Harper's Magazine*, 199:25-32 (Nov., 1949).

107   SNEE, JOSEPH M., S.J. "Religious Disestablishment and the Fourteenth Amendment," *Washington University Law Quarterly*, 1954:371-407 (Dec., 1954).

108   "Statement on Church and State," *Christianity and Crisis*, 8:90 (July 5, 1948).

> Twenty-seven Protestant leaders express their belief that "Jefferson's oft quoted words 'wall of separation'" are a "misleading metaphor" when used "in the interpretation of the Constitution."

109   SUTHERLAND, ARTHUR EUGENE, JR. "Due Process and Disestablishment," *Harvard Law Review*, 62:1306-1344 (June, 1949).

110   TINNELLY, JOSEPH T., C.M. "Preservation of American Institutions," *The Jurist*, 38:121-127 (April, 1958).

> Sermon delivered in Saint Matthew's Cathedral, Washington, D.C., Sunday, Jan. 26, 1958.

111   WAITE, EDWARD F. "Jefferson's 'Wall of Separation': What and Where?" *Minnesota Law Review*, 33:494-516 (April, 1949).

112   WECLEW, ROBERT G. "Church and State: How Much Separation?" *De Paul Law Review*, 10:1-26 (Autumn-Winter, 1960).

113   WEIGEL, GUSTAV, S.J. "Catholic and Protestant: End of War?" *Thought*, 33:383-87 (Autumn, 1958).

114   —————. "The Church and the Democratic State," *Thought*, 27:165-184 (Summer, 1952). Comment. John J. McLoughlin, 569-71 (Winter, 1952-53).

115 WEINTRAUB, RUSSELL J. "Religious Freedom," *Religious Education,* 55:418-423 (Nov.-Dec., 1960).

116 WHITE, ROBERT J. "Certain Aspects of the Legal Status of the Church in the United States," *The Jurist,* 1:20-49 (Jan., 1941).

117 ZWIERLEIN, FREDERICK JAMES. "Religious Freedom in the Bill of Rights: The Senate Subcommittee on Constitutional Rights," *Social Justice Review,* 48:267-72 (Nov., 1955).

II

Church-State Relationships in American Education

Note. The status of the Church-related private school, the role of the public school in dealing with religion and the issue of government aid to Church-related schools remain major areas of concern in the Church-State-school controversy.

Discussions covering more than one area were grouped in the following list along with material about specific issues not dealt with in subsequent units. This list supplements all other units.

Since the study of the 'school question' in American Church-State relationships would be very incomplete without access to the pertinent litigation, court decisions have been listed in this bibliography. Persons unaccustomed to interpreting citations and locating decisions should consult the notes in the two tables which precede unit I. Introductory materials in legal bibliography are suggested in *Appendix E*.

Studies on Church-related private schools, as such, are beyond the scope of this bibliography, but some useful references about this closely related field are suggested in the background material which follows.

A. BACKGROUND MATERIAL

1. BIBLIOGRAPHIES:

118 BRICKMAN, WILLIAM WOLFGANG. *Selected Bibliography on the History of Church-State Relations in Education in the United States.* New York: New York University School of Education, April, 1959. 16pp. (Mimeographed)

> See also his book review articles, Nos. 193-196 in this unit.

118a BURR, NELSON R. "Religion and Education," in James Ward Smith and A. Leland Jamison, eds., *A Critical Bibliography of Religion in America* (Religion in American Life, Vol. 4). Princeton, N.J.: Princeton University Press, 1961. Pp.654-677.

119 COHEN, IVA. *Church, State and Education; A Selected Bibliography,* 2d. rev. ed. New York: Library of Jewish Information, the American Jewish Committee, 1954. 28pp. (Mimeographed)

> Contents. "Church and State," 1-7. "Religious Education and Public Schools," 8-21. "Released Time," 21-24. "Federal Aid to Parochial Schools," 24-28.

2. SUMMARY MATERIAL AND LEGAL BACKGROUND:

120 AMERICAN JEWISH CONGRESS. COMMISSION ON LAW AND SOCIAL ACTION. *Digest and Analysis of State Attorney General Opinions Relating to Freedom of Religion and Separation of Church and State.* New York: the Congress, 1959. 89pp. (Mimeographed)

121 BEACH, FRED FRANCIS, and WILL, ROBERT F. *The State and Nonpublic Schools.* ... (U. S. Office of Education, Misc., No. 28, 1958). 152pp.

121a BRICKMAN, WILLIAM WOLFGANG. "Chronological Outline of Church-State Relations in American Education," in William W. Brickman and Stanley Lehrer, eds.,

Religion, Government and Education. New York: Society for the Advancement of Education, 1961. Pp.251-269.

122 EMERSON, THOMAS IRWIN, and HABER, DAVID (eds.). "Organized Religion and Education," in *Political and Civil Rights in the United States; A Collection of Legal and Related Materials.* 2d ed. Buffalo, N.Y.: Dennis & Co., 1958. Vol. II, pp.1130-1180.

> Contents. "History of Secular and Religious Education in the United States," 1130-1137. "Aid to Education," 1137-1157. "Released Time," 1157-1170. "Bible Reading," 1170-1176. "Flag Salute and Other Compulsory Practices Offensive to Certain Religions," 1176-1180.

123 LISCHKA, CHARLES NICHOLAS. *Private Schools and State Laws; The text as well as a Classified Summary of all State Laws Governing Private Schools, in force in 1924. Also, State Laws and State Supreme Court Decisions Governing Bible Reading in the Public Schools, with a Supplement for 1925.* (National Catholic Welfare Conference. Bureau of Education. Education Bulletins, No. 2, Jan., 1926). Washington, D.C.: The Conference. 296pp.

> N.B.: This compilation was also issued as *Education Bulletins, No. 4,* Oct., 1924. 220pp. and *Supplement: Education Bulletins, No. 3,* Jan., 1926. 76pp.

124 ZOLLMAN, CARL FREDERICK GUSTAV. "Religious Education," in *American Church Law.* Saint Paul, Minn.: West Publishing Co, 1933. Pp.68-101.

3. EARLIER STUDIES:

125 BROWN, SAMUEL WINDSOR. *The Secularization of American Education, as Shown by State Legislation, State Constitutional Provisions and State Supreme Court Decisions* (Teachers College, Columbia University, Contributions to Education, No. 49). New York: Teachers College, Columbia University, 1912. 160pp.

126 CONFREY, BURTON. *Secularism in American Education: Its History (Catholic University of America, Educational Research Monographs, Vol. 6, No. 1).* Wash-

ington, D.C.: Catholic University of America, 1931. 153pp.

4. CHURCH-RELATED SCHOOLS (Suggested Readings) :

127   BLAIR, BERTHA. "Church-related Elementary and Secondary Schools in Continental United States," National Council of the Churches of Christ in the United States of America, *Information Service*, Vol. 38, No. 1, Part 1 (January 3, 1959). 8pp.

See also "Religious Day Schools under Protestant Auspices," *Information Service*, Vol. 31, No. 18 (May 3, 1952). 4pp.

128   "The Catholic School System, 1900-1950," *Catholic School Journal*, 51:103-147 (April, 1951). A symposium in a special golden jubilee issue.

129   LOTZ, PHILIP HENRY (ed.). *Orientation in Religious Education*. New York: Abingdon-Cokesbury, 1950.

See: "Jewish Education in America," by Israel S. Chipkin, 501-518. "Roman Catholic Education," by Edward J. Heffron, 519-532.

130   LUTHERAN EDUCATION ASSOCIATION. *100 Years of Lutheran Education (Fourth Yearbook)*. River Forest, Illinois: Lutheran Education Association, 1947.

131   "Religion," *School and Society*, 82:98-110 (Oct. 1, 1955). (Special Issue).

Contents. "The Protestant Day School," D. Campbell Wyckoff, 98-101. "American Catholic Schools Today," John E. Wise, 101-104. "The Hebrew Day School Movement," Joseph Kaminetsky, 105-107.

132   RIAN, EDWIN HAROLD. *Christianity and American Education*. San Antonio, Texas: The Naylor Co., 1949. 272pp. Bibliography: 241-254.

See: "Roman Catholic Schools," 121-179. "Protestant Schools," 183-240.

133   STELLHORN, A. C. "Schools of the Lutheran Church, Missouri Synod," *School and Society*, 87:225-227 (May 9, 1959).

B. BOOKS AND PAMPHLETS

134 BELL, BERNARD IDDINGS. *Crisis in Education; a Challenge to American Complacency.* New York: McGraw Hill, 1949. 237pp.

> See pages 127-47, 148-77, 221-24. Excerpts. *Catholic Digest*, 13:73-77 (July, 1949).
>
> REVIEWS:
> *America*, 81:129 (Apr. 23, 1949) C. Keenan
> *Books on Trial*, 8:14-15 (May, 1949) Sister M. Teresa Francis
> *Catholic World*, 169-472 (Sept., 1949) E. B. Jordan
> *College and University*, 25:155-57 (Oct., 1949) S. A. Nock
> *Current History*, 17:162 (Sept., 1949)
> *High Points*, 32:76-77 (Sept., 1950) S. C. Lucey
> *Bulletin from Virginia Kirkus' Book Shop Service*, 17:146 (March 15, 1949)
> *New York Times Book Review*, p.7 (Apr. 24, 1949) Paul Ramsey
> *New Yorker*, 25:112 (May 7, 1949)
> *San Francisco Chronicle*, p.18 (Apr. 28, 1949)
> *Saturday Review of Literature*, 32:18 (Apr. 30, 1949) H. A. Overstreet
> *School and Society*, 69:286 (Apr. 16, 1949)
> *Survey Graphic*, 85:339 (June, 1949) H. W. Hintz

135 BENNETT, JOHN COLEMAN. "Church, State and Education," in *Christians and the State.* New York: Scribner, 1958. pp.236-251.

136 BLUM, VIRGIL CLARENCE, S.J. *Your Child's Religious Liberty.* St. Paul, Minn.: Cathechetical Guild, 1955. 64pp.

137 BOWER, WILLIAM CLAYTON. *Church and State in Education.* Chicago: University of Chicago Press, 1944. 103pp. Bibliography: pp.96-99.

> REVIEWS:
> *Annals of the American Academy of Political and Social Science*, 235:170 (Sept., 1944) Ephraim Fischoff
> *Catholic Historical Review*, 32:127-28 (Apr., 1946)
> *Catholic School Journal*, 44:273 (Nov., 1944)
> *Churchman*, 158:17 (June 1, 1944) W. P. Sears
> *Crozer Quarterly*, 21:260 (July, 1944) C. H. Moehlman
> *Education*, 64:578 (May, 1944)

Educational Administration and Supervision, 31:442 (Oct., 1945) L. E. Train
Elementary School Journal, 44:620 (June, 1944) R. W. Organ
Harvard Educational Review, 14:311 (Oct., 1944) P. J. Braisted
Journal of Religion, 24:282 (Oct., 1944) J. D. Russell
School and Society, 59:191 (March 11, 1944); 67:248-49 (March 27, 1948) W. W. Brickman
Thought, 19:504-07 (Sept., 1944)

138 BRADY, JOSEPH HUGH. *Confusion Twice Confounded; the First Amendment and the Supreme Court, an Historical Study.* 2d. ed. South Orange, N.J.: Seton Hall University Press, 1955. 192pp.

REVIEWS:
America, 93:48 (Apr. 9, 1955) P. Heffron
American Benedictine Review, 6:232 (Summer, 1955) J. Flynn
American Ecclesiastical Review, 132:212 (March, 1955) D. Granfield
Annals of the American Academy of Political and Social Science, 300:161 (July, 1955) J. W. Madden
Best Sellers, 14:190 (Feb. 1, 1955) E. Stanford, O.S.A.
Books on Trial, 13:335 (May, 1955) J. Noth
Catholic Historical Review, 41:178 (July, 1955) G. Kramer
Catholic Lawyer, 1:242 (July, 1955) W. White
Catholic University Law Review, 5:203 (May, 1955) F. J. Powers
Catholic World, 181:236 (June, 1955) M. M. Clarke
Dominicana, 40:205 (June, 1955)
Extension, 49:31 (May, 1955) P. Pruche, S.J.
Interracial Review, 28:107 (June, 1955) F. Quinn, S.J.
New York University Law Review, 30:1464 (Nov., 1955)
The Priest, 11:940 (Nov., 1955)
The Sign, 34:78 (Apr., 1955)
Thought, 30:272 (Summer, 1955) W. Frasca

Special comment. Robert E. Rodes. "Religious Education and the Historical Method of Constitutional Interpretation - A Review Article," *Rutgers Law Review,* 9:682-95 (Summer, 1955).

139 BRICKMAN, WILLIAM WOLFGANG, and LEHRER, STANLEY (eds.). *Religion, Government and Education.* New York: Society for the Advancement of Education, Inc., 1961. 292pp.

Contents. Preface, Stanley Lehrer, 7-8. Introduction, William W. Brickman, 9-12. Constitutional and Legal Aspects of the Church-State-School Problem, Harold H. Punke, 17-30. Public Aid to Religious Education, V. T. Thayer, 31-41. Religion and Public Education, Rolfe Lanier Hunt, 42-52. Public Service of the Lutheran School, Wm. A. Kramer, 53-63. The Controversy

Over Public Support to Parochial Schools, Bernard J. Kohlbrenner, 64-75. A Jewish Viewpoint on Church-State-School Relations, Philip Jacobson, 76-92. Religious Celebrations in School, J. Stephen Sherwin, 93-103. Baccalaureate in Broadhead: Interfaith Tension, William W. Boyer, 104-110. Debate Over Public Aid to Religious Schools, William W. Brickman, 111-143. Church, State and School in International Perspective, William W. Brickman, 144-247. Chronological Outline of Church-State Relations in American Education, William W. Brickman, 251-269. Selected Documents on the Church-State-School Issue, William W. Brickman, 270-283. Contributors and Their Biographical Background, Stanley Lehrer, 284-288.

Excerpts. "Church and State in Education," *School and Society*, 89:217-236 (May 6, 1961) and 237-251 (May 20, 1961).

140 BUTTS, ROBERT FREEMAN. *The American Tradition in Religion and Education (Beacon Press Studies in Freedom and Power, Vol. 5).* Boston: Beacon Press, 1950. 230pp. "Notes": pp.213-24.

Discussions. Robert Freeman Butts and John Courtney Murray. "Church, State and School: Discussion of American Tradition in Religion and Education," *Catholic School Journal,* 51:197-99 (June, 1951).

Thurston N. Davis. "Footnote on Church-State," *School and Society*, 81:180-82 (June 11, 1955). Reply. Robert Freeman Butts. "Say Nothing Of My Religion," *School and Society*, 81:182-84, 186-88 (June 11, 1955). Lee L. Rockwell, "Another Footnote on Church-State," 82:107-08 (Oct. 1, 1955). Comment. William F. Pashby, 82:172-73 (Nov. 26, 1955).

REVIEWS:

America, 83:579-81, 853 (Sept. 9, 1950) J. M. O'Neill
American Historical Review, 56:605-606 (April, 1951) W. W. Brickman
American Political Science Review, 44:1024 (Dec., 1950) David Fellman
Annals of the American Academy of Political and Social Science, 271:224 (Sept., 1950) F. J. Brown
Catholic Historical Review, 38:485 (Jan., 1953) E. M. Conners
Christian Century, 67:882 (July 5, 1950) Stanley Lichtenstein
College and University, 26:130-2 (Oct., 1950)
Crozer Quarterly, 27:268-70 (July, 1950) C. H. Moehlman
Educational Administration and Supervision, 37:125-28 (Feb., 1951) W. F. Bruce
Educational Forum, 15:121-22 (Nov., 1950) S. E. Frost, Jr.
Educational Research Bulletin, 30:134-35 (May, 1951) C. L. Foster
Elementary School Journal, 51:233-34 (Dec., 1950) E. J. Chave
George Washington Law Review, 19:114-18 (Oct., 1950) A. L. Scanlan
International Journal of Religious Education, 27:29 (Oct., 1950) E. L. Shaver

International Affairs, 26:587 (Oct., 1950) N. Micklem
Journal of Religion, 32:141-44 (Apr., 1952) S. E. Mead
Bulletin from Virginia Kirkus' Book Shop Service, 18:166 (March 15, 1950)
New York Times Book Review, p.24 (May 21, 1950) H. M. Kallen
Progressive Education, 28:100-03 (Jan., 1951) A. S. Clayton
Religious Education, 45:370 (Nov., 1950) H. C. Stuntz
San Francisco Chronicle, p.26 (May 21, 1950)
School and Society, 71:286 (May 6, 1950), 72:440 (Dec. 30, 1950) W. W. Brickman

141   CIARLANTINI, LINO ALDO. *The Liberty of the School and Family Education.* New York: Educational Publishers, 1954. 253pp.

REVIEWS:
Catholic Educational Review, 53:204-05 (March, 1955)
American Catholic Sociological Review, 17:166 (June, 1956)

142   COGLEY, JOHN (ed.). "The School Question," in *Religion in America; Original Essays on Religion in a Free Society.* New York: Meridian Books, 1958. Pp.118-167.

Contents. "Religion, Democracy and Public Education," Will Herberg, 118-147. "Religion and Education in a Free Society," James Hastings Nichols, 148-167.

N.B.: Another report of these papers and of the discussions which followed them was prepared by Donald McDonald. See "The School Question," in *Religion and Freedom; Report from a Seminar Sponsored by the Fund for the Republic (An Occasional Paper on the Role of Religion in the Free Society).* New York: Fund for the Republic, 1958. Pp.18-26.

Discussions of papers reported in this booklet are not given in *Religion in America.*

143   COLWELL, ERNEST C. "Protestantism: Opportunities in American Education," in William K. Anderson (ed.), *Protestantism, A Symposium.* Nashville, Tenn.: Commission on Courses of Study, The Methodist Church, 1944. Pp.250-59.

144   CURRAN, FRANCIS XAVIER, S.J. *The Churches and the Schools, American Protestantism and Popular Elementary Education.* Chicago: Loyola University Press, 1944. 152pp. Bibliography: pp.131-139.

Also: Protestant Parochial Schools," *Thought*, 28:19-38 (Spring, 1953).

145 DOYLE, JOHN. "Catholic Education and its Relation to the State," in Roy J. Deferrari (ed.), *Essays on Catholic Education in the United States.* Washington: Catholic University of America Press, 1942. Pp.25-40.

146 EDUCATIONAL POLICIES COMMISSION ("National Education Association of the United States" and "American Association of School Administrators"). *Public Education and the Future of America.* Washington, D.C.: National Education Association of the United States, 1955. 98pp.

> The Church-State implications of this report have been pointed out in a number of discussions.
> Brickman, William W. "Public and Religious Schools, *School and Society,* 82:108-09 (Oct. 1, 1955).
> Davis, Thurston N. "NEA Pulls a Boner," *America,* 93:348, 349, 352 (July 2, 1955).
> Fitzpatrick, Edward A. "A Program to Eliminate Private Schools?" *Catholic School Journal,* 55:123-25 (Apr., 1955) and 59:32-33 (Nov., 1959).
> Kane, John J. *Catholic-Protestant Conflicts in America.* Chicago, Henry Regnery Co., 1955. Pp.111-17.
> Ryan, William Granger. "No Place for Private Schools?" *Commonweal,* 62:33, 40, 42, 44 (Apr. 15, 1955).
> "There Went Forth Decrees from Educational Monopolists," *Catholic Educational Review,* 53:133-35 (Feb., 1955).
>
> *Educational Leadership,* 12:318-320 (Feb., 1955) P. M. Halverson
> *Nation's Schools,* 55:79 (March, 1955) K. E. Howe
> *Teacher College Record,* 56:412-413 (April, 1955) W. H. E. Johnson
> *Virginia Journal of Education,* 48:26-27 (Apr., 1955) W. Jansen

147 EDWARDS, NEWTON. *The Courts and the Public Schools.* Revised ed. Chicago: University of Chicago Press, 1955. 622pp.

> See: "State and Church in Relation to Education," pp.47-53.

148 EHLERS, HENRY. "Religion and Public Education," in *Crucial Issues in Education; An Anthology.* New York: Holt, 1955. Pp.118-178. Bibliography with each unit.

> Review: *Teachers College Record,* 57:52 (Oct., 1955) D. G. Scanlon

149 FUND FOR THE REPUBLIC. *Religion and the Schools*

(*Fund for the Republic Pamphlets*). New York: the Fund, 1959. 96pp.

Contents. "Foreword," John Cogley, 3. "Education for a Nation of Nations," Robert Gordis, 5-33. "A Case of Distributive Justice," William Gorman, 34-63. "A Problem of Culture," F. Ernest Johnson, 64-78. "An Unreligious View," Robert Lekachman, 79-96.

Replies. John Augustine Hardon, S.J., "Parochial Schools Under Fire; Reply to Robert Gordis." *Homiletic and Pastoral Review*, 59:1093-1098 (Sept., 1959).

John Augustine Hardon, S.J., "Catholics and Religion in the Public Schools; Gordis' and Lekachman's Positions Refuted," *Homiletic and Pastoral Review*, 60:23-28 (Oct., 1959)

Robert F. Drinan, S.J., "Catholic Schools and Public Funds," *Catholic Educator*, 30:131-33, 141 (Oct., 1959).

150 GANNON, ROBERT I., S.J. "Public Versus Private Schools," in *After Black Coffee*. New York: Declan X. McMullen Co., 1947. Pp.46-55.

151 GIBBONS, RAY. "The Relation of Church and State," in Philip Henry Lotz (ed.), *Orientations in Religious Education*. New York: Abingdon Cokesbury Press, 1950. Pp.479-490.

For an earlier summary, see Carl Zollman, "The Relation of Church and State," in Philip Henry Lotz, *Studies in Religious Education*. Nashville, Tenn.: Cokesbury, 1931. Pp.403-433.

152 HARTNETT, ROBERT CLINTON, S.J., and BOUSCAREN, ANTHONY. *The State and Religious Education*. Edited by Charles Keenan. New York: American Press, 1952. 47pp.

Contents. "McCollum Case: Government May Not Aid Religion." "Zorach Case: Retreat from McCollum." "Dr. Conant Raises the Divisive Bogy." "Community Relations of Catholic Schools." "California: Tax Exemption for Private Schools."

153 HERBERG, WILL. "Religion and Education in America," in James Ward Smith and A. Leland Jamison, eds., *Religious Perspectives in American Culture* (Religion in American Life, Vol. 2). Princeton, N.J.: Princeton University Press, 1961. Pp.11-51.

154 HUBER, RAPHAEL M. *The Part Played by Religion in the*

History of Education in the United States. Trenton, N.J.: MacCrellish & Quigley, 1951. 36pp.

155 JACOBSON, PHILIP, and MCLAUGHLIN, FRED. "Religion and American Education," in H. Gordon Hullfish (ed.), *Educational Freedom in an Age of Anxiety (Twelfth Yearbook of the John Dewey Society).* New York, Harper: 1953. Pp.108-32.

REVIEWS:
America, 89:53-54 (Apr. 11, 1953) W. Codd, S.J.
Educational Administration and Supervision, 40:121-24 (Feb., 1954) W. F. Bruce
Educational Forum, 18:367-68 (March, 1954) R. J. Poindexter
Harvard Educational Review, 23:145-46 (1953) F. E. Ellis
Journal of Higher Education, 25:49-50 (Jan., 1954) M. C. Otto
Religious Education, 49:58 (Jan., 1954) P. B. Maves
Teachers College Record, 55:59-60 (Oct., 1953) L. Suttell

156 KANE, JOHN JOSEPH. "The School Question," in *Catholic-Protestant Conflicts in America.* Chicago: Regnery, 1955. Chapter 8, pp.104-25.

157 LEHMANN, LEO HERBERT. *The Catholic Church and the Public Schools (Veripam no. 4).* New York: Agor Publishing Co., 1947. 23pp.

158 LOUGHERY, (Sister) M. BERNARD FRANCIS. *Parental Rights in American Educational Law, their Bases and Implementation.* 2d. ed. Washington, D.C.: Catholic University of America Press, 1957. 248pp. Bibliography: pp.221.235.

Revision of the author's doctoral dissertation.

REVIEW:
School and Society, 85:123 (Apr. 13, 1957) W. W. Brickman

159 MCCLUSKEY, NEIL GERARD, S.J. *Catholic Viewpoint on Education (Catholic Viewpoint Series,* John J. Delaney, Editor). Garden City, N.Y.: Hanover House, 1959. 192pp.

Foreword by Rt. Rev. Monsignor Frederick G. Hochwalt.

160 MCGRATH, (Sister) MARY BERNARD. *The Compatibility of Catholic Schools and Democratic Standards.* Washington, D.C.: Catholic University of America Press,

1948. 116pp. (Doctoral dissertation) Bibliography: pp.107-116.

161 MCLAUGHLIN, (Sister) RAYMOND. *A History of State Legislation Affecting Private Elementary and Secondary Schools in the United States, 1870-1945.* Washington, D.C.: Catholic University of America Press, 1946. 348pp. (Doctoral dissertation) Bibliography: pp.225-240.

"Constitutional provisions and state laws affecting private elementary and secondary schools in force in 1945," pp.241-341.

162 MARKE, DAVID TAYLOR. "Sectarian Education in America," in *Educational Law Simplified* (*Legal Almanac Series, No. 17*). New York: Oceana Publications, 1949. Pp.68-94. Same. *Phi Delta Kappan,* 31:234-247 (Jan., 1950).

The reissue of this number in the *Legal Almanac Series* (*Schools and the Law,* by Edmund Reutter, Jr., 1960) does not contain this special section.

163 MELBY, ERNEST OSCAR, and PUNER, MORTON (eds.). *Freedom and Public Education.* New York: Praeger, 1953. 314pp. "Selected references" at the end of each chapter.

An anthology. Some selections discuss aspects of church-state-school relationships.

REVIEWS:
America, 89:49-50 (Apr. 11, 1953) A. Farrell
American Association of University Women. Journal, 46:235-36 (May, 1953) C. Warren
American Catholic Sociological Review, 14:118 (June, 1950) J. O'Brien
American Teacher Magazine, 37:22 (May, 1953)
Annals of the American Academy of Political and Social Science, 289:204 (Sept., 1953) W. E. Givens
Catholic Educational Review, 51:422-23 (June, 1953) B. Rattigan
Childhood Education, 30:151 (Nov., 1953) W. A. Yauch
College and University, 29:116-17 (Oct., 1953) R. L. Taylor
Bulletin from Virginia Kirkus' Book Shop Service, 21:25 (Jan. 1, 1953)
Library Journal, 78:523 (March 15, 1953) H. H. Bernt
Michigan Education Journal, 30:442 (Apr., 1953)
National Association of Secondary School Principals Bulletin, 37:136 (Oct., 1953)
National Municipal Review, 43:267 (May, 1954) T. B. Mason

New York Herald Tribune, Book Review, p.8 (Aug. 9, 1953)
Theodore Brameld
Saturday Review, 36:30 (Sept. 12, 1953) J. S. Brubacher
School and Society, 77:392 (June 20, 1953) W. W. Brickman

164 MOEHLMAN, CONRAD HENRY. *The Church as Educator.*
New York: Hinds, Hayden & Eldredge, Inc., 1947.
184pp.

REVIEWS:

Adult Education Journal, 6:163 (July, 1947)
*Annals of the American Academy of Political and Social
Science,* 258:163-64 (July, 1948) R. H. Abrams
Christian Century, 64: 527 (Apr. 23, 1947) A. M. Motter
Churchman, 161:17 (March 15, 1947) K. M. Chworowsky
Clearing House, 21:567 (May, 1947) L. Mones
Crozer Quarterly, 24:266 (July, 1947) M. S. Enslin
Elementary School Journal, 48:398-99 (March, 1948) C. D.
Champlin
Nation's Schools, 39:32-33 (June, 1947) B. H. Bode
School (Elementary & Secondary Eds.), 36:152-53 (Nov.,
1947)
School and Society, 65:152 (Feb. 22, 1947); 67:248 (March
27, 1948) W. W. Brickman
Theology Today, 5:435-36 (Oct., 1948) J. D. Butler

165 MORRISON, CHARLES CLAYTON. "Protestantism and the
Public School" in *Can Protestantism Win America?*
New York: Harper, 1948. Pp.17-32.

Same. *Christian Century,* 63:490-93 (Apr. 17, 1946).
Same, abridged. Title: "Our Crop of Religious Illiterates,"
Readers' Digest, 49:127-28 (Aug., 1946). Discussion. *Christian
Century,* 63:593-94 (May 8, 1946).

REVIEWS:

Christian Century, 66:16 (Jan. 5, 1949) H. P. Van Dusen
Christian Science Monitor, p.11 (May 5, 1949) Neil Martin
Commonweal, 44:60-61 (May 3, 1946)
Crozer Quarterly, 26:147-48 (Apr., 1949) E. E. Aubrey
Theology Today, 7:266-67 (July, 1950) H. P. Douglass
U. S. Quarterly Book List, 5:173 (June, 1949)

166 MULLEN, ARTHUR FRANCIS. "The Fight for Educational
Freedom," in *Western Democrat.* New York: Wilfred
Funk, 1940. Pp.206-226. Condensed in the *Catholic
Digest,* 7:27-34 (May, 1943).

This is the story behind *Meyer v. State of Nebraska,* 262
U.S. 390; 43 Sup. Ct. 625 (1923), and the two state decisions which it reversed: *Meyer v. State of Nebraska,* 106 Neb.
657; 187 N.W. 100 (Neb., Feb. 16, 1922) and *Nebraska District of Evangelical Synod of Missouri, Ohio and Other States*

v. *McKelvie et al.*, 104 Neb. 93; 187 N.W. 927 (Neb., Apr. 19, 1922).

For additional information see "Parochial Schools and the State," in Orville Herman Zabel, *God and Caesar in Nebraska; A Study of the Legal Relationship of Church and State, 1854-1954 (Nebraska University. Studies: new series, no. 14).* University of Nebraska, 1955. Pp.130-159.

167   NETTLETON, TULLY. *Church, State and School (Beacon Reference Series).* Boston: Beacon Press, 1948. 37pp.

168   NOLL, JOHN FRANCIS. *Our National Enemy Number One: Education without Religion.* Huntington, Ind.: 1942. 312pp.

REVIEWS:

America, 67:275 (June 13, 1942)
American Ecclesiastical Review, 106:461 (June, 1942)
Ave Maria, 55:666 (May 23, 1942)
Extension, 37:15 (July, 1942)
Journal of Religious Instruction, 13:85 (Sept., 1942)
The Sign, 21:760 (July, 1942)
Social Justice Review, 36:285 (Dec., 1943)

169   O'BRIEN. JOHN ANTHONY. *Why the Catholic School? An Answer to a Common Question.* St. Paul, Minn.: Catechetical Guild, 1947. 31pp.

170   O'NEILL, JAMES MILTON. *The Catholic in Secular Education.* New York: Longman's Green, 1956. 172pp. Bibliography: pp.167-71.

REVIEWS:

America, 95:327 (June 30, 1956) N. McCluskey
Best Sellers, 16:141 (July 1, 1956) P. Lilly
Books on Trial, 14:428 (July, 1956) T. Bowdern
Catholic World, 184:238 (Dec., 1956) F. P. Kilcoyne
Dominicana, 41:266 (Sept., 1956)
Homiletic and Pastoral Review, 57:94 (Oct., 1956) F. Morriss
Interracial Review, 29:139 (Aug., 1956) A. O'Reilly
Jubilee, 4:49 (Oct., 1956)
Library Journal, 81:909 (Apr. 15, 1956) C. L. Higgins
Religious Education, 52:76 (Jan., 1957) Y. M. Fallandy
The Sign, 36:64 (Aug., 1956)
Thought, 32:160 (Spring, 1956) J. Donohue

171   ————. *Religion and Education Under the Constitution.* New York: Harper, 1949. 388pp. Bibliography: pp.319-325.

Special review. Leo Pfeffer, "Church and State: Something Less than Separation," *University of Chicago Law Review,* 19:1-29 (Autumn, 1951).

N.B.: Remarks about this article by Wilber G. Katz, "Freedom of Religion and State Neutrality," *University of Chicago Law Review,* 20:426-440 (Spring, 1953), at p.434.

REVIEWS:

America, 81:125 (Apr. 23, 1949) R. C. Hartnett
American Bar Association Journal, 35:758-61 (Sept., 1949) J. C. Hayes
Ave Maria, 69:506-07 (Apr. 16, 1949) T. Langley
Books on Trial, 8:14 (May, 1949) J. P. Kleinz
Catholic Educational Review, 47:425 (June, 1949) J. D. Hannan
Catholic Historical Review, 36:69-70 (Apr., 1950) W. E. McManus
Catholic School Journal, 49:18A (May, 1949)
Catholic World, 170:153 (Nov., 1949) J. McSorley
Christianity and Crisis, 12 no. 10:75-77 (1952) M. S. Bates
Christian Science Monitor, p.16 (June 16, 1949) Tully Nettleton
Churchman, 163:15 (Dec. 1, 1949) J. H. Titus
College and University, 25:469-71 (Apr., 1950) H. S. Fraser
Commonweal, 50:299 (July 1, 1949) B. W. Palmer
Educational Forum, 14:122-24 (Nov., 1949) S. E. Frost, Jr.
Fordham Law Review, 18:319-23 (Nov., 1949) F. X. Conway
Harvard Law Review, 63:729-32 (Feb., 1950) L. Clark
Historical Bulletin, 28:23-24 (Nov., 1949) P. Barrett
Homiletic and Pastoral Review, 49:846-52 (Aug., 1949) J. P. Donovan
International Journal of Religious Education, 25:28 (July, 1949) E. L. Shaver
Library Journal, 74:663 (Apr. 15, 1949) Nathaniel Stewart
New York Times Book Review, p.16 (July 10, 1949) B. F. Wright
Notre Dame Lawyer, 25:597-99 (Spring, 1959) C. Manion
Progressive Education, 28:100-03 (Jan., 1951) A. S. Clayton
St. John's Law Review, 24:343-45 (Apr., 1950) E. Fagan, Jr.
School and Society, 69:237 (March 26, 1949) ; 71:280 (May 6, 1950) W. W. Brickman
Sign, 28:60 (June, 1949) D. Bulman
Thought, 24:394-97 (Sept., 1949) J. L. Burke
University of Pittsburgh Law Review, 12:154-60 (Fall, 1950) W. Berg, Jr.

172 PRESBYTERIAN CHURCH OF THE U.S.A., BOARD OF CHRISTIAN EDUCATION. *The Church and the Public Schools, An Official Statement Approved by the 169th General Assembly of the Presbyterian Church in the United States of America.* Philadelphia, Pa.: The Board, 1957. 30pp.

COMMENTS:

Christianity and Crisis, 17:187-190 (Jan. 20, 1958) F. Ernest Johnson
Christianity Today, 2:3-7 (March 3, 1958) Carl Frederick Howard Henry
Christianity Today, 2:10-12 (May 12, 1958) Edward W. Greenfield
Commonweal, 66:243-44 (June 7, 1957)
Commonweal, 66:424 (July 26, 1957) John Cogley

173 PUNKE, HAROLD HERMAN. *Community Uses of Public School Facilities.* New York: King's Crown Press, 1951. 247pp. "Notes": pp.218-232.

A study of litigation. See units on the "Bible in the Schools," 35-89; "Arrangements between local school boards and denominational groups," 67-71; "Transportation," 72-83.

REVIEWS:

Clearing House, 26:247 (Dec., 1951) J. B. Greene
Educational Research Bulletin, 32:24 (Jan., 1953) R. E. Hubbard
Elementary School Journal, 53:423-24 (March, 1953) O. E. Peterson
Georgetown Law Journal, 40:642-43 (May, 1952) R. J. Zanard

174 REILLY, DANIEL FLAVIAN. *The School Controversy, (1891-1893).* Washington, D.C.: Catholic University of America Press, 1943. 302pp. (Doctoral dissertation) Bibliography: pp.277-290.

A brief account of this controversy is available in Patrick Henry Ahern, *The Life of John J. Keane, Educator and Archbishop, 1839-1918.* Milwaukee, Wisconsin: Bruce, 1955. Pp. 127-140.

REVIEWS:

Americas, 2:254-56 (Oct., 1945)
Dominicana, 29:197-99 (Sept., 1944)
Historical Bulletin, 23:46 (Jan., 1945)
Homiletic and Pastoral Review, 44:799 (July, 1944)
Review of Politics, 7:108 (Jan., 1945)
Thought, 20:561-63 (Sept., 1945)

175 RIAN, EDWIN HAROLD. *Christianity and American Education.* San Antonio, Texas: The Naylor Company, 1949. 272pp. Bibliography: pp.241-254.

See: "Public Schools," 3-117; "Roman Catholic Schools," 121-179; "Protestant Schools," 183-240.

REVIEWS:

America, 81:611-12 (Sept. 10, 1949) R. C. Hartnett
Catholic World, 170:319 (Jan., 1950) J. McSorley
International Journal of Religious Education, 26:32 (Nov., 1949)
Religious Education, 45:374-75 (Nov., 1950) J. C. Granbery
School and Society, 71:277 (May 6, 1950) W. W. Brickman
Thought, 25:562 (Sept., 1950) F. A. Ryan

176 *The Role of the Independent School in American Democracy*. Milwaukee, Wis.: Marquette University Press, 1956. 146pp.

Papers, delivered at a conference on education, the fifth in a series of anniversary celebrations commemorating the seventy-fifth anniversary of Marquette University (May 8, 9 and 10, 1956).

Contents: "The School Question in Mid-Twentieth Century," John Courtney Murray, S.J., 1-16. "Why American Catholics Conduct Schools," The Most Rev. Matthew F. Brady, 17-26. "The Partnership of the Independent and Public Schools in the Future of America—I," Msgr. Frederick G. Hochwalt, 27-36. "The Partnership of the Independent and Public Schools in the Future of America—II," by William G. Carr, 37-50. "The Partnership of the Independent and Public Schools in the Future of America—III," Arthur S. Adams, 51-60. "The Historical Background of the Independent School in the United States," William W. Brickman, 61-82. "The Contribution of Catholic Schools in America," Rev. James P. Shannon, 83-92. "Current Issues Facing the Independent Schools," Sister Mary Emil, I.H.M., 93-108. "Current Issues Facing Independent Colleges," Glenn L. McConagha, 109-18. "Philosophical Background of the Independent Schools," Jerome Kerwin, 129-36. "Constitutional and Legal Foundations of the Independent Schools," John W. McDonald, 137-46.

177 RUSSELL, JAMES EARL (ed.). "Religion in Education," in *National Policies for Education, Health and Social Services (Columbia University Bicentennial Conference Series)*. Garden City, N.Y.: Doubleday, 1955. Pp.412-99.

Contents: "Religion in American Life," Ralph H. Gabriel, 413-31. "Religion and General Education," F. Ernest Johnson, 432-36. "Constitutions, Churches and Schools," Arthur E. Sutherland, 437-55. "Report of the Recorder," Philip H. Phenix, 457-87. "Summing Up," Barbara Ward Jackson, 488-99.

REVIEWS:

American Sociological Review, 21:254 (Apr., 1956) A. M. Lee
Annals of the American Academy of Political and Social Science, 302:180 (Nov., 1955) C. H. Graton

Library Journal, 80:1594 (July, 1955) Paul Wasserman
Social Service Review, 30:215-16 (June, 1956) M. Hathway
U. S. Quarterly Book Review, 11:385 (Sept., 1955)

178 SCHACHNER, NATHAN. *Church, State and Education.*
New York: American Jewish Committee, 1947. 48pp.
(Reprinted from the *American Jewish Year Book,*
Vol. 49, 1947-48).

179 SPURLOCK, CLARK. *Education and the Supreme Court.*
Urbana, Ill.: University of Illinois Press, 1955.
252pp. Bibliography: pp.239-244.

Covers 39 cases decided from 1789 to 1953. Includes prac-
tically all those primarily concerned with education and other
representative cases on issues affecting it.

REVIEWS:
*Annals of the American Academy of Political and Social Sci-
ence,* 307:157 (Sept., 1956) R. J. Harris
Catholic Educational Review, 54:420-21 (Sept., 1956) T. O.
Martin
College and University, 31:366 (Jan., 1956) J. E. Flaherty
Journal of Higher Education, 28:56-57 (Jan., 1957) H. A.
Sprindt
Journal of Legal Education, 9:133 (1956) E. C. Bolmeier
Library Journal, 81:196 (Jan. 15, 1956) R. W. Johnson
National Elementary Principal, 35:46 (May, 1956) M. Remm-
lein
Nation's Schools, 57:120, 122 (March, 1956) L. O. Garber
Teachers College Record, 58:51-53 (Oct., 1956) D. Van Cleve

180 THAYER, VIVIAN TROW. *The Attack Upon the American
Secular School (Beacon Studies in Freedom and
Power).* Boston: Beacon Press, 1951. 257pp. Bibli-
ography: pp.239-49.

REVIEWS:
American Journal of Sociology, 57:605-06 (May, 1952) P. B.
Horton
American Political Science Review, 45:908 (Sept., 1951)
Christian Century, 68:740-71 (June 20, 1951) W. E. Garrison
Churchman, 166:16 (Aug., 1951) Joseph Fletcher
Bulletin from Virginia Kirkus' Book Shop Service, 19:221
(Apr. 15, 1951)
School and Society, 85:124-25 (Apr. 13, 1957) W. W. Brick-
man
Sign, 31:64 (Sept., 1951) D. Bulman
U. S. Quarterly Book Review, 7:266 (Sept., 1951)
Yale Review, new series, 41:142 (Autumn, 1951) W. L. Sperry

181 —————. *The Relationship of Church and State in*

Education. Horace Mann League of the United States of America, Inc., 1950. 18pp.

Address delivered at the twenty-seventh annual congress of the Horace Mann League, Atlantic City, N.J., Feb. 26, 1950.

182 —————. *Religion in Public Education.* New York: Viking Press, 1947. 212pp.

REVIEWS:
America, 77: (supplement) xxii, xxiii (Apr. 12, 1947) R. H. Mahoney
Best Sellers, 6:190-91 (Feb. 15, 1947)
Catholic Educational Review, 45:185-87 (March, 1947) E. V. Stanford
Catholic World, 165:131-35 (May, 1947) Joseph McSorley
Chicago Sun Book Week, p.4 (Feb. 16, 1947) J. T. Frederick
Current History, 12:373 (Apr., 1947)
Illinois Law Review, 43:903-04 (Jan.-Feb., 1949) C. Manion
International Journal of Religious Education, 24:31 (Jan. 1948)
Bulletin from Virginia Kirkus' Book Shop Service, 15:65 (Feb. 1, 1947)
Nation, 164:309 (March 15, 1947) Albert Guerard
Nation's Schools, 40:27 (Aug., 1947) E. J. Chave
New York Times Book Review, p.22 (June 22, 1947) Leo Chapiro
Progressive Education, 25:249 (Oct., 1947) U. Reinhardt
Saturday Review of Literature, 30:12 (March 1, 1947) G. E. Shipler
School and Society, 67:249 (March 27, 1948) W. W. Brickman
Springfield Union, p.2 (June 21, 1947) H. H. Wagner

183 —————. "Sectarian Attacks upon Public Education," in *Public Education and its Critics* (*Kappa Delta Pi lecture series*). New York: Macmillan, 1954. Pp.30-72.

Revised and expanded from a previous article in *Educational Theory,* April, 1953.

REVIEWS:
Cleveland Open Shelf, p.23 (Aug., 1954)
Current History, 29:195 (Sept., 1955) D. Denker
Educational Forum, 19:374 (March, 1955) W. H. Congdon
Educational Leadership, 12:62 (Oct., 1954) P. M. Halverson
Quarterly Journal of Speech, 40:325-31 (Oct., 1954) R. Murphy
Saturday Review, 37:29 (Sept. 11, 1954) Benjamin Fine
School and Society, 80:139 (Oct. 30, 1954) W. W. Brickman

184 WHITE HOUSE CONFERENCE ON EDUCATION, WASHINGTON, 1955. *A Report to the President.* The Committee for the White House Conference on Education. Wash-

ington, D.C.: U. S. Government Printing Office, 1956. 126pp.

The report includes a few statements about nonpublic schools (pp.10, 20, 103). The Church-State aspect was discussed in the literature about the conference.

COMMENTS:

Edward A. Fitzpatrick, "The White House Conference on Education and the Bishops," *Catholic School Journal*, 56:11-12 (Jan., 1956).

Neil G. McCluskey, S.J., "Inside the White House Conference," *America*, 94:326-28 (Dec. 17, 1955).

Charles James McNeil, "What Should our Schools Accomplish?" *Catholic School Journal*, 56:40-43 (Feb., 1956).

Clint Pace, "The White House Conference on Education," *National Catholic Educational Association Bulletin*, 52:49-51 (Aug., 1955).

James Shappelle, "Two-way Interpretation of Schools through the White House Conference," *Catholic Educational Review*, 54:1-3 (Jan., 1956).

"White House Conference on Education—Four Reports," *Religious Education*, 51:5-17 (Jan.-Feb., 1956). Reports by Gerald E. Knoff, Neil G. McCluskey, John Slawson, Jordan L. Larson.

N.B.: Numerous reports and reactions are listed in the *Education Index*, Vol. 10 (June, 1955-May, 1957), pp.1484-1486.

185 WILLIAMS, JERRE STOCKTON. *The Supreme Court Speaks.* Austin: University of Texas Press, 1956. 465pp.

Relevant cases in "Part 6," the Gobitis, Barnette, Everson and Zorach decisions.

186 WITKOWIAK, STANISLAU BENEDICT. *Limitations Imposed upon the Rights and Powers of Respective States over Education by the United States Supreme Court.* Washington, D.C.: Catholic University of America Press, 1942. 174pp. Bibliography: pp.162-170. (Doctoral dissertation)

C. PERIODICAL ARTICLES

187 BADGER, WILLIAM V. "Parental Rights: A Child's Curriculum," *Educational Administration and Supervision*, 39:88-102 (Feb., 1953).

188 BLUM, VIRGIL CLARENCE, S.J. "The Baptists Revive Parochial Schools," *Catholic World*, 191:246-252 (July, 1960).

189 BOEHNING, RUSSELL M., S.J. "Why Catholics Pay Twice," *Catholic School Journal*, 47:266-67 (Oct., 1947).

190 BOLMEIER, EDWARD CLAUDE. "What the Courts Say about Church and Public School Relationships," *Yearbook of School Law*, 1953, pp.83-106.

191 BRADY, WILLIAM O. "Church and State and School," *Catholic Digest*, 14:1-5 (Dec., 1949). Condensed from the *Daily Argus Leader*, Sioux Falls, S.D., Oct. 3, 1949.

192 BRANT, IRVING. "Church and State in America," *American Mercury*, 67:685-92 (Dec., 1948).

193 BRICKMAN, WILLIAM WOLFGANG. "Religion and Education," *School and Society*, 67:245-53 (March 27, 1948).

194 ——————. "The School and the Church-State Question," *School and Society*, 71:273-82 ((May 6, 1950).

195 ——————. "Religious Education," *School and Society*, 76:262-67 (Oct. 25, 1952).

196 ——————. "Church, State and School," *School and Society*, 85:122-27, (Apr. 13, 1957).

197 BROOKE, WALTER. "The Case for Christian Day Schools," *Christianity Today*, 3:11-12 (August 31, 1959).

198 BRUSTAT, AUGUST W. "The Case for Religious Schools," *The Freeman,* 6:43-47 (May, 1956).

Reprinted by the Foundation for Economic Education, Irvington-on-the-Hudson, N.Y.

199 BURKE, JAMES L., S.J. "Busses, Released Time and the Political Process," *Marquette Law Review,* 32:179-87 (Dec., 1948).

200 BURNHAM, PHILIP. "Double Fight for Schools," *Commonweal,* 71:14 (Oct. 2, 1959).

201 BUTLER, EUGENE J. "Legislation Affecting Catholic Schools," *Catholic Educational Review,* 39:3-11 (Jan., 1941).

202 BUTTS, ROBERT FREEMAN. "Church and State in American Education," *Teachers College Record,* 52:145-57 (Dec., 1950.)

203 —————. "James Madison, the Bill of Rights and Education," *Teachers College Record,* 60:121-128 (Dec., 1958).

204 —————. "States' Rights and Education," *Teachers College Record,* 58:189-97 (Jan., 1957).

205 CAESAR, J. HAROLD. "A United Front for Church and School," *Religious Education,* 37:366-70 (Nov.-Dec., 1942).

206 CATHOLIC CENTRAL UNION (VEREIN) OF AMERICA. "Declaration of Principles Adopted by the 104th Convention of the Catholic Central Union (Verein) of America, Conducted at San Francisco, Cal., July 31 to August 5, 1959. *Social Justice Review,* 52:176-179 (Sept., 1959) and following issues.

Pertinent topics: "The Crisis in Education," p.179 (Sept.), "Discrimination Against Private Schools," pp.214-215 (Oct.).

207 CALVERT, WALTER DUDLEY. "When Parochial Schools Failed," *Christian Century,* 74:1349, 1350 (Nov. 13, 1957).

208   "Church and State—Religion and Politically Organized Society," *Catholic University Law Review,* 1:89-92 (Jan., 1951).

209   "The Church and the School," *Phil Delta Kappan,* 40: 301-317, 333-338 (May, 1959) ; 347-358 (June, 1959).

A series of articles.

Contents. (May) "Christian and Public Schools: Some Specific Problems," 302-304, 333-338. "Student Value Judgements Do Differ in Public, Religious and Private Schools," Richard Prince, 305-307. "The Role of Religion in a Private University," Carroll V. Newsom, 308-310. "Teaching Religion in the State University," John William Ashton, 311-313. "A Five Year Study of Teacher Education and Religion," Avis Leo Sebaly, 314-317.

Contents. (June) "Voluntary Religious Isolation—Another School Segregation Story," Maurice Jacob Thomas, 347, 348, 354-358. "Academic Freedom and Tax Support for Independent Education," Virgil Clarence Blum, S.J., 349-353.

210   COGLEY, JOHN. "The School Question," *Commonweal,* 66:424 (July 26, 1957).

CONANT, JAMES BRYANT. See *Appendix D.*

211   CONNELL, EDWARD A. "The Missing Ingredient," *The Sign,* 28:58-60 (Dec., 1948).

212   CORWIN, EDWARD S. "The Supreme Court as the National School Board," *Thought,* 23:665-683 (Dec., 1948).

Revised in *Law and Contemporary Problems,* 14:3-22 (Winter, 1949).

213   COSTANZO, JOSEPH F. "Thomas Jefferson, Religious Education and Public Law," *Journal of Public Law,* 8:81-108 (Spring, 1959).

214   COSWAY, RICHARDS, and TOEPPER, ROBERT A. "Religion and the Schools," *University of Cincinnati Law Review,* 17:117-43 (March, 1948).

215   CUNNEEN, JOSEPH E. "Catholics and Education," *Commonweal,* 58:437-41 (Aug. 7), 461-464 (Aug. 14, 1953).

216 DAWSON, CHRISTOPHER. "Education and the State," *Commonweal,* 65:423-27 (Jan. 25, 1957). Discussion. 512-13 (Feb. 15, 1957).

217 DONAHUE, CHARLES. "Freedom and Education, the Pluralist Background," *Thought,* 27:542-60 (Winter, 1952-53). Comment. Joseph W. Evans, "Pluralism," pp.571-74.

218 DONOVAN, CHARLES F., S.J. "October 1942, or October 1875?" *Homiletic and Pastoral Review,* 43:97-104 (Nov., 1942).

219 ——————. "Have These United States of Ours an Established Religion?" *Homiletic and Pastoral Review,* 52:413-19 (Feb., 1952). Discussion. 52:652-54 (Apr., 1952)

The two preceding articles refer to a speech delivered by the Honorable Edmund F. Dunne, Chief Justice of the Territorial Court of Arizona, at Tucson, Feb. 2, 1875, before a joint session of the Arizona legislature. It was printed in several editions. References follow.

Our Public Schools: Are they Free for All or Are they Not? 3rd ed. New York: T. D. Egan, 1875. 40pp.

Same text. *Brownson's Quarterly Review,* pp.516-38 (Oct., 1875).

220 DRINAN, ROBERT F., S.J. "Parental Rights and American Law: the Oregon School Case—Twenty-five Years After," *Catholic World,* 172:21-26 (Oct., 1950).

Remarks about the case of *Pierce v. Society of Sisters,* 268 U.S. 510; 45 S. Ct. 571 (1925).

The complete record was printed as *Oregon School Cases,* Baltimore, Maryland: Belvedere Press, 1925. 943pp.

221 ——————. "Pressure Groups and Church-State Relations," *Homiletic and Pastoral Review,* 50:996-1,000 (Aug., 1959).

A review of briefs *amici curiae* in the Everson and McCullum cases.

222 DYKSTRA, JOHN W. "Parochial Divisions in American Life," *Christian Century,* 75:465-67 (Apr. 6, 1958).

223   "The Educational Battleground," *The Wall Street Journal,* August 25, 1959, p.8, Cols. 1 and 2.

> Comment. Edward A. Fitzpatrick. *Catholic School Journal,* 59:32-33 (Nov., 1959).
>
> Remarks in reply to statements made at a conference of public school administrators, meeting at Teachers College, Columbia University, during which private secondary schools were termed "wasteful" and "inherently undemocratic."

224   EDWARDS, NEWTON. "Scope of Federal Authority over Education," *Yearbook of School Law,* 1955, pp.79-90.

225   ELLIS, FREDERICK EUGENE. "Aspects of the Relations of the Roman Catholic Church to Public Education," *The Educational Forum,* 19:65-74 (Nov., 1954).

226   ENSLEY, (Bishop) FRANCIS GERALD, and BUFORD, JOHN LESTER. "Why don't Methodists Have Parochial Schools?" *Together: The Midmonth Magazine for Methodist Families,* 2:30-32 (Nov., 1958).

> Contents. "Methodist Postal System Just as Logical," Bishop Francis Gerald Ensley, 30, 32. (Text reprinted by Protestants and Other Americans United for the Separation of Church and State, Washington, D.C.). "We Have Public Schools: Let's Back Them!" John Lester Buford, 31,32.

227   FARRELL, ALLAN PETER, S.J. "Relationships of Government, Religion and Education," *National Catholic Educational Association Bulletin,* 46:164-68 (Aug., 1949).

228   —————. "Two Systems—Parochial and Public," *America,* 76:15-16 (Oct. 5, 1946).

229   FELLMAN, DAVID. "Separation of Church and State in the United States: a Summary View," *Wisconsin Law Review,* 1950:427-78 (May, 1950).

230   FERRIER, MARTIN K. "Judicial Control of the School Program," *Yearbook of School Law,* 1956, pp.81-105.

> Bible reading, prayer, released time, flag salute and pledge of allegiance considered with other aspects.

231   FISHER, ROGER J. "Separation of Church and State," *Boston University Law Review,* 33:68-80 (Jan., 1953).

232　FISHMAN, JOSHUA AARON (Compiler). "Subsidized
　　　Pluralism in American Education," edited by Wil-
　　　liam W. Brickman and Stanley Lehrer, *School and
　　　Society,* 87:245-268 (May 23, 1959).

　　　　　Issued as a supplement.

　　　　　Contents. "Publicly Subsidized Pluralism: The European
　　　and the American Context," Joshua A. Fishman, 246-248.
　　　"Quality and Freedom Through Pluralism," Robert Francis
　　　Creegan, 248-251. "The Segregational Aspects of Publicly Sub-
　　　sidized Pluralism," Richard L. Plaut, 251-253. "Religion and
　　　State Power: The American Pattern," Charles Donahue, 253-
　　　256. "Subsidized Pluralism: Its Implications for Intergroup
　　　Relations," Martin Philip Chworowsky, 257-260. "Ethnic-
　　　Religious Groups and Publicly Subsidized Pluralism," Marshall
　　　Sklare, 260-263. "The American Dilemma of Publicly Sub-
　　　sidized Pluralism," Joshua A. Fishman, 264-267.

233　FITZPATRICK, EDWARD AUGUSTUS. "Federal Government
　　　and the Schools," *Catholic School Journal,* 59:67-69
　　　(March, 1959).

234　——————. "The Right to Educate," *Catholic School
　　　Journal,* 58:27-29 (March, 1958).

235　"Forbidden Establishment of Religion," *The Jurist,*
　　　10:98-103 (Jan., 1956).

236　FRASCA, WILLIAM R. "Confusion in the Supreme Court,"
　　　Thought, 28:545-70 (Winter, 1953-1954).

237　FULLER, EDGAR. "Public Schools and Separation of
　　　Church and State," *School Executive,* 68:11-18 (Feb.,
　　　1949). Same, condensed. *Education Digest,* 14:3-6
　　　(May, 1949).

238　GABEL, RICHARD JAMES. "Religion After the Adoption
　　　of the Federal and State Constitutions," *Catholic
　　　Educational Review,* 38:385-99 (Sept., 1940).

　　　　　Deals mainly with religion in education.

239　GANNON, ROBERT IGNATIUS, S.J. "Relationships of
　　　Government, Religion and Education," *National
　　　Catholic Educational Association Bulletin,* 46:52-57
　　　(Aug., 1949).

240   GARDNER, GEORGE KNOWLES. "Liberty, the State and
      the School," *The Catholic Lawyer,* 1:285-96 (Oct.,
      1955).

241   GIBBONS, RAY. "Protestantism and Public Education,"
      Social Action, 15:4-27 (Feb. 15, 1949).

242   HARPSTER, JAMES E. "Religion, Education and the Law,"
      Marquette Law Review, 36:24-66 (Summer, 1952).

243   HARTNETT, ROBERT CLINTON, S.J. "Is Religious Educa-
      tion Divisive?" *Thought,* 24:17-22 (March, 1949).
      Same. *Catholic Mind,* 47:321-24 (July, 1949), and
      *The Right to Educate; Democracy and Religious
      Education,* New York: American Press, 1949. Pp.43-
      48.

244   ——————. "Religion and American Democracy,"
      America, 77:569-71 (Aug. 23, 1947). "Congress and
      the School Question," *America,* 77:599-602 (Aug. 30,
      1947). "The Courts and Aid to School," *America,*
      77:683-86 (Sept. 20, 1947).

      N.B.: These titles form part of a series.

245   ——————. "Revolution and Counterrevolution in the
      School Controversy," *Vital Speeches,* 16:560-62
      (July 1, 1950). Same, abridged, with title "Are
      Religious Schools American?" *Catholic Digest,* 14:
      79-81 (Sept., 1950).

      Reply. Gordon C. Lee. "Catholic Educational Policy Ex-
      amined," *National Education Association Journal,* 40:47-48
      (Jan., 1951).

      Rejoinder. Robert C. Hartnett. "Mr. Lee Examines Catholic
      School Policy," *America,* 84:581-83 (Feb. 17), 635-36 (March
      3, 1951).

246   HAYES, JOHN C. "Law and the Parochial School: a
      Formulation of Conflicting Positions," *Catholic Law-
      yer,* 3:99-111 (Apr., 1957).

247   HEALY, CLETUS, S.J. "Catholic and Public Schools,"
      Catholic World, 169:451-55 (Sept., 1949).

248   HENLE, R. J., S.J. "American Principles and Religious
      Schools," *Saint Louis University Law Journal,* 3:237-

51 (Spring, 1955). Same (without footnotes), *Catholic Mind*, 54:301-09 (June, 1956).

249 HILLBRAND, EARL KANSAS. "Cooperation between School and Church," *Kentucky School Journal*, 22:14-16 (Jan., 1944).

250 HUNT, ROLFE LANIER. "Education of a Neophyte," *National Council Outlook*, 8:15, 16 (Sept., 1958).

Comment. *America*, 100:59 (Oct. 18, 1958).

251 INGRAM, T. ROBERT. "Education and Faith: A Plea for Christian Day Schools," *Christianity Today*, 5:3-5 (Feb. 27, 1961).

252 "The Issue of Sectarianism," *Progressive Education*, (Special issue), 26:97-128 (Feb., 1949).

Contents. "Let's Make the Sectarian Issue Clear, an Editorial," B. Othanel Smith, 97-98. "Religion in Education: the Issues," William Heard Kilpatrick, 98-102; "Church-State Separation and the Public Schools," R. Lawrence Siegel, 103-11; "New Threats to the Principle of Separation," John L. Childs, 112-15; "How Sectarian Schools Receive Public Aid," Thomas E. Benner, 115-17; "The Public Schools Build Moral Character," Hazel Flett & Alice Pittman, 119-20; "What do Sectarians Want?" B. Othanel Smith, 121-24; "Fanning the Fires of Freedom—A Review of Two Recent Books," A. S. Clayton, 125-27.

REVIEW:
School and Society, 71:278 (May 6, 1950) W. W. Brickman.

253 JENNET, RAYMOND JAMES. "America Needs the Catholic School," *Catholic School Journal*, 51:234 (Sept., 1951).

254 JOHNSON, FREDERICK ERNEST. "Issues Emerging in Religion and General Education," *Religious Education*, 37:356-58 (Nov.-Dec., 1942).

255 JOHNSON, GEORGE. "Government and Education," *Catholic Educational Review*, 38:321-29 (June, 1940). (Address delivered at the Eighth American Scientific Congress, Washington, D.C., May 16, 1940.)

256 JOHNSON, LEIGHTON H. "Unemphasized Aspects of the

Independent-School Question," *School and Society,* 87:239-240 (May 23, 1959).

Includes remarks about the charge that independent schools are "undemocratic."

257 KATZ, WILBER GRIFFITH. "Freedom to Believe," *Atlantic Monthly,* 192:66-69 (Oct., 1953).

257a KAUPER, PAUL G. "Church and State: Cooperative Separation," *Michigan Law Review,* 60:1-40 (Nov., 1961).

258 KNIGHT, DAVID M. "State Regulation of Independent Schools," *America,* 93:263-65 (June 4, 1955).

259 KOHLBRENNER, BERNARD JOHN. "Some Practical Aspects of the Public Character of Private Education," *School and Society,* 86:348-351 (Oct. 11, 1958).

260 KONVITZ, MILTON RIDVAS. "Whittling Away Religious Freedom; the Current Threat to Separation of Church and State," *Commentary,* 1:5-13 (June, 1946).

Replies. R. Lawrence Siegel, "Religion in the Public Schools," 2:188-89 (Aug., 1946); Abraham L. Feinberg, 2:388-89 (Oct., 1946).

261 MCDEVITT, JOHN. "Aspects of Canon and Civil Law Relative to Parochial Schools," *The Jurist,* 14:481-503 (Oct., 1954).

262 MCINTYRE, JAMES FRANCIS (Cardinal). "The Spirit of America—Freedom Under God," *Vital Speeches,* 22: 57-59 (Nov. 1, 1955).

263 MCKEOUGH, MICHAEL JOHN, O. Praem. "The State, the Church and the School," *Catholic Educational Review,* 47:291-302 (May, 1949).

264 MCMANUS, WILLIAM E. "Are Catholic Schools Divisive?" *Interracial Review,* 29:100-03 (June, 1953).

265 ——————. "Relations of Government, Religion and Education," *National Catholic Educational Association Bulletin,* 46:291-99 (Aug., 1949).

266 —————. "A Summary Report of School Legislation," *Catholic Educational Review*, 44:323-28 (June, 1946). Also: "As Congress Went Home," 44:398-405 (Sept., 1946).

267 McNICHOLAS, JOHN TIMOTHY, O.P., "No Wall Between God and the Child," *National Catholic Educational Association Bulletin*, 44:53-64 (Aug., 1947).

268 MAHONEY, CHARLES JOSEPH. "Face the Issue: Vital Need of Religious Education for American Democratic Society," *Vital Speeches*, 17:658-63 (Aug. 15, 1951).

269 MAHONY, THOMAS HARRISON. "A Legal Inquiry on the Church-State Problem in the U.S.A." *Catholic Educational Review*, 48:75-95 (Feb., 1950).

270 —————. "The State and Religion for the Past Fifty Years," *Catholic School Journal*, 51:134-37 (Apr., 1951).

271 MALONEY, CORNELIUS. "An Evaluation of Present Opposition to Parochial Schools," *Catholic Educational Review*, 44:162-68 (March, 1946).

272 MILNER, LUCILLE B. "Church, State and Schools," *New Republic*, 113:177-80 (Aug. 13, 1945).

　　　Reply. Howard L. Parsons, 113:440-41 (Oct. 1, 1945).

273 MOLLOY, THOMAS E. "Church and State in Education," *Catholic Mind*, 33:366-76 (Oct. 8, 1935).

274 MONTAVON, WILLIAM FREDERICK. "Liberty of Education," *Catholic Mind*, 41:16-19 (Dec., 1943).

275 MORGAN, JOY ELMER. "Our American Heritage of Religious Freedom," *National Education Association Journal*, 40:91 (Feb., 1950).

　　　Reply. "N.E.A. Doubts our Wisdom," *America*, 84:635-36 (March 3, 1951).

276 MORKOVSKY, JOHN L. "The Welfare of the Child by Government, Religion, Education," *Catholic Action*, 32:6-7 (Feb., 1950).

277   MUENCH, ALOYSIUS J. "Religion in Education," *Social Justice Review*, 48:19-22 (Apr.), 54-56 (May), 90-92 (June), 140-42 (July-Aug.), 212-14 (Sept., 1955).

278   MURPHY, WILLIAM J. "Religion in Democratic Education," *Vital Speeches*, 6:397-99 (Apr. 15, 1940).

279   MURRAY, JOHN COURTNEY, S.J. "The Religious School in a Pluralistic Society," *The Catholic Mind*, 54:502-11 (Sept., 1956). Same. *The Role of the Independent School in American Democracy*, Milwaukee, Wis.: Marquette University Press, 1956. Pp.1-16.

THE NATION (Periodical). See *Appendix A.*

280   NATIONAL CATHOLIC EDUCATIONAL ASSOCIATION. "The Right to Educate—The Role of Parents, Church, State," *National Catholic Educational Association, Bulletin* (Proceedings issue), 55:1-416 (August, 1958).

A symposium in the proceedings of the 55th annual meeting.

Contents. "The Right to Educate—The Role of Parents, Church, State," Rev. Joseph T. Tinnelly, 35-46. "Some Canonical and Theological Aspects of Church-State Relations," Rev. James A. O'Donohoe, 54-60. "The Catholic Obligation to Educate," Rev. Neil G. McCluskey, S.J., 176-181. "The Right to Educate and the Correlative Duty," Harold G. Reuschlein, 182-188. "The Right to Educate: Home," John I. McEnerney, 189-191. "The Right of the Church to Educate," Rt. Rev. Msgr. Joseph G. Cox, 192-193. "The Right to Educate: State," John B. Taulane, 194-196. "The Importance of Religion in American Education," Joseph C. Duggan, 236-242. "The State's Right to Educate" (Summary), Very Rev, Thomas O. Martin, 243. "The Parents' Right to Educate," John G. Gallen, 244-246. "The Right to Educate—The Role of the Church," Most Rev. Stephen A. Leven, 300-302. "The Right to Educate—The Role of the State," Randolph E. Wise, 303-306. "The Right to Educate—The Role of the Parent," Miriam Theresa Rooney, 307-311.

Some addresses of this symposium were reprinted in the *Catholic Lawyer*, 4:196-243 (Summer, 1958).

The address of Rev. Thomas O. Martin is given only in summary here. The full text may be read in the *Catholic Lawyer*, 4:218-224 (Summer, 1958).

281   NATIONAL CATHOLIC WELFARE CONFERENCE. "The Place of the Private and Church-Related Schools in Ameri-

can Education," Statement issued by the Catholic
Bishops of the United States, Nov. 20, 1955. *Catholic
Mind,* 54:111-116 (Feb., 1956).

Comment. George Axtelle, "A Reply to the Bishops of the
United States," *Progressive Education,* 33:155, 160 (Sept.,
1956).

282 ————————. "The Teaching Mission of the Church,"
Statement issued by the Catholic Bishops of the
United States, November 16, 1958. *Catholic Mind,*
57:181-185 (March-April, 1959). Same. *Catholic
School Journal,* 59:49-51 (January, 1959).

Comment. Reinhold Niebuhr, *Christianity and Crisis,* 18:178
(Dec. 22, 1958).

283 NATIONAL EDUCATION ASSOCIATION OF THE UNITED
STATES. "The State and Sectarian Education," *National Education Association, Research Bulletin,* 24:
1-44 (Feb., 1946).

Reply. William E. McManus and Vincent C. Allred, *A
Review of "The State and Sectarian Education,"* Washington,
D.C.: National Catholic Educational Association, 1946. 24pp.

New Report. "The State and Sectarian Education," *National
Education Association, Research Bulletin,* 34:169-215 (Dec.,
1956).

284 NELSON, CLAUD. "Public Education and Protestant Concensus," *Christianity and Crisis,* 19:130-132 (Sept.
21, 1959).

285 O'KEEFE, WILLIAM J. "The Status of Parochial and
Private Schools Under the Law," *National Catholic
Educational Association Bulletin,* 55:291-97 (Aug.,
1958).

286 O'NEILL, JAMES MILTON. "Church, Schools and the
Constitution," *Commentary,* 3:562-70 (June, 1947).

287 OXNAM, GARFIELD BROMLEY. "Church, State and
Schools," *Nation,* 168:67-70 (Jan. 15, 1949).

288 "Parents' Right to Prescribe Religious Education of
Children," *De Paul Law Review,* 3:83-89 (Autumn-
Winter, 1953).

289 PARSONS, WILFRID, S.J. "Dangerous Trends in American Education," *Catholic Digest,* 13:83-86 (Oct., 1949). Condensed from *Cor,* Sacred Heart Monastery, Hale Corner, Wisconsin (Sept., 1949).

290 PFEFFER, LEO, and O'NEILL, JAMES MILTON. "The Meaning of the Establishment Clause—A Debate: No Law Respecting an Establishment of Religion (Leo Pfeffer), Nonpreferential Aid to Religion is not an Establishment of Religion (J. M. O'Neill)," *Buffalo Law Review,* 2:225-78 (Spring, 1953).

291 PFEFFER, LEO. "Religion, Education and the Constitution," *Lawyers Guild Review,* 8:387-99 (May-June, 1948).

292 PIERCE, DONALD J. "Parents' Rights in Public Education," *America,* 84:747-49 (March 31, 1951).

293 PITT, FELIX NEWTON. "Parochial Schools and the Public," *America,* 77 (section two): iv-viii (Apr. 12, 1947).

294 PUNKE, HAROLD HERMAN. "Religious Issues in American Public Education," *Law and Contemporary Problems,* 20:138-68 (Winter, 1955).

295 REINERT, PAUL C., S.J. "Freedom in American Education," *School and Society,* 87:472-473 (November 21, 1959).

296 "Religion and Education," *Commonweal,* 63:247-48 (Dec. 9, 1955).

297 "Religion and Education," *Progressive Education* (Special Issue), 33:129-60 (Sept., 1956).

> Contents. "A General Interpretation of Separation of Church and State and its Implications for Public Education," Myron Lieberman, 129-34, 160; "Religion and Educational Progressivism," Ward Madden, 135-38. Religion and Education, a Symposium: "Some Issues in Religion and Education," William H. Kilpatrick, 139-40; "The Relation Between Religion and Education," Robert Freeman Butts, 140-42; "Religion and Education," F. Ernest Johnson, 143-48; "Religion and Public Education," G. H. Reavis, 148-50; "Religion in Public Education," Jerome Nathanson, 151, 160; "The Place

of the Private and Church-Related Schools in American Education," National Catholic Welfare Conference, 152-54; "A Reply to the Bishops of the United States, American Humanist Association," George Axtelle, 155, 160.

298 "Religion and the State," *Law and Contemporary Problems,* 14:1-169 (Winter, 1949).

The studies in this issue center on the school question.

Contents. "The Supreme Court as National School Board," Edward S. Corwin, 3-22; "Law or Prepossession?" by John Courtney Murray, 23-43; "Separation of Church and State: The First Freedom," Milton R. Konvitz, 44-60; "Educational Cooperation Between Church and State," Alexander Meiklejohn, 61-72; "Religion, Education and the Supreme Court," Charles Fahy, 73-91; "Religious Education in the Schools," Russell N. Sullivan, 92-112 "Religion and Federal Aid to Education," William A. Mitchell, 113-43; "Preferment of Religious Institutions in Tax and Labor Legislation," Monrad G. Paulsen, 144-59.

The essay by John Courtney Murray listed above was reprinted, with introductory remarks, in Robert Green McCloskey (ed.), *Essays in Constitutional Law*, New York: Knopf, 1957. Pp.316-347. Editorial remarks, pp.310-316.

299 ROSSI, PETER HENRY, and ROSSI, ALICE SCHAERR. "Background and Consequences of Parochial School Education," *Harvard Educational Review,* 25:168-99 (Summer, 1957).

300 RYAN, CARL J. "Educators Forget the Need for God," *America,* 65:37-38 (Apr. 19, 1941).

Remarks on the occasion of the annual meeting of the American Association of School Administrators, 1941.

301 SHEERIN, JOHN B., C.S.P. "Are Catholic Schools Divisive?" (Editorial), *Catholic World,* 193:69-71 (May, 1961).

302 SHOCKLEY, GRANT. "Church, State and Education," *Journal of Religious Thought,* 8:125-33 (Spring-Summer, 1951).

303 SKEMP, THOMAS H. "Freedom of Religious Worship," *Marquette Law Review,* 25:19-22 (Dec., 1940).

304 SOPHRIN, ALAN. "The First Amendment and the Schools," *Ohio Bar,* 30:1003-10 (Nov. 25, 1957).

A review essay of cases.

305 STOUT, DAVID WILLIAM. "The Establishment of Religion under the Constitution," *Kentucky Law Journal,* 37:220-39 (March, 1949).

306 SUTHERLAND, ARTHUR E. "Constitutions, Churches and Schools," *Religious Education,* 51:64-70 (Jan., 1956) Bibliography included.

307 —————. "The Supreme Court and the Public School," *Harvard Educational Review,* 24:71-85 (Spring, 1954). "The Supreme Court and the Private Schools," *Harvard Educational Review,* 25:127-31 (Summer, 1955).

308 TIESZEN, D. W. "Legal Concepts Concerning Religious Influences in Public Education as Defined by State Courts of Last Resort," *Teachers College Record,* 55:61-69 (Nov., 1953).

309 UTHE, EDWARD W. "The State and Religious Education in the United States," *Lutheran Quarterly,* 2:324-35 (Aug., 1950).

310 WALSH, JOHN E., C.S.C. "The Parochial School: Partner or Pariah?" *School and Society,* 71:257-62 (Apr. 29, 1950).

311 ZWEIRLEIN, FREDERICK JAMES. "The Cauldron Continues to Boil," *Social Justice Review,* 42:363-66 (March, 1960).

D. UNPUBLISHED DISSERTATIONS

312 BADGER, WILLIAM V. "A Systematic Analysis of the United States Supreme Court Cases Dealing with Education: 1790-1951." Tallahassee, Fla.: Florida State University, 1953. (Unpublished doctoral dissertation)

313 BAYLES, LEWIS ALLEN. "Freedom and Power in a Multigroup Society as Related to the Control of Education." Columbus, Ohio: Ohio State University, 1957. (Unpublished doctoral dissertation)

314 BROWN, GEORGE W. "Sectarian Education in the United States, 1917-47." Chicago, Ill.: University of Chicago, 1949. (Unpublished doctoral dissertation)

315 BRUNNER, JAMES C. "A Critical Analysis of the Development of Arguments against Non-public Schools from the Oregon School Case to 1960." Washington, D.C.: Catholic University of America, 1960. (Unpublished master's dissertation)

316 BURGESS, JOHN A. "An Historical Review of the Interpretation of the First Amendment as Applied to Education." Boston, Mass.: Boston University, 1953. (Unpublished master's dissertation)

317 CARBIN, (Sister) MARY ANGELA, O.S.U. "The Attitude of the Republican Party toward Religious Schools, 1875-1880." Washington, D.C.: Catholic University of America, 1948. (Unpublished master's dissertation)

318 DOHERTY, JOHN F. "Developments of the Policies of the National Education Association of the United States." Washington, D.C.: Catholic University of America, 1957. (Unpublished master's dissertation)

A general study of N.E.A. See Policies: "Federal Aid," pp. 52-58; "Relationship with Private Schools," pp.74-82.

319   ELEFANTE, ANGELA MARIE. "The Rights and Duties of
the Independent School in the United States." Washington, D.C.: Catholic University of America, 1959.
(Unpublished doctoral dissertation)

> Abstract. (Same title) Catholic University of America
> Press, 1959. 26pp. Bibliography: pp.13-26.

320   ELLIS, FREDERICK E. "The Attitude of the Roman Catholic Church towards the Problem of Democratic
Freedom and American Public Education as Shown
in Selected Writings in Philosophy, the Philosophy
of History and the Philosophy of Education." Cambridge, Mass.: Harvard University, 1950. (Unpublished doctoral dissertation)

321   FARRINGTON, CHARLES A., S.J. "An Application of the
United States Office of Education to Catholic Edu-
cation." Washington, D.C.: Catholic University of
America, 1947. (Unpublished master's dissertation)

322   FOWERBAUGH, RAYMOND. "Requirements and Aids of the
Forty-Eight States Relative to Non-Public Elementary Schools." Washington, D.C.: Catholic University of America, 1955. (Unpublished master's dissertation)

323   HARRINGTON, ELEANOR M. "Non-School Use of Public
School Property: Its Legal Basis." New York, N.Y.:
Fordham University, 1941. (Unpublished doctoral
dissertation) Abstract. *Yearbook of School Law,*
1942. P.186.

> One division is entitled: "Religious and Sectarian Uses."

324   JOHNSON, JOSEPH N. "The Development of Certain
Legal Issues Concerning the Relationship Between
Public and Sectarian Education." Pittsburgh, Pa.:
University of Pittsburgh, 1953. (Unpublished doc-
torial dissertation)

> Abstract. *Yearbook of School Law,* 1954, pp.115-16.

> Issues discussed: public funds for non-public schools, sec-
> tarianism in public schools, flag salute.

325   MCCORMICK, ROBERT J. "An Analysis of U.S. Supreme
Court Cases Affecting Education Between 1942 and

1956." Washington, D.C.: Catholic University of America, 1956. (Unpublished master's dissertation)

326 MAYER, (Sister) MARY MARCIANA, O.P. "Twentieth Century Trends in Church-State Educational Relationships in the United States and England." Washington, D.C.: Catholic University of America, 1950. (Unpublished master's dissertation)

327 NICOLETTI, JAMES F. "The Attitude of the Church toward the Public School System." Washington, D.C.: Catholic University of America, 1951. (Unpublished master's dissertation)

328 OVERTON, PAUL D. "The Role of the Non-Public School in American Education with Especial Reference to Favorable and Unfavorable Criticisms." Macomb, Ill.: Western Illinois State College, 1955. (Unpublished master's dissertation)

329 ROCHE, (Rev.) WILLIAM M. "A Critical Analysis of the National Catholic Welfare Conference News Releases in the Field of Education." Washington, D.C.: Catholic University of America, 1958. (Unpublished master's dissertation)

330 SCANLAN, JOHN WILLIAM. "The State and the Non-State School Including a Consideration of the Support of the Non-State School." Evanston, Ill.: Northwestern University, 1940. (Unpublished doctoral dissertation)

Abstract. *Yearbook of School Law*, 1941, pp.192-93.

331 SMITH, DASIL A. "The Legal Status of the Private Schools as Determined by Court Decisions." Los Angeles, Calif.: University of Southern California, School of Education, 1950. (Unpublished doctoral dissertation)

Brief abstract. *Yearbook of School Law*, 1953, p.114.

332 TAYLOR, SALLIE R. "The Public and the Parochial School: a Personal and Social Adjustment Study." Gainesville, Fla.: University of Florida, 1955. (Unpublished master's dissertation)

333 TRAGER, FRANK N. "The Relation of Religion to Public Education in America," New York, N.Y.: New York University, 1952. (Unpublished doctoral dissertation)

E. STATE MATERIAL (With cases)

California:

334 HURLEY, MARK JOSEPH. *Church-State Relationships in Education in California.* Washington, D.C.: Catholic University of America Press, 1948. 189pp. Bibliography: pp. 168-180. (Doctoral dissertation)

335 "State, Church and Child—Statutory Provisions for School Permit," *Stanford Law Review,* 1:316-25 (Jan., 1949).

Connecticut:

336 MASON, (Sister) MARY PAUL. *Church-State Relationships in Education in Connecticut, 1633-1953.* Washington, D.C.: Catholic University of America Press, 1953. 324pp. Bibliography: pp.301-316. (Doctoral dissertation)

REVIEW:
School and Society, 85:123 (Apr. 13, 1957) W. W. Brickman

337 STEWART, GEORGE, JR. *A History of Religious Education in Connecticut to the Middle of the Nineteenth Century (Yale Studies in the History and Theory of Religious Education, I).* New Haven, Conn.: Yale University Press, 1924. 402pp. Bibliography, pp.371-384.

Hawaii:

338 DENVER, DANIEL J. "The Legal Status of Catholic Schools under the Constitutional and Statutory Law

of Hawaii." Washington, D.C.: Catholic University of America, 1953. (Unpublished master's dissertation)

Illinois:

339 KUCERA, DANIEL WILLIAM, O.S.B. *Church-State Relationships in Education in Illinois.* Washington, D.C.: Catholic University of America Press, 1955. 252pp. Bibliography: pp.234-47. (Doctoral dissertation)

Covers from the time of the French Missionaries to 1954.

REVIEW:

School and Society, 85:123 (Apr. 13, 1957) W. W. Brickman

Indiana:

340 WATSON, CARLOS. "Legal Status of Religion in Indiana Common Schools," *Teachers College Journal*, 22:57-61 (Dec., 1950).

Kansas:

341 GARDNER, HENRY. "Catholic Elementary and Secondary Education Under Kansas State Law." Washington, D.C.: Catholic University of America, 1954. (Unpublished master's dissertation)

Maryland:

342 BURNS, JOHN J. "Freedom of Private Schools in Maryland." St. Louis, Mo.: St. Louis University, 1955. (Unpublished master's dissertation)

343 MCCORMICK, LEO JOSEPH. *Church State Relationships in Education in Maryland.* Washington, D.C.: Catholic University of America Press, 1942. Bibliography: pp. 277-287. (Doctoral dissertation)

Massachusetts:

344 SMITH, SHERMAN MERRITT. *The Relation of the State to Religious Education in Massachusetts.* Syracuse, N.Y.: Syracuse University, 1926. 350pp. Bibliography: pp.323-339.

Based on the author's doctoral dissertation, Clark University, 1925.

Michigan:

345 DRACHLER, NORMAN. "The Influences of Sectarianism, Non-sectarianism, and Secularism upon the Public Schools of Detroit and the University of Michigan, 1837-1900." Ann Arbor, Mich.: University of Michigan, 1951. (Unpublished doctoral dissertation)

> Abstract. *Religious Education*, 47:215-16 (May-June, 1952) and *Dissertation Abstracts*, 11, no. 2:291-92. Microfilm. University Microfilms, Ann Arbor, Mich., Publication No. 2398.

346 LEWIS, THOMAS F. "A Study of an Attempt to Abolish Private Schools in Michigan in 1920 by Amending the Michigan State Constitution." Detroit, Michigan: University of Detroit, 1953. (Unpublished master's dissertation)

347 MCLEAN, WILLIAM MAURICE. "The Constitutional and Legal Basis for Undivided School Support and Current Practice in Michigan." Ann Arbor, Mich.: University of Michigan, 1950. (Unpublished doctoral dissertation)

> Abstract. "Michigan Public Schools and Religion; Summary of Doctoral Dissertation," *Michigan Education Journal*, 28:299-302 (Jan., 1951).

348 MARTIN, FRANK T. "The Michigan School Controversy." Washington, D.C.: Catholic University of America, 1949. (Unpublished master's dissertation)

> A history of the "Hamilton Amendment," an attempt to eliminate private schools, 1920 and 1924.

349 PELLETIER, ROBERT JOHN. "Educational Legislation Affecting Elementary and Secondary Schools in the State of Michigan." Washington, D.C.: Catholic University of America, 1950. (Unpublished master's dissertation)

Mississippi:

350 PICKARD, (Sister) M. GRACE. "The History and Present Status of Legal Relationships between the State of Mississippi and Private Elementary and Secondary Schools." Washington, D.C.: Catholic University of America, 1955. (Unpublished master's dissertation)

Nebraska:

351 ZABEL, ORVILLE HERMAN. *God and Caesar in Nebraska; a Study of the Legal Relationship of Church and State, 1854-1954 (Nebraska University. Studies: new series, no. 14).* University of Nebraska, 1955. 198pp. Bibliography: pp.187-190. (Doctoral dissertation)

REVIEW:
Catholic Historical Review, 42:493 (Jan., 1957)

New Hampshire:

352 KINNEY, CHARLES B., JR. *Church and State, the Struggle for Separation in New Hampshire, 1630-1900 (Columbia University. Teachers College. Studies in Education).* New York: Teachers College, 1955. 198 pp. Bibliography: pp.179-186.

REVIEW:
School and Society, 85:124 (Apr. 13, 1957) W. W. Brickman

New Jersey:
(Case Material)

353 *Board of Education of Mountain Lakes v. Maas, 56 N.J. Super. 245; 152 A.2d 394 (New Jersey, 1959).*

Decision upholding the practice of compulsory vaccination of school children against objections for reasons of conscience.

New York:

354 CAREY, ELIZABETH BRENNOCK. "The State and Non-public Schools." New York, N.Y.: New York University, 1949. (Unpublished doctoral dissertation)

Abstract. *Dissertation Abstracts,* 10, no. 1:25-27 (1950). Microfilm. Ann Arbor, Mich.: University Microfilms. Publication no. 1528.

A discussion of the problem in New York State, 1777-1948.

355 CONNORS, EDWARD MICHAEL. *Church-State Relationships in Education in the State of New York.* Washington, D.C.: Catholic University of America Press, 1951. 187pp. (Doctoral dissertation)

Abstract. *Catholic Educational Review,* 49:546-47 (Oct., 1951).

Covers 1825-1940.

REVIEW:
School and Society, 85:122-23 (Apr. 13, 1957) W. W. Brickman

356 MAHONEY, CHARLES JOSEPH. *The Relation of the State to Religious Education in Early New York, 1633-1825.* Washington, D.C.: Catholic University of America Press, 1941. 225pp. (Doctoral dissertation)

357 SERKO, DAVID. "Religion and the New York Public Schools," *Intramural Law Review* (New York University School of Law), 12:235-49 (May, 1957).

North Carolina:

358 GOBBEL, LUTHER LAFAYETTE. *Church State Relationships in Education in North Carolina Since 1776 (Duke University Publications).* Durham, N.C.: Duke University Press, 1938. 251pp. Bibliography: pp.229-241.

Based on the author's doctoral dissertation, Yale University.

REVIEW:
Catholic Historical Review, 26:134 (Apr., 1940)

North Dakota:

359 SCHNEIDER, HENRY W. "North Dakota Legislation Relative to Elementary and Secondary Schools." Washington, D.C.: Catholic University of America, 1954. (Unpublished master's dissertation)

Abstract. *Catholic Educational Review,* 53:40-41 (Jan., 1955).

N.B.: Special attention given to private schools and the problem of religion.

Ohio:
(1. Case Material)

-- 1958 --

360 *State v. Hersberger,* 150 N.E.2d 671 (Ohio, 1958).

Decision upholding compulsory education law against Amish parents who wanted to educate children of high school age at home for religious reasons.

361 CARLEY, WILLIAM. "Parental Rights Under Fire," *Catholic World*, 189:137-142 (May, 1959).

362 HAIGHT, JAMES T. "The Amish School Controversy," *Ohio Bar*, 31:846-59 (Oct. 6, 1958).

(2. Other Literature)

363. OTTE, LOUIS E. "The Educational Policy of the Methodist Episcopalian Church in Ohio during the Nineteenth Century." Columbus, Ohio: Ohio State University, 1946. (Unpublished doctoral dissertation)

Oregon:

364 GURR, JOHN E., S.J. "The Civil Rights of Handicapped Children," *Social Order*, 4:170-72 (Apr., 1954).

> Court decision affirming the right of children registered in non-public schools to be admitted to special public school speech correction classes. (N.B.: the philosophy of the decision).

Pennsylvania:

(1. Case Material)

-- 1950 --

365 *Commonwealth (Pennsylvania) v. Bey,* 166 Pa. Super. 136; 70 A.2d 693 (Pa., 1950).

> Compulsory education law upheld in this decision against Mohammedan parents who objected to the attendance of children at school on Friday for religious reasons.

-- 1951 --

366 *Commonwealth (Pennsylvania) v. Beiler,* 168 Pa. Super. 462; 79 A.2d 134 (Pa., 1951).

> Decision upholding compulsory education law against Amish parents who wanted to educate children at home for religious reasons.

-- 1955 --

367 *Commonwealth (Pennsylvania) v. Smoker,* 177 Pa. Super. 435; 110 A.2d 740 (Pa., 1955).

Decision upholding compulsory education law in the case of a Superintendent of Public Instruction refusing work permit to a child of Amish parents who wanted to educate children away from school for religious reasons.

(2. Other Literature)

368   HUNTER, MARGARET A. "Education in Pennsylvania Promoted by the Presbyterian Church of the United States of America, 1726-1837." Philadelphia, Pa.: Temple University, 1937. (Unpublished doctoral dissertation)

369   SECKINGER, RICHARD KARL. "Relation of the State to Religious Education in Pennsylvania, 1776-1874." New York, N.Y.: Columbia University, Teachers College, 1952. (Unpublished doctoral dissertation)

370   SHEA, JEREMIAH P. "The Extent of State Control over Catholic Elementary and Secondary Education in Pennsylvania." Washington, D.C.: Catholic University of America, 1948. (Unpublished master's dissertation)

Texas:

371   SACKETT, FREDERICK D., O.M.I. "A History of Legislation Affecting Religious Education in the Elementary and Secondary Schools of Texas." Washington, D.C.: Catholic University of America, 1952. (Unpublished master's dissertation)

Utah:

372   CLARK, JAMES RATCLIFFE. "Church and State Relationships in Education in Utah." Logan, Utah: Utah State University, 1958. (Unpublished doctoral dissertation)

Virginia:
(1. Case Material)

-- 1948 --

373   *Rice v. Commonwealth,* 188 Va. 224; 49 S.E.2d 342 (Va., 1948).

Decision upholding compulsory education law against parents who wanted to educate children at home for religious reasons.

(2. Other Literature)

374   BELL, SADIE. *The Church, the State and Education in Virginia.* Philadelphia, Pa.: Science Press Printing Co., 1930. 796pp. Bibliography: pp.661-735. (Doctoral dissertation, University of Pennsylvania, 1929)

Washington:

(1. Case Material)

375   *State ex. rel. Shoreline School District No. 412 v. Superior Court for King County, Juvenile Court,* 155 Wash. Dec. 175; 346 P.2d 999 (Washington, 1959)

Decision upholding compulsory education law against parents who believed that children should be educated at home for religious reasons.

REVIEW:

Washington Law Review, 35:151-159 (Summer, 1960) Timothy R. Clifford

(2. Other Literature)

376   TRIESCH, NORMAN. "Catholic Elementary and Secondary Schools under Washington State Law." Washington, D.C.: Catholic University of America, 1954. (Unpublished master's dissertation)

Wisconsin:

377   "We Fight for this Freedom Too," *Catholic Mind,* 49: 390-91 (June, 1951)

Reprinted from the *Catholic Herald Citizen,* Milwaukee, Wisconsin, Jan. 13, 1951.

III

Religion In Public Education

Note. The attempts of educators to recognize the importance of religion in education have opened a number of problem areas in public education, including Bible reading, the recitation of prayer and released time. The display of religious emblems, religious graduation exercises in churches, flag saluting, teaching the germ theory of disease and a variety of other practices have been objected to for reasons of conscience. General discussions and literature covering more than one issue have been grouped in this unit. The material on special issues given in IV to VII completes this general list. Many entries in I and II provide additional coverage.

Difficulties in the interpretation of the First Amendment, conflicting attitudes about the importance of religion in general education and the unavoidable dilemmas accompanying any recognition of religion in a pluralistic society remain causes of misunderstanding.

The collision between believers and nonbelievers is always with us. While the latter oppose any religious influence, large groups of parents, without advocating compulsion, want their desires recognized at least to the extent that the desires of nonbelievers are not given priority.

Controversies in the philosophy of education underlie the conflict. The abundant literature provided on the subject by the philosophers of education is beyond the scope of this bibliography but the reading of a few formulations expressing a broad variety of viewpoints is suggested with the following background material.

A. BACKGROUND MATERIAL

1. BIBLIOGRAPHIES:

378   BLAKEMAN, EDWARD W. "Religious Education and the Public School; a Bibliography," *Religious Education,* 43:39-50 (Jan.-Feb., 1948).

379   COHEN, IVA. "Religious Education and the Public Schools," in *Church, State and Education; A Selected Bibliography,* 2d. rev. ed. New York: Library of Jewish Information, American Jewish Committee, 1954. pp.8-20. (Mimeographed)

380   COLE, STEWART G. and BLAKEMAN, EDWARD W. "Selected Bibliography: Moral and Spiritual Values in Education," *Religious Education,* 48:163-165 (May-June, 1953).

381   LITTLE, LAWRENCE C. "A Selected Bibliography on Religion and Public Education," *Religious Education,* 44:177-180 (May-June, 1949), and 46:251-256 (July-August, 1951).

382   POLITELLA, JOSEPH. *Religion in Education, An Annotated Bibliography.* Oneonta, N.Y.: American Association of Colleges for Teacher Education, 1956. 90pp.

> A book list. Much of the material deals with the philosophy of the problem as well as with methodology and content, but many entries concern religion in public education. See sections I and II.

383   POPE, JAMES D. *Moral, Spiritual and Religious Values in Public Education (Bibliography, No. 31).* Gainesville, Fla.: University of Florida Education Library, 1958. 40pp. (Mimeographed)

2. SUMMARY MATERIAL AND LEGAL BACKGROUND:

384   CONWAY, DON. "Religious and Public Education in the United States," *International Journal of Religious Education,* 32:34-40 (March, 1956).

Includes a summary of "State Regulations Concerning Religion and Public Education," and a chart: "Summary Statement of Legal References Relating to Problems of Religion and Public Education," pp.36-37.

385 HUNT, ROLFE LANIER. "Religious and Education," *American Academy of Political and Social Science, Annals,* 332:89-100 (Nov., 1960).

386 KEESECKER, WARD W. *Legal Status of Bible Reading and Religious Instruction in Public Schools (U.S. Office of Education. Bulletin, 1930, No. 14).* Washington, D.C.: U.S. Government Printing Office, 1930. 29pp.

387 "Legal Status of Religious Teaching in Various States, 1949-1950," *Nation's Schools,* 48:65 (Sept., 1951).

A summary chart.

388 NATIONAL EDUCATION ASSOCIATION OF THE UNITED STATES. RESEARCH DIVISION. *The Status of Religious Education in the Public Schools.* Washington, D.C.: The Association, 1949. 35pp. (Offset)

Reviews previous studies and summarizes findings from inquiries sent to 5,100 local superintendents of schools in December, 1948.

3. EARLIER STUDY:

389 BEMAN, LAMAR TANEY (comp.). *Religious Education in the Public Schools (The Reference Shelf, Vol. 5, No. 2).* New York: H. W. Wilson Co., 1927. 170pp.

4. PHILOSOPHIES OF EDUCATION (Suggested readings):

390 FULLER, EDMUND (ed.). *The Christian Idea of Education; Papers and Discussions by William G. Pollard, E. Harris Harbinson, Alan Paton, Massey H. Shepherd, Jr., John Courtney Murray, S.J., Jacques Maritain, Georges Flirovsky, Reinhold Niebuhr, Stephen F. Bayne, Jr.* New Haven: Yale University Press, 1957. Includes bibliographical references.

391 "Images of Man," *Religious Education,* 53:83-150 (March-April, 1958).

Contents. "Secular Images of Man," "Sacred Images of Man," "What Image of Man Should Education Foster?" "Images and Morals in the Mass Manipulation of Behavior," "Strategy of Religion for Nurturing Sacred Images of Man."

392 NELSON, HENRY B. (ed.). *Modern Philosophies and Education (National Society for the Study of Education, 54th Yearbook, Part 1)*. Chicago, Ill.: Chicago University Press, 1955. 374pp.

Contributions from John S. Brubacker, John Wild, Jacques Maritain, Theodore M. Greene, George R. Geiger, Robert S. Cohen, Ralph Harper, Kenneth Burke, Herbert Feigl, James K. Feibleman.

393 "Religious Education and General Education—A Symposium," *Religious Education*, 48:135-157 (May-June, 1953).

Contents. "A Jewish Point of View," Will Herberg. "Another Jewish Point of View," Philip Jacobson. "A Protestant Point of View," Erwin L. Shaver. "A Catholic Point of View," Gerald S. Sloyan.

394 "The Child: Citizen of Two Worlds," Statement Issued by the Catholic Bishops of the United States, November, 1950. Text in Raphael M. Huber (ed.), *Our Bishops Speak, National Pastorals and Annual Statements of the Hierarchy of the United States, 1919-1951*. Milwaukee, Wisc.: Bruce, 1952. Pp.161-69. Same. *Catholic Mind*, 49:137-44 (Feb., 1951).

A summary statement of the Catholic philosophy of education.

B. BOOKS AND PAMPHLETS

395 AMERICAN COUNCIL ON EDUCATION. (CONFERENCE ON RELIGION AND PUBLIC EDUCATION, Princeton, N.J.,

1944.) *Religion and Public Education; Proceedings of a Conference (American Council on Education. Studies. Series I, Reports of Committees and Conferences, No. 22, Vol IX, Feb., 1945.)* Washington, D.C.: the Council, 1945. 76pp.

> Report of a conference sponsored by the American Council on Education. To show the relationships between the initiatives taken by the Council to further the study of problems in the relation of religion to public education, reports of conferences and studies are listed chronologically here.

396 AMERICAN COUNCIL ON EDUCATION. COMMITTEE ON RELIGION AND EDUCATION. *The Relation of Religion to Public Education; The Basic Principles (American Council on Education. Studies. Series I, Reports of Committees and Conferences, No. 26, Vol. XI, April, 1947).* Washington, D.C.: the Council, 1947. 54pp.

> DISCUSSIONS:
> Nevin Cowger Harner. *Religion's Place in General Education, Including "The Relation of Religion to Public Education . . ."* Richmond, Va.: John Knox Press, 1949. 167pp. (The text of the report prepared by the American Council on Education is included, pp.87-167).
> "Religion in Public Education," *Religious Education,* 42:129-190 (May-June, 1947), and 42:365-67 (Nov.-Dec., 1947).
> Walter George Muelder. "The Basic Strategy of Religion in Public Education," *Christendom,* 12:370-80 (Summer, 1947).

> REVIEWS:
> *America,* 77:113 (May 3, 1947)
> *American School Board Journal,* 115:31-33 (July, 1947) Edward A. Fitzpatrick
> *Catholic Mind,* 46:80-85 (Feb., 1948) Sister M. Madeleva
> *Christendom,* 13, no. 3:414-16 (1948) H. C. Bohn
> *International Journal of Religious Education,* 23:33-34 (June, 1947) E. L. Shaver
> *Nation's Schools,* 40:23-24 (July, 1947) V. T. Thayer
> *School and Society,* 66:53 (July 26, 1947) I. L. Kandel
> *School and Society,* 67:249-50 (March 27, 1948) W. W. Brickman
> *Theological Studies,* 8:716 (Dec., 1947)

397 AMERICAN COUNCIL ON EDUCATION. COMMITTEE ON RELIGION AND EDUCATION. *The Function of the Public Schools in Dealing With Religion; A Report on the Exploratory Study made by the Committee on Religion and Education.* Washington, D.C.: the Council, 1953. 145pp. Bibliography: pp.125-145.

COMMENTS AND REVIEWS:
"The Function of the Public Schools in Dealing with Religion," *Religious Education*, 48:67-80 (March-Apr., 1953), and 48:169-70 (May-June, 1953). Critiques by Louis Finkelstein, Frederick G. Hochwalt, Paul H. Vieth, William Clayton Bower.
America, 89:52-53 (Apr. 11, 1953) G. McCabe
American School Board Journal, 126:33-34 (June, 1953) Edward A. Fitzpatrick
Childhood Education, 30:48 (Sept., 1953) E. C. Williams
Elementary School Journal, 53:531-32 (May, 1953) V. Henry
International Journal of Religious Education, 29:33 (May, 1953) E. L. Shaver
The Jurist, 14:96-98 (Jan., 1954) Edward Roelker
National Elementary Principal, 32:46 (May, 1953) R. Barnes
The Priest, 9:335-340 (May, 1953)
School and Society, 85:125 (April 13, 1957) W. W. Brickman
School Executive, 73:86-88 (March, 1954) Clarence Linton, William C. Bower

398 AMERICAN COUNCIL ON EDUCATION. (CONFERENCE ON RELIGION AND PUBLIC EDUCATION, Harriman, N.Y., 1957.) *The Study of Religion in the Public Schools: An Appraisal.* Edited by Nicholas C. Brown. Washington, D.C.: American Council on Education, 1958. 229pp.

Report of a Conference on Religion and Public Education sponsored by the American Council on Education at Arden House, Harriman, N.Y., March 10-12, 1957.

Contents (Papers). "Summary of Policies and Recommendations of the American Council on Education, Committee on Religion and Education," F. Ernest Johnson, 5-18. "Public Authority and Religious Education: a Brief Survey of Constitutional and Legal Limits," Arthur E. Sutherland, 33-47. "Religion in the History of American Ideas," Bert James Loewenberg, 77-96. "Religious Matter in the Teaching of American History," John Thomas Farrell, 97-113. "The Study of Religion in High School American History," Jack Allen, 122-32. "Some Religious Aspects of Elementary American History," Sister Mary Nona, O.P., 139-53. "The Next Decade of Research and Experimentation Relating to Religion and Public Education," Eugene E. Dawson, 184-200.

Text of papers also available in *Religious Education*, 52:247-307 (July-Aug., 1957).

399 AMERICAN JEWISH COMMITTEE. *Religion in Public Education.* New York: the Committee, 1955. 20pp.

REVIEW:
School and Society, 85:126 (Apr. 13, 1957) W. W. Brickman

400 ───────. *Religion in Public Education; a Statement of Views.* Rev. ed., New York: American Jewish Committee, 1957. 22pp.

401 BOWER, WILLIAM CLAYTON. *Moral and Spiritual Values in Education.* Lexington, Ky.: University of Kentucky Press, 1952. 214pp.

REVIEWS:
America, 87:548-49 (Sept. 6, 1952) C. Donovan
Annals of the American Academy of Political and Social Science, 282:164 (July, 1952) Galen Jones
Childhood Education, 29:194-95 (Dec., 1952) R. E. Curry
Christian Century, 69:853 (July 23, 1952)
Churchman, 166:15 (June, 1952) Roger Shaw
Educational Forum, 17:240-41 (Jan., 1953) A. R. Mead
International Journal of Religious Education, 28:36 (March, 1952) E. L. Shaver
National Parent-Teacher, 46:32 (May, 1952)
Religious Education, 47:235 (May, 1952) S. G. Cole
Review and Expositor, 49:365-66 (July, 1952) F. Edge
San Francisco Chronicle, p.24 (Apr. 13, 1952)
School and Society, 75:159 (March 8, 1952)
School and Society, 76:266 (Oct. 25, 1952) W. W. Brickman
U. S. Quarterly Book Review, 8:149 (June, 1952)

402 BRAITERMAN, MARVIN. *Religion and the Public Schools* (Issues of Conscience, No. 1). New York: Commission on Social Action of Reform Judaism. Copyright, the Union of American Hebrew Congregations, 1958. 73pp. Bibliography: pp.70-71.

403 BROWN, KENNETH IRVING. *Not Minds Alone; Some Frontiers of Christian Education.* New York: Harper, 1954. 206pp.

REVIEWS:
Association of American Colleges. Bulletin, 40:553-56 (Dec., 1954) E. A. Fitzpatrick
Christian Century, 71:494 (Apr. 21, 1954) P. E. Gresham
Christian Scholar, 37:152-54 (June, 1954) M. Cunninggim
Springfield Republican, p.7c (Apr. 18, 1954) G. B. Affleck

404 BRUBACKER, JOHN SEILER (ed.). *The Public Schools and Spiritual Values* (Seventh Yearbook of the John Dewey Society). New York: Harper, 1944. 222pp.

REVIEWS:
American Association of Collegiate Registrars. Journal, 21:106-07 (Oct., 1945) E. K. Feaver

American Teacher, 29:10-11 (Dec., 1944) G. E. Axtelle
Childhood Education, 22:150 (Nov., 1945) D. W. Lefever
Christian Century, 61:1229 (Oct. 25, 1944) W. E. Garrison
Clearing House, 19:518 (Apr., 1945) P. W. L. Cox
Educational Administration and Supervision, 31:313-15 (May, 1945) W. F. Bruce
Educational Forum, 9:375-76 (March, 1945) W. J. Gifford
International Journal of Religious Education, 21:32-33 (May, 1945) E. L. Shaver
North Central Association Quarterly, 19:361-62 (Apr., 1945) W. E. Drake
School and Society, 61:398-99 (June 16, 1945) F. E. Johnson; 67:249 (March 27, 1948) W. W. Brickman
School Executive, 64:40 (Dec., 1944) C. M. Dannelly
School Review, 53:183-84 (March, 1945) J. W. Reynolds
Social Education, 9:187-88 (Apr., 1945) W. H. Mohr
Social Studies, 36:87-88 (Feb., 1945) R. H. McFeely

405   BUTLER, NICHOLAS MURRAY. "Religion and Faith in Education," in *Liberty—Equality—Fraternity; Essays and Addresses on the Problems of Today and Tomorrow*. New York: Scribner's, 1942. Pp.145-51.

CONFERENCE ON RELIGION IN PUBLIC EDUCATION
1) Princeton, N.J., 1944.
2) Harriman, N.Y., 1957.

See no. 395 and no. 398. Both conferences were sponsored by the American Council on Education. Reports are listed with its publications.

406   DUNN, WILLIAM KAILER. *What Happened to Religious Education? The Decline of Religious Teaching in the Public Elementary School, 1776-1861*. Baltimore: Johns Hopkins Press, 1958. 361pp. Bibliography: pp.311-38.

"A condensation and a rewriting in some parts" of the author's doctoral dissertation completed at Johns Hopkins University in 1956. (Dissertation: "The Decline of the Teaching of Religion in the American Public Elementary School in the States Originally the Thirteen Colonies, 1776-1861." Baltimore: Johns Hopkins University, 1956. 461pp.)

Abstract. *Religious Education*, 52:184 (May-June, 1957).

407   *Education and the Faith of America; Addresses Given During the Centennial Celebration of the Packer Collegiate Institute*. Brooklyn, N.Y.: Packer Collegiate Institute, 1945. 77pp.

408 EDUCATIONAL POLICIES COMMISSION ("National Education Association of the United States" and "American Association of School Administrators"). *Moral and Spiritual Values in the Public Schools.* Washington, D.C.: National Education Association of the United States, 1951. 100pp.

REVIEWS:
America, 84:745-47 (March 31, 1951) R. C. Hartnett
Catholic Educational Review, 21:201-202 (Dec., 1950)
Childhood Education, 28:136 (Nov., 1951) W. E. Bain
Educational Research Bulletin, 32:26 (Jan., 1953) R. E. Jewett
International Journal of Religious Education, 27:32 (June, 1951) E. L. Shaver
National Education Association Journal, 40:177-78 (March, 1951) William G. Carr
Review and Expositor, 49:223 (Apr., 1952) F. Edge
School and Society, 76:266 (Oct. 25, 1952) W. W. Brickman
Science Education, 35:225 (Oct. 1, 1951)

Neil Gerard McCluskey, S.J., *Public Schools and Moral Education.* New York: Columbia University Press, 1958. See pp.4-7, 259-60, 269-71.

"Moral and Spiritual Values in the Public Schools—A Symposium," *Religious Education,* 46:195-237 (July-August, 1951). Contains critiques by William G. Carr, F. Ernest Johnson, William C. Bower, Nathan Brilliant, John S. Brubacker, Ernest J. Chave, Israel G. Chipkin, Stewart G. Cole, J. B. Edmonson, Martin W. Essex, Solomon B. Freehof, Robert S. Gilchrist, Ernest A. Becker, Jr., Hugh Hartshorne, Thomas J. Quigley, B. Othanel Smith, Paul H. Vieth, Lawrence C. Little.

409 ELLIS, FREDERICK E. "Religion in the Public Schools," in Robert Holmes Beck, *The Three R's Plus.* Minneapolis: University of Minnesota Press, 1956. Pp. 354-59.

410 FLEMING, WILLIAM SHERMAN. *God in Our Public Schools.* 3d ed. Pittsburgh, Pa.: National Reform Association, 1947. 248pp.

REVIEWS:
Christian Century, 61:1229 (Oct., 25, 1944) W. E. Garrison
Religious Education, 40:178 (May, 1945) L. A. Stidley

411 GAEBELEIN, FRANK ELY. *Christian Education in a Democracy, the Report of the National Association of Evangelicals.* New York: Oxford University Press, 1951. 305pp.

REVIEWS:

Christian Century, 68:1017 (Sept. 5, 1951) J. B. Miller
Elementary School Journal, 52:304-05 (Jan., 1952) E. J. Chave
Library Journal, 76:864 (May 15, 1951) R. W. Henderson
Religious Education, 46:367-68 (Nov., 1951) M. T. Hopper
Review of Politics, 14:141 (Jan., 1952) L. R. Ward
School and Society, 73:270 (Apr. 28, 1951)
Theological Studies, 12:603-05 (Dec., 1955) E. L. Hirsh
Yale Review, new series, 41:142 (Autumn, 1951) W. L. Sperry

412   HARNER, NEVIN COWGER. *Religion's Place in General Education, including "The Relation of Religion to Public Education: The Basic Principles. A Committee Report of the American Council on Education".* Richmond, Va.: John Knox Press, 1949. 167pp. Notes: 82, 83.

REVIEW:

School and Society, 71:277 (May 6, 1950) W. W. Brickman

413   HAUSER, CONRAD AUGUSTINE. *Latent Religious Resources in Public School Education (A Study in Correlation on the Curriculum Side).* Philadelphia, Pa.: Heidelberg Press, 1924. 319pp.

414   —————. *Teaching Religion in the Public Schools.* New York: Round Table Press, 1942. 319pp.

A sequel to *Latent Religious Resources in Public School Education.*

REVIEWS:

Christian Century, 59:562 (Apr. 29, 1942)
Churchman, 156:31 (June 1, 1942) William Grime
Educational Outlook, 16:189-90 (May, 1942) O. F. Noble
International Journal of Religious Education, 18:36 (March, 1942) E. L. Shaver
Religious Education, 37:123 (March, 1942) C. E. Butler
School and Society, 55:224 (Feb. 21, 1942)
School Review, 50:572-74 (June, 1942) E. J. Chave

415   HAY, CLYDE LEMONT. *The Blind Spot in American Public Education.* New York: Macmillan, 1950. 110pp.

REVIEWS:

Books on Trial, 9:175 (Dec., 1950) W. Mang
Commonweal, 53:405 (Jan. 26, 1951) W. E. McManus
Christian Century, 69:16-17 (Jan. 2, 1952) J. V. Thompson

Crozer Quarterly, 28:178 (Apr., 1951) F. R. Morey
International Journal of Religious Education, 27:32 (March, 1951) E. L. Shaver
Bulletin from Virginia Kirkus' Book Shop Service, 18:407 (July 15, 1950)
Library Journal, 75:1399 (Sept. 1, 1950)
Religious Education, 45:371-72 (Nov., 1950) L. Stidley
Saturday Review of Literature, 34:16 (Sept. 8, 1951) W. Taeusch
School and Society, 72:175 (Sept. 9, 1950); 85:125 (Apr. 13, 1957) W. W. Brickman
Science Education, 35:224 (Oct., 1951)
Springfield Republican, p.5C (Sept. 24, 1950)
Survey, 87:40 (Jan., 1951) O. Tead

416 HENRY, VIRGIL. *The Place of Religion in Public Schools; a Handbook to Guide Communities.* New York: Harper, 1950. 164pp. Bibliography: pp.151-60.

REVIEWS:
America, 79:473-74 (Aug. 28, 1948) E. Morgan
America, 82:495 (Jan. 28, 1950) R. C. Hartnett
Catholic Educational Review, 48:286-87 (Apr., 1950) J. A. Gorham
Commonweal, 48:619-21 (Oct. 8, 1948) A. Fremantle
Educational Research Bulletin, 29:164 (Sept., 1950) J. E. Jewett
International Journal of Religious Education, 26:33 (March, 1950)
Review of Politics, 14:142 (Jan., 1952) L. R. Ward
School and Society, 71:277 (May 6, 1950) W. W. Brickman

417 HORTON, MILDRED MCAFEE, and CLOTHIER, ROBERT C. *Moral and Spiritual Values in Education; Addresses . . . before the Eighty-Fifth Convocation of the Board of Regents of the University of the State of New York, October twenty-sixth, nineteen hundred and fifty-one.* Albany, N.Y.: University of the State of New York, 1951. 21pp.

418 HUBNER, (Sister) MARY OF SAINT MICHAEL. *Professional Attitudes Toward Religion in the Public Schools of the United States Since 1900.* Washington, D.C.: Catholic University of America Press, 1944. 208pp. Bibliography: pp.184-204. (Doctoral dissertation)

REVIEW:
Catholic School Journal, 44:273 (Nov., 1944)

419 JOHNSON, FREDERICK ERNEST (ed.). *American Education and Religion: The Problem of Religion in the Schools. A series of Addresses.* Published by the Institute for Religious and Social Studies, Jewish Theological Seminary of America. Distributed by Harper, 1952. 211pp. Bibliographic notes.

Addresses by: Vivian T. Thayer, Simon Greenberg, Frederick G. Hochwalt, Nevin C. Harner, J. Hilles Miller, Ordway Tead, Roscoe L. West, Mildred McAfee Horton, Samuel L. Hamilton, Mathew P. Gafney, F. Ernest Johnson.

REVIEWS:

America, 88:358 (Dec. 27, 1952) G. A. Kelly
American Teacher, 38:23 (May, 1954) H. Merritt
Annals of the American Academy of Political and Social Science, 186:223 (March, 1953) C. H. Moehlman
Chicago Sunday Tribune, p.48 (Dec. 7, 1952) L. T. Heron
Christian Century, 70:576 (May 13, 1953)
International Journal of Religious Education, 29:31 (Apr., 1953) E. L. Shaver
Journal of Bible and Religion, 21:213-14 (July, 1953) W. G. Ross
Journal of Higher Education, 25:54-55 (Jan., 1954) O. Tead
Journal of Religious Thought, 11 no. 1:85 (1953-54) E. M. Baxter
Religious Education, 48:284 (July, 1953) J. S. Armentrout
New York Times Book Review, p.7 (Jan. 18, 1953) A. P. Stokes
Saturday Review of Literature, 36:56 (Feb. 21, 1953)
School and Society, 85:125 (Apr. 13, 1957) W. W. Brickman
Springfield Republican, p.4D (Jan. 11, 1953) J. F. Rooney
Teachers College Record, 54:350 (March, 1953) J. G. Chamberlin

420 KELLER, JAMES GREGORY. *All God's Children; What Your Schools Can Do for Them.* Garden City: N.Y., Hanover House, 1953. 292pp.

REVIEWS:

Ave Maria, 78:26 (Dec. 5, 1953) J. O'Shea
Bulletin from Virginia Kirkus' Book Shop Service 21:576 (Aug. 15, 1953)
Mission Digest, 12:38 (Apr., 1954)
New York Times Book Review, p.22 (Dec. 6, 1953) N. K. Burger
San Francisco Chronicle, p.29 (Oct. 18, 1953) J. H. Jackson
Shield (College Ed.), 33:15 (Apr. 15, 1954)
Sign, 33:75 (Jan., 1954)
Springfield Republican, p.5C (Feb. 14, 1954)
Religious Education, 49:173 (March, 1954) J. T. Foudy

421   LEE, UMPHREY. "Religion and the Public Schools," in
      Render Unto the People (The Cole Lectures, Vander-
      bilt University, 1946). New York: Abingdon Cokes-
      bury Press, 1947. Pp.65-90.

422   MCCLUSKEY, NEIL GERARD, S.J. *Public Schools and
      Moral Education: the Influence of Horace Mann,
      William Torrey Harris and John Dewey.* New York:
      Columbia University Press, 1958. 315pp. Bibli-
      ography: pp.277-304.

      From the author's doctoral dissertation: "Three Historical
      Influences on the Public School Philosophy of Values," New
      York: Columbia University, 1957. Abstract. *Religious Educa-
      tion,* 53:270-72 (May-June, 1958).

      REVIEW:
      Social Order, 9:186-187 (April, 1959) John L. Blewett, S.J.

423   MARTIN, RENWICK HARPER. *The Fourth R in American
      Education.* Pittsburgh: The Author, 1957. (Dr. R.
      H. Martin, Grant Bldg., Pittsburgh 19, Pa.)

424   —————. *Our Public Schools, Christian or Secular?*
      Pittsburgh: National Reform Association, 1952. 152
      pp.

      REVIEW:
      Religious Education, 49:174 (March-Apr., 1954) J. Meade
      Letts

425   MASON, ROBERT EMMETT. *Moral Values and Secular
      Education.* New York: Columbia University Press,
      1950. 155pp. Bibliography: pp.137-46. (Doctoral dis-
      sertation, Columbia University)

      REVIEWS:
      College and University, 26:130-32 (Oct., 1950)
      Crozer Quarterly, 27:377 (Oct., 1950) H. M. Gehr
      Journal of Philosophy, 48:221 (March 29, 1951) H. A. Larabee
      Religious Education, 46:126 (March, 1951) L. W. Norris
      School and Society, 72:279 (Oct., 28, 1950) W. W. Brickman
      School Review, 58:557-58 (Dec., 1950) C. D. Champlin
      Social Service Review, 25:259-60 (June, 1951) C. H. Lyttle

426   MATTOX, FOUNT W. *The Teaching of Religion in the
      Public Schools* (Contribution to Education, no. 396).
      Nashville, Tenn.: George Peabody College for Teach-
      ers, 1948. 133pp. Bibliography: pp.130-133. (Doc-
      toral dissertation)

REVIEWS:
Religious Education, 44:311 (Sept., 1949) L. Stidley
School and Society, 76:266 (Oct. 25, 1952) W. W. Brickman

427 METHODIST CHURCH. NEW YORK EAST METHODIST CON-
FERENCE. *Second Church and State Assembly:Reli-
gion and Public Education*. Reports. (Processed)

Assembly held at Tuxedo Park, N.Y., April 16-18, 1959.

(Copyright, 1959, Board of Social and Economic Relations
of the Methodist Church, 740 Rush St., Chicago, Ill.)

Contents. Preface. I, "How Can Christianity be Taught?"
Ross Sudger, critique by Marie Alice Jones. II, "Community
Conflicts and Reconciliation," Arthur Gilbert. III, "Current
Litigation Involving Church and State," Phil Baum and Phil
Jacobson. IV, "The Place of Religion in General Education,"
A) Jewish Position, Phil Jacobson, B) The Catholic School,
Neil G. McCluskey, S.J., C) Protestant Position, Gerald E.
Knoff. V, "Will Public Schools Survive?" R. Lanier Hunt.
Supplement: "Why Not Reserved Time?" Claud D. Nelson.
Supplement: "Are Public Schools a Luxury?" Dean M. Kelley.
Summary of Discussion. Directory of Participants. (Papers
are individually paginated.)

428 MOEHLMAN, CONRAD HENRY. *School and Church: the
American Way; an Historical Approach to the Problem of Religious Instruction in Public Education*.
New York: Harper, 1944. 178pp. "Notes": pp.139-
61; Bibliography: pp.163-73.

REVIEWS:
America, 71:538 (Sept. 2, 1944)
*Annals of the American Academy of Political and Social Sci-
ence*, 235:169 (Sept., 1944) Ephraim Fischoff
Catholic Educational Review, 44:121-123 (Feb., 1946) W. E.
McManus
Catholic Historical Review, 30:308-310 (Oct., 1944)
Commonweal, 40:164 (June 2, 1944) Emerson Hynes
Crozer Quarterly, 21:339 (Oct., 1944) A. J. Jones
Educational Administration and Supervision, 31:380-81 (Sept.,
1945) W. F. Bruce
High Points, 26:73 (Dec., 1944) M. Wolfson
Journal of Religion, 25:214-15 (July, 1945) S. E. Mead
Bulletin from Virginia Kirkus' Book Shop Service 12:166
(Apr. 1, 1944)
Progressive Education, 22:11-13 (Oct., 1944) H. S. Elliott
Religious Education, 39:349 (July, 1944) E. J. Chave
Review of Religion, 9:396-99 (May, 1945) E. B. Greene
Saturday Review of Literature, 27:10-11 (June 3, 1944) H. M.
Kallen

School and Society, 59:288 (Apr. 22, 1944) ; 67:247-48 (March 27, 1949) W. W. Brickman
Social Education, 9:187-88 (Apr., 1945) W. H. Mohr
Survey, 81:31 (Jan., 1945) F. Ernest Johnson

429 NOLDE, O. FREDERICK, and HILL, GEORGE E. *Religious Education and the Public Schools (University of Pennsylvania, School of Education, Educational Service Bureau, Publication No. 1).* Philadelphia: 1942. 16pp.

430 PFEFFER, LEO. *Religion and the Public Schools (Jewish Affairs, Vol. 2, no. 3).* Revised, edited. New York: American Jewish Congress, 1949. 26pp.

431 PHENIX, PHILIP HENRY. "Religion in American Public Education," in George Zygmunt F. Bereday and Luigi Volpicelli (eds.), *Public Education in America; A New Interpretation of Purpose and Practice.* New York: Harper, 1958. pp.91-99.

432 "Religious Stewardship for Today's Children," *American Association of School Administrators. Official Report,* 1952. Washington, D.C.: the Association. pp.7-38.

> Contents. "Religious stewardship for today's children," Arthur L. Miller, first general session, St. Louis, Feb. 24, 1952, 9-20. "Religious stewardship for today's children," Louis Evans, first general session, Los Angeles, March 9, 1952, 21-38. "An affirmative climate for today's young people," Abraham L. Sacher, first general session, Boston, April 6, 1952, 39-49.

433 SCOTT, CECIL WINFIELD, and HILL, CLYDE M. (eds.). "Religion," in *Public Education Under Criticism (Prentice-Hall Education Series).* New York: Prentice-Hall, 1954. pp.128-48. An anthology.

434 SELLERS, HORACE B. *The Constitution and Religious Education.* Boston: Christopher Publishing House, 1950. 146pp.

435 SPERRY, WILLIAM LEAROYD (ed.). *Religion and Education (Religion in the Post-War World, Vol. 4)* by Alexander Meiklejohn and others. Cambridge, Mass.: Harvard University Press, 1945. 114pp.

Contents. "From Church to State," Alexander Meiklejohn, 3-31. "The Public Schools and Religious Education," Payson Smith, 32-56. "Religious Education in the State Universities," Howard Mumford Jones, 57-71. "Religion in the Liberal Colleges," Victor L. Butterfield, 72-96. "The Teaching Office of the Church," Theodore Parker Ferris, 97-114.

REVIEW:

School and Society, 67:248 (March 27, 1948) W. W. Brickman

436   THAYER, VIVIAN TROW. "Freedom of Inquiry and Secular Education," in H. Gordon Hullfish (ed.). *Educational Freedom in an Age of Anxiety (Twelfth Yearbook of the John Dewey Society)*. New York: Harper, 1953. pp.82-107.

REVIEWS:

America, 89:53-54 (Apr. 11, 1953) W. J. Codd, S.J.
Educational Administration and Supervision, 40:121-24 (Feb. 1954) W. F. Bruce
Educational Forum, 18:367-68 (March, 1954) R. J. Poindexter
Harvard Educational Review, 23 no. 2:145-46 (1953) F. E. Ellis
Journal of Higher Education, 25:49-50 (Jan., 1954) M. C. Otto
Religious Education, 49:58 (Jan., 1954) P. B. Maves
Teachers College Record, 55:59-60 (Oct., 1953) L. Suttell

437   ————. "Religion and Morals in the Public Schools," in Percy Friars Valentine (ed.), *Twentieth Century Education*. New York: Philosophical Library, 1946. pp.558-83.

REVIEWS:

Catholic Educational Review, 44:622-23 (Dec., 1946) E. B. Jordan
Childhood Education, 23:437 (May, 1947) I. A. Hammer
Educational Forum, 11:375 (March, 1947)
Elementary School Journal, 47:236-37 (Dec., 1946) O. D. Froe
Journal of Physical Education, 44:70 (March, 1947) R. C. Taylor
School and Society, 64:192 (Sept. 14, 1946)
School and Society, 65:93 (Feb. 1, 1947) J. J. Jelinek
Social Studies, 37:335 (Nov., 1946)

438   ————. *Religion in Public Education (Ethical Foundation Series)*. New York: New York Society for Ethical Culture, 1946. 20pp.

439   ————. "Religion in the Public Schools," in *American Education Under Fire*. New York: Harper, 1944. pp.97-115.

Reply. W. F. Cunningham, "American Education Under Fire," *Catholic Educational Review,* 43:129-38 (March, 1945).

REVIEWS:

Arizona Teacher-Parent, 35:17- (Oct., 1946)
Baltimore Bulletin of Education, 22:135-36 (Apr., 1945) T. A. VanSant
Book Week (Chicago Sun), p.5 (Dec. 24, 1944) S. I. Hayakawa
Christian Century, 61:1503 (Dec. 27, 1944) K. I. Brown
Clearing House, 19:517 (Apr., 1945) P. W. L. Cox
Current History, 8:72 (Jan., 1945)
Educational Administration and Supervision, 31:182-85 (March, 1945) W. F. Bruce
Educational Forum, 9:483-84 (May, 1945) H. R. Becker
Elementary School Journal, 45:533-54 (May, 1945) C. D. Champlin
International Journal of Religious Education, 21:30 (Apr., 1945) H. J. Sweet
Junior College Journal, 15:330 (March, 1945)
Bulletin from Virginia Kirkus' Book Shop Service, 12:419 (Sept. 15, 1944)
New York Herald Tribune Weekly Book Review, p.28 (Dec. 3, 1944) Hiram Haydn
North Central Association Quarterly, 19:363 (Apr., 1945) H. Harap
Pennsylvania School Journal, 93:153 (Dec., 1944)
Progressive Education, 23:150 (Feb., 1946) U. R. Reinhardt
Religious Education, 40:368-69 (Nov., 1945) W. A. R. Leys
School and Society, 60:320 (Nov. 11, 1944)
School Executive, 64:42 (March, 1945) W. G. Carr
Social Education, 9:185-86 (Apr., 1945) A. K. Loomis
Springfield Republican, p.4D (Nov. 26, 1944)
Thought, 20:145-46 (March, 1946)

440 VAN DUSEN, HENRY PITNEY. *God in Education; A tract for the times (The Rockwell Lecture, 1950).* New York: Scribner, 1951. 128pp. Bibliography: pp.119-23.

Condensed with title "Protestant Looks at the Schools," *Catholic Digest,* 15:21-5 (Aug., 1951).

REVIEWS:

Association of American Colleges. Bulletin, 37:395-97 (Oct., 1951) C. E. Diehl
Christian Century, 68:844 (July 18, 1951) W. E. Garrison
Churchman, 165:17 (Aug., 1951) W. L. Caswell
Crozer Quarterly, 28:355 (Oct., 1951) C. H. Moehlman
Bulletin from Virginia Kirkus' Book Shop Service, 19:181 (March 15, 1951)
New York Times Book Review, p.14 (May 27, 1951) Paul Ramsey
Religious Education, 46:375 (Nov., 1951) F. McKibben
Saturday Review of Literature, 34:33 (June 30, 1951) K. D. Miller

School and Society, 74:223 (Oct. 6, 1951)
School and Society, 76:263 (Oct. 25, 1952) W. W. Brickman
Sign, 30:74 (June, 1951)
Time, 57:78-80 (May 14, 1951) "Replace the Keystone."

441   WILLIAMS, JOHN PAUL. *The New Education and Religion, A Challenge to Secularism in Education.* New York: Association Press, 1945. 198pp.

REVIEWS:

Christian Century, 62:551 (May 2, 1945) Evelyn Luchs
Christendom, 11 no. 1:85-89 (1946) S. L. Hamilton
Churchman, 159:15 (Oct. 1, 1945) W. L. Caswell
Educational Outlook, 20:93 (Jan., 1946) Z. Klain
International Journal of Religious Education, 21:31 (May, 1945) H. J. Sweet
Library Journal, 70:265 (March 15, 1945) G. W. Wakefield
Religious Education, 40:180-83 (May, 1945) G. A. Coe
School and Society, 61:92 (March 24, 1945); 67:250 (March 27, 1948) W. W. Brickman

442   —————. "The Relation of Religion and Public Education," in Philip Henry Lotz (ed.), *Orientation in Religious Education.* New York: Abingdon Cokesbury Press, 1950. Pp.491-500.

For an earlier summary see Edward R. Bartlett, "The Character Education Movement in the Public Schools," in Philip Henry Lotz and Leonidas Wakefield Crawford (eds.), *Studies in Religious Education.* Nashville, Tenn.: Cokesbury, 1931. Pp.450-471.

443   WORRELL, EDWARD K. *Restoring God to Education.* Wheaton, Illinois: Van Kampen Press, 1950. 110pp.

REVIEW:

School and Society, 76:263 (Oct. 25, 1952) W. W. Brickman

C. PERIODICAL ARTICLES

444   AMATORA, S. M. "Educate the Whole Child," *Education,* 71:393-96 (Feb., 1951).

445 AXELROD, JOSEPH. "The Public Educator's Dilemma in the Communication of Values," *Religious Education*, 49:325-32 (Sept.-Oct., 1954).

446 BALLOU, RICHARD BOYD. "Religious Values in Public Education," *Religious Education*, 49:317-24 (Sept.-Oct., 1954).

447 BARNES, JOHN B. "Can We Teach Silently?" *Educational Forum*, 22:289-291 (March, 1958).

448 BARTKY, JOHN A. "Theology, Science and Philosophy in Teaching Democratic Behavior," *School and Society*, 85:54-56 (Feb. 16, 1957).

449 BATTRICK, DELMER H. "How are Schools Including Moral and Spiritual Values in the School Program?" *National Association of Secondary School Principals Bulletin*, 39:141-46 (Apr., 1955).

450 BELL, BERNARD IDDINGS. "Know How vs. Know Why," *Life*, 29 no. 16:89-99 (Oct. 16, 1950).

> See pp.97, 98, "A Nation of Religious Illiterates." Same, abridged, with title "Our Schools; their Four Grievous Faults," *Reader's Digest*, 58:123-26 (Jan., 1951).
>
> COMMENTS:
> *Catholic World*, 173:98-104 (May, 1951) M. W. Hess., "Canon Bell: Crusader for Religious Education."
> *Christian Century*, 67:1287-89 (Nov. 1, 1950)

451 BENNETT, JOHN C. "When Christmas Becomes Divisive," *Christianity and Crisis*, 18:162-163 (Nov. 24, 1958).

452 BILLING, SHERRY. "Religion is an Everyday Affair," *Texas Outlook*, 43:26-27 (April, 1959).

453 BISHOP, RAYMOND JOHN, S.J. "American Public Schools in Catholic Focus," *Catholic School Journal*, 53:112-13 (Apr., 1953).

454 "Bishop Corson Comforts Foes of Schools," *Christian Century*, 66:1446 (Dec., 1949). Reply, 67:19 (Jan., 1950).

455 BLAIR, PAXTON. "The Need for New Directions in Education," *Vital Speeches*, 19:372-81 (Apr. 1, 1953). See pp.379-81, "Teaching Spiritual Values."

456 BODE, BOYD HENRY. "Religion and the Public Schools," *School and Society*, 67:225-229 (March 27, 1948). Replies. Edmund Baumeister, *School and Society*, 67:473-475 (June 26, 1948). S. Raymond, "The Principles of Pragmatism and the Teaching of Religion in the Public School," *Catholic Educational Review*, 47:365-379 (June, 1949).

457 BOLMEIER, EDWARD CLAUDE. "Legality and Propriety of Religious Instruction in the Public Schools," *Educational Forum*, 20:473-82 (March, 1956).

458 BOWER, WILLIAM CLAYTON. "Taking Account of Religion," *Kentucky School Journal*, 34:12-13 (Apr., 1956).

459 ——————. "Trends in Moral and Spiritual Values in the Public Schools." *Religious Education*, 48:22-25 (Jan.-Feb., 1953).

460 BRACKETT, RUSSELL D. "Are We Respecting Religious Rights?" *Minnesota Journal of Education*, 36:23 (March, 1956).

461 BRADSHAW, EMERSON O. "Can Religion be Taught in our Public Schools?" *Religious Education*, 35:32-39 (Jan.-March, 1940).

462 BRICKMAN, BENJAMIN. "Reflections on the Issue of Religion and American Public Education," *Educational Outlook*, 30:79-84 (March, 1956).

463 BROWN, FRANCIS J. "Studies of Religion in Public Education," *Phi Delta Kappan*, 36:252-56 (Apr., 1955).

464 BROWN, KENNETH I. "American Education as a Mirror," *Vital Speeches*, 15:245-51 (Feb. 1, 1949).

465 BRUBACHER, JOHN S. "The Public Schools and the Crisis in Spiritual Values," *New York State Education*, 33:531-34 (Apr., 1946).

466 —————. "Why Force Religious Education?" *Nation's Schools,* 36:23-24 (Nov., 1945).

467 BUDDY, CHARLES F. "Bring the Ten Commandments Back into the Schools," *America,* 93:613-15 (Sept. 24, 1955).

468 BURNHAM, PHILIP. "Double Fight for Schools," *Commonweal,* 71:14 (Oct. 2, 1959).

469 BURROWS, ALBERT H. "Public Schools and the Teaching of Religion," *School and Society,* 88:179, 182-83 (April 9, 1960).

470 BUTLER, NICHOLAS MURRAY. "The Place of Religious Instruction in Our Educational System," *Vital Speeches,* 7:167-68 (Jan. 1, 1941).

471 BUTLER, WILLIAM J. "No Lamb of God in School," *Catholic World,* 167:203-11 (June, 1948).

472 BYRD, OLIVER ERASMUS. "Religion and the School Health Program," *California Journal of Secondary Education,* 30:66-69 (Feb., 1955).

473 "Can Our Public Schools Do More About Religion?" *Journal of Education,* 125:245-47 (Nov.), 273-75 (Dec., 1942).

> Answers by: Rev. F. Ernest Johnson, 245. Rev. Israel S. Chipkin, 245-46. Rev. Everett R. Clinchy, 246-47. Rev. J. Elliot Ross, C.S.P., 272. Rev. Harold J. Ockenga, 273-74. Rt. Rev. William A. Scully, 274-75.

474 CANAVAN, FRANCIS P. "The State as Educator," *Thought,* 25:487-96 (Sept., 1950).

475 CARMICHAEL, A. MAX. "What Shall Be Done about Religion in the Public Schools," *Progressive Education,* 30:161-65 (Apr., 1953).

476 CASWELL, HOLLIS L. "Are the Public Schools Irreligious?" *Vital Speeches,* 19:399-402 (Apr. 15, 1953). Same. *Teachers College Record,* 54:357-65 (Apr., 1953).

477　CHAMBERLIN, J. GORDON. "The Dilemma of the Christian Teacher," *Teachers College Record*, 54:38-42 (Oct., 1952).

478　CHILDS, JOHN L. "Spiritual Values in Public Education," *Teachers College Record*, 48:367-73 (March, 1947).

479　"The Church and Public Schools," *International Journal of Religious Education*, 34:3-52 (May, 1958). (Special issue).

　　　Contents. "God in the classroom," Charles M. Laymon, 3. "Beyond moral and spiritual values," Lawrence C. Little, 45-46. "Multiply your effectiveness," Leonard Grindstaff, 6, 7, 52. "Grouping and grading," Ruth Strang, 8, 9, 46. "Home, Church and School," George C. Chamis, 10, 11. "A short reading list on religion and public education," 11. "Weekday Church school—a bridge," Alice L. Goddard, 12-13 "An educational platform for the public schools," George H. Reavis, 14-27. "Live issues; a guide to the use of an educational platform, either individually or in groups," Gerald E. Knoff, 27-30.

480　CLARK, SAMUEL I. "Religion in Public Education," *American Association of University Professors, Bulletin*, 40:645-56 (Winter, 1954-55).

481　CLAYTON, JOHN WESLEY. "The 'Gray Ghosts' of the PTA," *Christianity Today*, 3:15 (May 11, 1959).

482　CLEARY, CATHERINE B. "Putting God in a School System," *America*, 85:595-96 (Sept. 22, 1951).

　　　Plaques with motto 'In God We Trust' placed in the public schools of Stamford, Conn., through the efforts of a housewife.

483　COE, GEORGE A., and JOHNSON, F. ERNEST. "Religion in Public Education? A Forum," *International Journal of Religious Education*, 18:4, 36 (Sept.), 4, 34 (Oct.), 4, 18 (Nov.), 4, 32 (Dec., 1941).

484　COE, GEORGE A. "Religion, Education, Democracy," *Religious Education*, 35:131-37 (July-Sept., 1940).

485　——————. "Shall the State Teach Religion?" *School and Society*, 51:129-33 (Feb. 3, 1940). Reply. C. E. Hagie, "Religion in the Schools?-Yes!" *School and Society*, 51:677-79 (May 25, 1940).

486 ——————. "What Sort of Religion?" *International Journal of Religious Education,* 17:13-14 (Nov., 1940).

487 ——————. "The Word 'Religion,' " *School and Society,* 70:17-19 (July 9, 1949).

488 COLE, STEWART G., and TREPP, LEO. "Religion and the Public Schools—A Symposium," *Religious Education,* 48:158-68 (May-June, 1953).

> Contents. "The Dilemma of the Public School Educator," Stewart G. Cole, pp.158-65.
>
> "A Report on Teacher Attitudes Regarding Moral and Spiritual Values in Public Education," Leo Trepp, pp.166-68.

489 CONNELL, FRANCIS J., C.S.S.R. "Religious Instruction in the Public Schools," *American Ecclesiastical Review,* 135:199-201 (Sept., 1956).

> Answer to a question about the problem of teaching a common core of religious values.

490 COOGAN, J. E. "That Wall of Separation and the Public School," *Catholic World,* 172:252-55 (Jan., 1951). Same. *Catholic Mind,* 46:317-71 (June, 1951).

491 COSTANZO, JOSEPH F. "Religion in Public School Education," *Thought,* 31:216-44 (Summer, 1956).

492 COURTIS, STUART A. "Religion Has No Place in Public Schools," *Nation's Schools,* 39:22-23 (June, 1947).

493 COUSINS, NORMAN. "Religion and the Schools," *Saturday Review,* 34:16 (Dec. 29, 1951). Discussion. 35:23 (Jan. 19), 24 (Feb. 2), 26 (Feb. 16, 1952).

> Reflections based on a decision of the New York State Board of Regents to omit questions on the germ theory of disease in order not to offend Christian Scientists.

494 CURRY, L. C. "Education and Religion," *Kentucky School Journal,* 21:15-16 (Dec., 1942).

495 ——————. "How Godless is Public Education?" *Kentucky School Journal,* 22:43-44 (Feb., 1944).

496　DANA, ELLIS H. "Education for What?" *Christian Education*, 30:323-29 (Dec., 1947).

497　DAVIS, HAROLD L. "Dealing with Religious Differences," *The National Elementary Principal*, 37:83-87 (Sept., 1957) (36th yearbook).

498　DONOVAN, CHARLES F., S.J. "Need We Fear the Public Schools?" *Catholic Educational Review*, 48:299-305 (May, 1950).

499　DONOVAN, JOSEPH P. "Are our Tax-Supported Schools Public?" *Homiletic and Pastoral Review*, 46:419-26 (March, 1946).

500　DURGIN, LAWRENCE L. "Honest Talk in Churches," *Social Action*, 22:18-26 (March, 1957).

501　EDMONSON, JAMES B. "Do the Public Schools Emphasize Moral and Spiritual Values?" *Kentucky School Journal*, 32:10-12 (Dec., 1953).

　　　Same. *Virginia Journal of Education*, 47:9-10 (Dec., 1953). *Ohio Schools*, 32:12-13 (Jan., 1954). *Michigan Education Journal*, 31:274-75 (Feb., 1954). *Michigan Schools*, 68:20-1 (Apr., 1954).

502　───────. "Sectarian Pressure on Public Schools," *Nation's Schools*, 40:29 (Oct., 1947).

503　───────. "Teachers' Opinions on Religion and the Public Schools," *Religious Education*, 42:330-32 (Nov.-Dec., 1947).

504　ELLIOTT, HARRISON S., and COLE, STEWART G. "Religious Education and Public Education, a Suggested Syllabus," *Religious Education*, 35:195-209 (Oct.-Dec., 1940).

　　　Contents: "The Place of Religion in Elementary and Secondary Education," by Harrison S. Elliott, pp.195-204.

　　　"The Place of Religion in Higher Education," by Stewart G. Cole.

505　FADENRECHT, JOHN H. "Moral and Spiritual Values in Public Education," *Educational Administration and Supervision*, 43:49-58 (Jan., 1957).

506 FAHS, SOPHIA LYON. "Religion in the Public Schools. Values at Stake," *University of Pennsylvania Bulletin*, 41:122-31 (June 26, 1941).

This issue: University of Pennsylvania, School of Education. "Roads to the Future." (Twenty-Eighth Annual Schoolmen's Week, Proceedings, March 26-29, 1941.)

507 FEY, HAROLD E. "Religion in Public Education," *Christian Century*, 66:231-33 (Feb. 23, 1949).

508 FOSDICK, HARRY E. "Shall American School Children be Religiously Illiterate?" *School and Society*, 66:401-06 (Nov. 29, 1947).

Same. Condensed. *Readers Digest*, 54:97-100 (Feb., 1949). Discussion. *School and Society*, 67:140-41 (Feb. 21, 1948), R. H. Beck, 240-41 (March 27, 1948).

509 FOX, GEORGE G. "Religious Education, but not in Public Schools," *Religious Education*, 36:212-19 (Oct.-Dec., 1941).

510 GARBER, LEE O. "Display of Ten Commandments, Saying Grace, Ruled Illegal," *Nation's Schools*, 60:45-46 (Dec., 1957).

Same. Condensed. *Education Digest*, 23:17-19 (March, 1958).

511 GAUERKE, WARREN E. "Religion and the Public Schools: Some Legal Problems," *School and Society*, 75:401-04 (June 28, 1952).

512 GOLDIN, JUDAH. "Spiritual Values in Public Education," *National Education Association Journal*, 41:588-89 (Dec., 1952).

513 GRANT, DOROTHY FREMONT. "Services Rendered for Taxes Paid," *Ave Maria*, 70:391-97 (Sept. 24, 1949).

514 HARDON, JOHN AUGUSTINE, S.J. "Religion in the Public Schools," *Catholic Educational Review*, 56:289-98 (May, 1958).

515 HARTNETT, ROBERT CLINTON, S.J. "Alternatives to Released Time," *America*, 80:37-39 (Oct. 16, 1948).

516 HAUSER, CONRAD AUGUSTINE. "Hands Off the Public Schools?" *Religious Education*, 37:99-104 (March-Apr., 1942).

517 HAY, CLYDE LEMONT. "Our Bifurcated Educational System," *Religious Education*, 43:72-74 (March-Apr., 1948).

518 HENRY, CARL F. H. "Christian Responsibility in Education," *Christianity Today*, I:11-14 (May 27, 1957).

519 HILL, HENRY H. "Public Schools Must be Secular," *Atlantic Monthly*, 190:75-77 (Oct., 1952). Discussion, 190:20 (Dec., 1952).

520 HOGAN, G. STUART. "Underprivileged Children of the Public Schools," *Catholic Mind*, 38:126-37 (Apr. 8, 1940).

Comments about the "Friends of the Public Schools," and their attitude about religion in public education.

521 HOLMES, HENRY W. "God in the Public Schools," *Atlantic Monthly*, 166:99-105 (July, 1940).

522 HOWE, MARK DeWOLFE. "Religion and Race in Public Education," *Buffalo Law Review*, 8:242-250 (Winter, 1959).

N.B.: "Religion," pp.242-247.

523 "How Should Public Schools Celebrate Holidays—or Should They? Superintendents Disagree on the Answer," *Nation's Schools*, 59:92,94 (Feb., 1957).

An opinion poll.

524 HUNT, HEROLD C. "Are Public Schools Godless?" *School Executive*, 71:19-22 (May, 1952).

525 HUNT, ROLFE LANIER. "Christian Concern for the Public Schools," *Social Action*, 24:4-10 (Feb., 1958).

526 —————. "How Far Can Public Schools Go?" *International Journal of Religious Education*, 30:20-22 (Apr., 1954).

527 —————. "How Shall Public Schools Deal with Religion?" *International Journal of Religious Education,* 32:8-10 (Oct., 1955).

528 —————. "Religion in Public Education," *Phi Delta Kappan,* 36:243-44, 256 (Apr., 1955).

529 —————. "Religion: Its Relation to Public Education," *Nation's Schools,* 67:59-65, 106, 108, 110, 112 (March, 1961).

An interview reported by Arthur H. Rice.

530 JARMAN, BERNICE HERMAN. "Religious Education and the Public School," *School and Society,* 67:44-46 (Jan. 17, 1948).

531 JOHNSON, F. ERNEST. "Church, State and School," *Education,* 71:353-57 (Feb., 1951).

532 —————. "The Place of Religion in Public Education," *Education,* 64:521-23 (May, 1944).

533 —————. "Religion and Education," *Teachers College Record,* 57:378-85 (March, 1956).

534 —————. "Religion and Public Education," *National Association of Secondary-School Principals, Bulletin,* 31:95-102 (Apr., 1947).

535 —————. "Religion and Public Education," *Social Action,* 24:11-14 (February, 1958).

Abstract (prepared by the author) of an address delivered at a conference on public education held at Mansfield, Ohio, by the social action agencies of the Evangelical and Reformed Church and the Congregational Christian Churches in February, 1957.

536 —————. "Religion and Public Education; a major force in history and contemporary life," *Vital Speeches,* 16:311-14 (March 1, 1950).

537 —————. "Religion and the Philosophy of Education," *Vital Speeches,* 7:35-39 (Nov. 1, 1940).

538 —————. "Religious Education in Public Schools," *Contemporary Jewish Record*, 3:459-69 (Sept.-Oct., 1940).

539 —————. "Spiritual Values in the Secondary School Program," *National Association of Secondary-School Principals, Bulletin,* 35:47-52 (Apr., 1951).

540 —————. "The Wall of Secularism," *Social Action,* 19:30-32 (Dec., 1952).

541 KALLEN, HORACE MEYER. "Churchmen's Claims on the Public School," *Nation's Schools,* 29:49-50 (May), 52-53 (June, 1942).

> For a formulation of the author's religious views, see "Democracy's True Religion," *Saturday Review of Literature,* 34:6-7, 29-30 (July 28, 1951). Discussion. 34:26-27 (Sept. 1), 25 (Sept. 22, 1951).

> Horace M. Kallen is the author of *Secularism is the Will of God, An Essay in the Social Philosophy of Democracy and Religion.* New York: Twayne Publishers, 1954. 233pp.

542 KEPNER, CHARLES W. "The School Challenges the Church," *School and Society,* 52:215-19 (Sept. 21, 1940).

543 KILPATRICK, HAROLD. "Texas Teachers in Religious Re-training," *National Council Outlook,* 9:20-21 (May, 1959).

544 KING, LAUREN ALFRED. "How Far: Not Whether but How; the Teacher's Religious Opinions in the Classroom," *Journal of Higher Education,* 26:361-65 (Oct., 1955).

545 KIZER, ELMER W. "Spiritual Values in the Secondary School Program," *National Association of Secondary-School Principals, Bulletin,* 35:53-59 (Apr., 1951).

546 KUIPER, RIENK BOURKE, and MULLER, RALPH L. "Our Public School System is Fallacious" (by R. B. Kuiper); "Our Public School System is Sound" (by Ralph L. Muller), *Nation's Schools,* 37:26-28 (June, 1946).

547 LEIBSON, BERNARD. "The Public Schools: Are they 'Godless' or Ethical?" *Clearing House,* 27:3-7 (Sept., 1952).

548 LEWIS, JOSEPH. "More Objections to Religion and the Bible in Public Schools," *Teachers College Journal,* 15:52-53 (Jan., 1944).

549 LITTLE, LAWRENCE C. "Syllabus on Religion and Public Education," *Religious Education,* 44:163-80 (May-June, 1949). Selected bibliography, pp.177-180.

550 LUCKS, HENRY A. "Integrating Religious Instruction and Public School Studies," *Catholic Educational Review,* 52:26-35 (Jan., 1954).

551 LUM, CHEONG, KAGHEHIRO, GEORGE, and LARM, EDWIN. "Some Thoughts on Moral and Spiritual Values and the Secular Public School," *Progressive Education,* 30:166-71 (Apr., 1953).

552 LYNN, ROBERT W. "The Public Schools and Protestant Faith," *Social Action,* 19:2-29 (Dec., 1952).

553 McCAFFREY, KENNETH J. "Hanukkah and Christmas," *Commonweal,* 67:289-290 (Dec. 13, 1957).

554 McCASLAND, S. VERNON. "Our Secularized Education," *Christian Century,* 58:1576-78 (Dec. 17, 1941).

555 McCLUSKEY, NEIL GERARD, S.J. "Spiritual Values in the Public Schools," *America,* 95:619-20 (Sept. 29, 1956). Note, p.606.

556 MADIGAN, LAWRENCE M. "Religion in the Public School," *Catholic World,* 189:201-207 (June, 1959). Reprinted in the *Catholic Mind,* 58:315-322 (July-August, 1960).

557 MARTIN, ALLYE A. "Keep God in our Public Schools," *Texas Outlook,* 43:24-25 (April, 1959).

558 MARTIN, RENWICK HARPER. "Fourth R in American Education," *Christianity Today,* 1:11-12 (Sept. 2, 1957).

559   MAYER, FREDERICK. "Education and Religion," *Phi Delta Kappan,* 36:245-48 (Apr., 1955).

560   MATER, MILTON. "The Vestige of God," *Commonweal,* 52:11-15 (Apr. 14, 1950).

561   MEYER, AGNES E. "The Public School and Sectarian Religion," *Educational Forum,* 12:435-50 (May, 1948). Same. Condensed. *School Executive,* 67:37-38 (Feb., 1948), *Readers' Digest,* 52:65-69 (March, 1948).

      Reply. Ralph J. Dyer, S.M., "Sorry, Lady, We were there First," *Catholic Educator,* 19:24-25 (Sept., 1948).

562   MEYER, CARL S. "Religion in the Public Schools," *Concordia Theological Monthly,* 28:81-109 (Feb., 1957).

563   MILLER, WILLIAM LEE. "The Fight Over America's Fourth 'R,'" *The Reporter,* 14:20-26 (March 22, 1956).

      Reprinted by the American Jewish Committee.

564   MILLIGAN, JOHN P. "Think on These Things When you Hear Someone Say the Schools are Godless," *National Education Association Journal,* 41:587 (Dec., 1952).

565   MOEHLMAN, ARTHUR B. "Sectarian Attitudes toward Public Schools," *Nation's Schools,* 38:19 (Dec., 1946).

566   MONES, LEON. "The Problem of Religious and Moral Education in our Public Schools," *Education,* 74:250-56 (Dec., 1953).

567   MORRISON, CHARLES CLAYTON. "The Inner Citadel of Democracy," *Christian Century,* 58:617-19 (May 7), 652-54 (May 14, 1941).

568   MULFORD, HERBERT B. "As Public Education Defaults on Religion," *School and Society,* 64:443-44 (Dec. 21, 1946).

569   ————. "A New Spiritual Chapter in Public Education," *American School Board Journal,* 131:29-30 (July, 1955).

570 ————. "A Pattern for Religion in Public Education," *Religious Education,* 49:333-36 (Sept.-Oct., 1954).

571 ————. "Public School Boards Face Dilemma in Religious Education," *Religious Education,* 43:68-71 (March-Apr., 1948).

572 ————. "This is a Religious Nation," *American School Board Journal,* 124:39-40 (Feb., 1952).

573 ————. "Toward a New Spiritual Formula for Public Education," *American School Board Journal,* 128:33-34 (May, 1954).

574 MUNN, MERTON DEMING, and YODER, DAYTON T. "Teaching Religion in Public Schools? Yes." M. D. Munn. "Teaching Religion in Public Schools? No." D. T. Yoder, *Religious Education,* 37:213-20 (July-Aug., 1942).

575 MURPHY, JOHN L. "Religious Education and Democracy; The Moral Training of our Young People," *Vital Speeches of the Day,* 26:30-32 (Oct. 15, 1959).

576 NACHLAS, MORTON deCORCEY. "A Study of Attitudes of School Administrators Toward Religious Instruction in the High School," *National Association of Secondary-School Principals, Bulletin,* 36:95-100 (Oct., 1952).

577 NATHANSON, JEROME. "Foot in the Door," *Nation,* 173: 423-25 (Nov. 17, 1951). Same in Theodore Brameld (ed.), *Battle for Free Schools (Beacon Reference Series).* Boston: Beacon Press, 1951. Pp.39-46.

578 NATIONAL CATHOLIC WELFARE CONFERENCE. "Secularism," Statement issued by the Catholic Bishops of the United States, Nov. 14, 1947. In Raphael M. Huber (ed.), *Our Bishops Speak; National Pastorals of the Hierarchy of the United States.* Milwaukee, Wis.: Bruce, 1952. Pp.137-145. Same. *Catholic Mind,* 46:1-8 (Jan., 1948).

Statement often referred to in the literature about religion in public education.

579 NATIONAL CONFERENCE ON RELIGION AND PUBLIC EDU-
CATION. "Public Education and Religion; A Study
Document for Churches on the National Conference
on Religion and Public Education," *International
Journal of Religious Education*, 32:21-52 (March,
1956). Edited by Rolfe Lanier Hunt.

Report on the "National Conference on Religion and Public
Education," held at Saint Louis, Mo., Nov. 6-8, 1955. The
conference was sponsored by the National Council of the
Churches of Christ in the U.S.A., Committee on Religion and
Public Education.

State regulations concerning religion and public education
are given on pp.34-40, in a summary prepared by Don. Conway.

COMMENTS:
Eugene Carson Blake, "Why does the National Council of
Churches Sponsor a Conference on Religion in Public Education?" *Religious Education*, 51:259-65 (July, 1956). John
Augustine Hardon, S.J., "National Council Considers Religion
and Public Education," *Catholic Educator*, 27:594-595 (May,
1957).

580 NATIONAL COUNCIL OF THE CHURCHES OF CHRIST IN
THE UNITED STATES OF AMERICA. "Relation of Religion to Public Education; Study Document," *International Journal of Religious Education*, 36:21-36
(April, 1960).

Text reprinted by the National Council.

COMMENTS:
Religious Education, 55:265-296 (July-August, 1960). Contents. "Relation of Religion to Public Education," by Rolfe
Lanier Hunt, 265-69. "A Protestant Looks at the Study Document," by John C. Bennett, 269-273. "Observations from a
Catholic Viewpoint," by Neil G. McCluskey, S.J., 273-278.
"Public Aid to Religious Schools?" by William W. Brickman,
279-288. "A New Trend in Weekday Religious Education,"
by Alice L. Goddard, 288-292. "Religious Holiday Observance
in Public Schools," by J. Leonard Azneer, 293-296.

Frederick Ernest Johnson. "Religion and Public Education,"
Christianity and Crisis, 20:127-128 (Sept. 19, 1960).

581 NORTON, ALBERT CHARLES. "Christianity and our
Schools," *Christianity To-day*, 2:8-10 (May 12, 1958).

Comment on the hundreth anniversary (1857-1957) of the
National Education Association of the United States.

582 "Our Public Schools—A Masonic Monopoly?" *Social
Justice Review*, 51:268-269 (Dec., 1958).

583 PALMER, RAYMOND RODERICK. "Should Religion be Taught in the Public Schools?" *Social Studies, 49*: 17-20 (Jan., 1958).

584 "Parents Please Read," by a Public School Teacher, *The Sign,* 22:301 (Dec., 1942).

585 PARKER, ALFRED E. "Consensus on Religion in the Schools," *Phi Delta Kappan,* 38:145-47 (Jan., 1957).

586 PATTERSON, CECIL H. "Religion in Education: Its Status Under Federal Law," *Progressive Education,* 31:22-25 (Oct., 1953).

587 PAYNE, ELIZABETH CARAMAN. "Moses is Nobody," *Christian Century,* 68:106-08 (Jan. 24, 1951).

588 PHENIX, PHILIP H. "Religion in American Public Education," *Teachers College Record,* 57:26-31 (Oct., 1955).

589 POPE, LISTON. "Religion and our Schools," *American Magazine,* 153:24-25, 110-14 (May, 1952).

590 POWERS, FRANCIS J. "Current Decisions on Religious Education and Observances in Public Schools," *Catholic Educational Review,* 49:217-27 (Apr., 1951).

591 "Public Schools Can Teach Religion!" *Christian Century,* 65:374-76 (Apr. 28, 1948).

592 PUNKE, HAROLD H. "Religion in American Public Schools," *Religious Education,* 52:113-40 (March-Apr., 1957).

593 QUIGLEY, A. E. "Catholic Teachers in Public Schools; How Much do a Teacher's Religious Convictions Affect Her Work in the Classroom?" *Commonweal,* 31:426-28 (March 8, 1940). Reply. E. Sheridan, 31: 493 (March 29, 1940).

594 READ, GERALD. "Concerns for Religion and Education," *Phi Delta Kappan,* 36:267-68 (Apr., 1955).

595　"Religion and Public Education—A Symposium," *Religious Education,* 44:323-47 (Nov.-Dec., 1949).

Contents. "An Opportunity for Public Education," Samuel P. Franklin, 323-26. "Legal Aspects of Religious Education on Released Time," Thomas West, 327-31. "Religion and the Public Schools—Trends in Protestant Thinking," Erwin L. Shaver, 332-35. "The Faith of Youth as Shown by a Survey in Public Schools in Los Angeles," Erma Pixley and Emma Beekman, 336-42. "Religious Education in British Schools," Herbert L. Ewin, 343-47.

596　"Religion and the Public Schools—Symposium," *Religious Education,* 51:243-75 (July-Aug., 1956).

Contents. "Different Approaches in Dealing with Religion in the Public School," William Clayton Bower, 243-45. "Kentucky Pioneers," J. Mansir Tydings, 245-49. "Things To Be Done," Leo R. Ward, 250-54. "The Schools and Religion," G. H. Reavis, 255-58. "Why Does the National Council of Churches Sponsor a Conference on Religion in Public Education?" Eugene Carson Blake, 259-65. "The AACTE Teacher Education and Religion Project at Mid-Passage," A. L. Sebaly, 266-69. Three Case Studies. "Education About Religion," H. L. Shibler, 270-71. "Teaching of Moral and Spiritual Values in the Cincinnati Public Schools," Claude V. Courter, 270-71. "A Brief Sketch of the Development of Moral and Spiritual Values in the Los Angeles City Schools," Erma Pixley, 272-75.

597　"Religion in Education," *America,* 91:394 (July 17), 414 (July 24), 434 (July 31), 454 (Aug. 7, 1954).

598　"Religion in Public Education," *Catholic Action,* 29: 13-15 (Dec., 1947).

599　"Religion in the Public Schools," *Christian Century,* 58:384-85 (March 19, 1941).

600　"Religion in the Public Schools—A Symposium," *Religious Education,* 50:211-46 (July-Aug., 1955).

Contents. "A Proposed Program for Achieving the Role of Religion in Education," William Clayton Bower, 211-18. "Religion and Public Education—A Personalist Viewpoint," Charles Donahue, 219-24. "A Workshop on Religion in the Public Schools," Arthur Gilbert, 225-31. "Religion in Public Education," American Jewish Committee, 232-37. "Religion in Teacher Education," Eugene E. Dawson, 238-42. "Teaching Spiritual Values in the Public Schools," Herbert F. A. Smith, 243-46.

601 "Religion in the Schools: Does God Belong?" *America,* 94:296-97 (Dec. 10, 1955).

602 "Religious Education and the Public Schools—A Symposium," *Religious Education,* 43:193-228 (July-Aug., 1948).

> Contents. "The Language of the Problem," Samuel P. Franklin, 193-97. "Major Issues in the Proposals to Make Agencies of Public Education Responsible for Teaching Religion," Harrison S. Elliott, 198-200. "Religion and the Schools—What Can We Hope For?" F. Ernest Johnson, 201-06. "Religion and the Public Schools—What to Guard Against," Solomon B. Freehof, 207-10. "The Legal Situation Resulting From the Recent Supreme Court Decision," Madaline Kinter Remmlein, 211-16. "The Relationship Between Government and Church-Sponsored Education," Thomas J. Quigley, 217-22. "To Reduce Tensions Between Government and Church-Sponsored Education," Ernest W. Kuebler, 223-28.

603 "Religious Education in the Public Schools," *National Education Association, Research Bulletin,* 35:169-71 (Dec., 1957).

604 "Religious Teaching in Public Schools?" *U. S. News and World Report,* 45:78 (Dec. 26, 1958).

605 RICE, ARTHUR H. "What Shall Schools Teach about Religion?" *Nation's Schools,* 44:20 (July, 1949).

606 ROGERS, VIRGIL M. "Are the Public Schools 'Godless'?" *Christian Century,* 74:1065-67 (Sept. 11, 1957). Discussion. 74:1204 (Oct. 9, 1957).

607 RYAN, CARL J. "Democracy as a Religion," *School and Society,* 83:217-19 (June 23, 1956). Reply. F. C. Neff, 85:133-34 (April 13, 1957). Reply. C. Reed, 85:298 (Oct. 12, 1957).

608 ————. "Religion and Public Education," *Catholic Educational Review,* 57:532-536 (Nov., 1959).

609 SCHISLER, JOHN Q. "Religion and the Public Schools," *Religion in Life,* 21:83-93 (Winter, 1951-52).

610 SEITZ, W. C. "Religious Education in Homogeneous School Districts," *Religious Education,* 37:49-51 (Jan.-Feb., 1942).

611 SERAMUR, (Sister) CLARITA. "The Place Religion Holds in Our Public School System Today," *Catholic Educational Review,* 41:347-53 (June, 1943).

612 SHATTUCK, GEORGE E. "Religious Education in the Schools?" *School and Society,* 53:372-73 (March 22, 1941).

613 SHERWIN, J. STEPHEN. "Christmas in the Schools," *School and Society,* 85:331-33 (Nov. 9, 1957). Reply. E. J. Kammer, 86:66 (Feb. 1, 1958).

614 SISSON, EDWARD O. "Teaching Religion in Public School is Playing with Fire," *Nation's Schools,* 35: 43-44 (June, 1945).

615 SMITH, CHARLES BUNYAN. "American Public Schools Must Remain Secular," *Journal of Teacher Education,* 8:201-206 (June, 1957).

616 SOUTHCOTT, LYALL W. "Religion and Education—Past, Present and Future," *Teachers College Journal,* 15: 68-69 (Jan., 1944).

   Critique: Edward R. Bartlett. "Teaching Religion in a Democracy," 15:70-71 (Jan., 1944).

617 SOUTHWORTH, WILLIAM D. "Religion and the Public Schools," *Clearing House,* 32:515-516 (May, 1958).

618 "Spiritual Values and Public Education," *New York State Education,* 33:529-45 (Apr., 1956) (special issue).

   Contents. "A Moral and Spiritual Reawakening," Harry S. Truman, 528. "Spiritual Values and Public Education," W. Earl Ledden, 529-30. "Public Schools and the Crisis in Spiritual Values," John S. Brubacher, 531-34. "We Learn What We Live," William Heard Kilpatrick, 535-37. "Teaching Values in American Schools," Ruth Cunningham, 538-40. "Spiritual Values in Secondary Education," Harry J. Linton, 541-44. "Spiritual Values in Education," Mary B. Henderson, 545.

619 "Spiritual Values in the Elementary School," *National Elementary Principal,* 27:1-351 (Sept., 1947).

   This issue is the twenty-sixth yearbook of the Department of Elementary School Principals of the National Education Association of the United States.

620 STEWART, JOHN T. "Teaching 'About' Religion," *Christian Century,* 72:1360-61 (Nov. 23, 1955).

621 SUTTON, WILLIS A. "Let's Teach Religion in the Public Schools," *International Journal of Religious Education,* 17:12, 40 (Nov., 1940).

622 SWEET, WILLIAM W. "Our Educational Dilemma," *International Journal of Religious Education,* 17:6, 7, 14 (Nov., 1940).

623 TAFT, CHARLES P. "Religion and the Public Schools," *National Education Association Proceedings,* 1952: 81-85. Same. *Christian Century,* 69:944-46 (Aug. 20, 1952).

624 THAYER, VIVIAN TROW. "Our Secular Schools and Religion," *Phi Delta Kappan,* 34:394-98 (June, 1953).

625 ————————. "Religion and the Public Schools," *Harper's Magazine,* 188:458-66 (Apr., 1944).

626 TIESZEN, D. W. "Legal Concepts Concerning Religious Influences in Public Education as Defined by State Courts of Last Resort," *Teachers College Record,* 55:61-69 (Nov., 1953).

627 TRAGER, FRANK N. "The Big Blooming Buzzing Confusion—Religion in Public Education," *Religious Education,* 46:82-89 (March-Apr., 1951).

628 TUTTLE, CHARLES H. "Public Schools and Religious Education; the Child is not the Mere Creature of the State," *Vital Speeches,* 7:279-80 (Feb. 15, 1941).

629 VANDER WERF, LESTER. "Symbols of our Concern," *Educational Leadership,* 13:117-23 (Nov., 1955). See also "Religion and Education," pp.121, 122.

630 VAN DUSEN, HENRY P., and NORTON, JOHN K. "What Should be the Relation of Religion and Public Education?" *Teachers College Record,* 56:1-15 (Oct., 1954).

    Two answers to a question.

631 "Wall or Wavy Line?" *Christian Century*, 78:35-36 (Jan. 11, 1961).

632 WEIGLE, LUTHER A. "The Crisis of Religion in Education; Schools Cannot be Neutral as to God," *Vital Speeches*, 20:147-49 (Dec. 15, 1953).

633 ————. "Public Education and Religion," *Religious Education*, 35:67-75 (Apr.-June, 1940).

634 ————. "Religion in Public Education," *University of Pennsylvania Bulletin*, 42:340-52 (June 26, 1942). This issue: University of Pennsylvania School of Education. "Education in a Nation at War." Twenty-Ninth Annual Schoolmen's Week, Proceedings, March 18-21, 1942.

635 "What Shall Public Schools Teach about Religion?" *School Executive*, 70:57-66 (Dec., 1950).

636 "Where Theology and Politics Meet" (Editorial), *National Council Outlook*, 9:18 (Jan., 1959).

Comment on Christmas observances in the public schools.

637 WILLIAMS, GEORGE HUNSTON. "Church-State Separation and Religion in the Schools of our Democracy," *Religious Education*, 51:369-77 (Sept.-Oct., 1956).

638 ————. "The Church, the Democratic State, and the Crisis in Religious Education," *Harvard Divinity School Bulletin*, 46:35-61 (1949).

639 WILLIAMS, H. V. "What Can Be Done, About Teaching Religion in the American Public School?" *Nation's Schools*, 48:64-66, 68 (Sept., 1951).

Summary of the legal status of religious education in the public schools. Table of provisions by state.

640 WILLIAMS, J. PAUL. "The Schoolmen and Religion," *School and Society*, 70:97-100 (August 13, 1949).

641 WITHEY, RAYMOND A. "A Neglected Area of Education," *Educational Administration and Supervision*, 38:76-82 (Feb., 1952).

642 WORTH, CHARLES L. "The Public Schools and Religious Education," *School and Society*, 52:252-56 (Sept. 28, 1940).

643 WRIGHT, JOHN J. "The Religious Inspiration of Our Legal Tradition," *Religious Education*, 49:309-16 (Sept.-Oct., 1954).

644 ZWIERLEIN, FREDERICK J. "Opposition to Religious Education in Public Schools," *Social Justice Review*, 41: 114-17 (July-Aug.), 149-52 (Sept., 1948).

645 —————. "Religion in Schools?" *Social Justice Review*, 46:293-96 (Jan.), 327-29 (Feb.), 365-68 (March, 1954). 47:1-5 (Apr.), 46-48 (May), 228-29 (Nov.), 261-64 (Dec., 1954), 297-99 (Jan., 1955).

D. UNPUBLISHED DISSERTATIONS

646 ANDERSON, HENRIETTA. "Some Aspects of Religious Education and the Public Schools." Grand Forks, N.D.: University of North Dakota, 1953. (Unpublished master's dissertation)

647 BEAULIEU, LOUIS P. "A Discriminative Survey of Leading Theories and Practices for Giving Due Recognition to Religion in the Public Schools." Los Angeles, Calif.: University of Southern California, 1958. (Unpublished master's dissertation)

648 BLACKSTON, HELEN G. "Moral and Spiritual Values in Public Education: Primary Grades." Austin, Texas: University of Texas, 1954. (Unpublished master's dissertation)

649 BORTNER, ROSS L. "Teaching Spiritual Values in the Elementary Public School." Philadelphia, Pa.: University of Pennsylvania, 1956. (Unpublished doctoral dissertation)

650 CAMPBELL, (Sister) MARGARET. "Religious Instruction and Public Education." Chicago, Ill.: De Paul University, 1953. (Unpublished master's dissertation)

651 COLEMAN, H. GERTRUDE. "An Inquiry into the Function of Religion in the Public Schools of America." Providence, R.I.: Rhode Island College of Education, 1954. (Unpublished master's dissertation)

652 COLLINGON, (Sister) M. ROSE RITA. "Views of Public School Educators on Moral and Spiritual Values as Evidenced in Selected Educational Periodicals." Washington, D.C.: Catholic University of America, 1958. (Unpublished master's dissertation)

653 CROUCH, HUGH C. "Religious Education in Certain Tax-Supported, Teacher Education Institutions." Macomb, Ill.: Western Illinois State College, 1956. (Unpublished master's dissertation)

654 DALIN, GALEN E. "Some Legal Aspects of Religion in Public Schools of the United States." Mankato, Minn.: Minnesota State Teachers College, 1956. (Unpublished master's dissertation)

655 DANNEKER, CARL J. "The Concept of Religion as Held by Recent Non-Catholic Educational Writers." Washington, D. C.: Catholic University of America, 1950. (Unpublished master's dissertation)

656 DE BOER, RAY L. "Historical Study of Mormon Education and the Influence of Its Philosophy on Public Education in Utah." Denver, Colo.: University of Denver, 1952. (Unpublished doctoral dissertation)

657 DIERENFIELD, RICHARD BRUCE. "An Examination of the Current Relationships Between Religion and American Public Schools." Greely, Colo.: Colorado College of Education, 1958. (Unpublished doctoral dissertation)

658 DOWNIE, PAUL S. "The Relation of Religion to Public School Education." Ann Arbor, Mich.: University of Michigan, 1957. (Unpublished master's dissertation)

659 DUFFY, EUGENE. "Evaluation of the Teaching of Religion in the Secondary Schools of the United States." Los Angeles, Calif.: Immaculate Heart College, 1957. (Unpublished master's dissertation)

660 DUFFY, JANET. "Religion in the Public Schools." Garden City, N.Y.: Adelphi College, 1958. (Unpublished master's dissertation)

661 ESCH, I. LYND. "The Appreciation of Religious Values in the Public Schools." Los Angeles, Calif.: University of Southern California, 1942. (Unpublished doctoral dissertation)

662 FITZGIBBONS, MARK. "A Study of Certain Plans Relative to Religious Instruction as a Part of the Education of School Children, with Particular Reference to New York State." Syracuse, N.Y.: Syracuse University, 1949. (Unpublished doctoral dissertation)

663 FORCINELLI, JOSEPH. "School Administration and Religious Education in the Public Schools of America." Claremont, Calif.: Claremont College, 1955. (Unpublished master's dissertation)

664 GOADRICK, EDWARD W. "Religion, the Fourth 'R' in the American Public School Curriculum." Dillon, Mont.: Western Montana College of Education, 1956. (Unpublished master's dissertation)

665 HAYWOOD, MARIE W. "Meeting the Need for Moral and Character Training in the Public Elementary School." Detroit, Mich.: University of Detroit, 1954. (Unpublished master's dissertation)

666 HERDMAN, DONALD L. "Conceptions of Moral Education in the American Public Schools, 1865-1917." New Haven, Conn.: Yale University, 1950. (Unpublished doctoral dissertation)

667 HULSER, JOHN V. "Factors of Religion and Social Class in the Support of Public Schools." Storrs, Conn.: University of Connecticut, 1957. (Unpublished doctoral dissertation)

668 HUZICA, (Sister) MARY P. "Some of the Founding Fathers and their Ideas of Religion in Education." Cleveland, Ohio: St. John College, 1955. (Unpublished master's dissertation)

669 INCH, MORRIS ALTON. "Teaching About Religion in the Public Schools of the United States." Boston, Mass.: Boston University School of Theology, 1955. 291pp. (Unpublished doctoral dissertation)

> Abstract. *Dissertation Abstracts*, 15 no. 8:1453. Microfilm. Ann Arbor, Mich.: University Microfilms, Publication no. 12,297.

670 JEWETT, JAMES P. "Moral Education in American Public Schools, 1800-1860." Chicago, Ill.: University of Chicago, 1950. (Unpublished doctoral dissertation)

671 JOHNSON, ALVIN D. "Religion in Public Education." Storrs, Conn.: University of Connecticut, 1955. (Unpublished master's dissertation)

672 JOHNSON, DUANE L. "The Meaning of Moral and Spiritual Values in Contemporary Public Education." Fresno, Calif.: Fresno State College, 1956. (Unpublished master's dissertation)

673 JONES, ATTWOOD J. JR. "Southern Baptist Attitudes toward Church-State Cooperation in Religious Instruction, 1930-1952." Louisville, Ky.: Southern Baptist Theological Seminary, 1957. (Unpublished doctoral dissertation)

674 JORDAN, CHARLES F. "Views of the National Education Association on the Relation of the Public Schools to Religious Education." Baltimore, Md.: Loyola College, 1954. (Unpublished master's dissertation)

675 KRAMER, JOHN G. "A Critical Analysis of the Major Arguments against the Teaching of Religion in the Public Schools." Columbus, Ohio: Ohio State University, 1954. (Unpublished doctoral dissertation)

676 LIVINGSTON, ISAAC. "A Program for the Development of Moral and Spiritual Values in School Curricula." Claremont, Calif.: Claremont College, 1955. (Unpublished master's dissertation)

677 MALONE, HOWARD E. "A Review of the Laws Pertaining to Religion in the Public Schools of the United States." Claremont, Calif.: Claremont College, 1953. (Unpublished master's dissertation)

678 MARTIN, WILLIAM M. "Some Legal Aspects of Religion and the Public Schools." Morehead, Ky.: Morehead State College, 1952. (Unpublished master's dissertation)

679 MAXSON, WILLIAM E. "The Administration of Moral Education in the Public Secondary School." Medford, Mass.: Tufts College, 1953. (Unpublished master's dissertation)

680 MEAD, GERTRUDE F. "The Teaching of Moral and Spiritual Values." Macomb, Ill.: Western Illinois State College, 1955. (Unpublished master's dissertation)

681 MILLER, JAMES BLAIR. "Patterns of Disagreement Concerning Religion in Relation to Public Education in the United States." Bloomington, Ind.: Indiana University, 1955. (Unpublished doctoral dissertation)

682 MILLER, RAYMOND R. "The Legal Status of Religion in the Public Elementary and Secondary Schools of the United States." Bloomington, Ind.: Indiana University, 1949. (Unpublished doctoral dissertation)

683 MURRA, WILBUR F. "An Inquiry into the Role of Religion in the Public Schools of a Secular State." Minneapolis, Minn.: University of Minnesota, 1958. (Unpublished doctoral dissertation)

684 NORTON, EDWARD J. "A Critical Analysis of Plans for Teaching Moral and Spiritual Values in Public Schools." Washington, D.C.: Catholic University of America, 1954. (Unpublished master's dissertation)

Abstract. *Catholic Educational Review*, **53**:40 (Jan., 1955)

685 PEPPER, RAY E. "Religion in Public Education." Columbus, Ohio: Ohio State University, 1957. (Unpublished master's dissertation)

686 PFLUG, HAROLD E. "Theistic Religion in Missouri Public School Textbooks." New Haven, Conn.: Yale University, 1950. (Unpublished doctoral dissertation)

687 POLLARD, MARJORIE Y. "The Legal Aspects of Teaching Religion in the Public Schools." San Marcos, Texas: Southwest State Teachers College, 1957. (Unpublished master's dissertation)

688 REYNOLDS, CLARENCE ELIOT. "Basis of Cooperation in Religious Education Between Religion and the Public Schools." Stanford, Cal.: Stanford University, 1946. (Unpublished doctoral dissertation)

689 RITTS, JOE. "A Guide to Moral and Spiritual Values in the Elementary School." San Francisco, Cal.: San Francisco State College, 1955. (Unpublished master's dissertation)

690 SCHOLL, CAROLYN S. "Religion and Public Education: An Investigation of Existing Policies." Garden City, N.Y.: Adelphi College, 1955. (Unpublished master's dissertation)

691 SEYFERT, FREDERICK, JR. "Religion in Public Education." Meadville, Pennsylvania: Allegheny College, 1958. (Unpublished master's dissertation)

692 SLAUGHTER, JIM J., JR., "The Case for Religious Instruction in the Public High School." Austin, Texas: University of Texas, 1956. (Unpublished master's dissertation)

693 STUMP, LAWRENCE M. "Present Tendencies in the Teaching of Religion in the Public Schools of the United States." Tucson, Arizona: University of Arizona, 1946. (Unpublished doctoral dissertation)

694 THIMM, FRED. "The Need for Religious Education in American Public Schools." Detroit, Michigan: Wayne State University, 1957. (Unpublished master's dissertation)

695 TILL, JACOB E. "An Inquiry into Religious Values in the Public School Curriculum." Omaha, Neb.: University of Omaha, 1957. (Unpublished master's dissertation)

696 VICKERY, CHARLES E. "An Investigation of Religious Training in Tax-Supported Institutions for Delinquent Juveniles." Louisville, Ky.: Southern Baptist Theological Seminary, 1954. (Unpublished doctoral dissertation)

697 WARREN, HAROLD C. "Changing Conceptions in the Religious Elements in Early American School Readers." Pittsburgh, Pa.: University of Pittsburgh, 1951. (Unpublished doctoral dissertation)

698 WILSON, KARL K. "Historical Survey of the Religious Content of American Geography Textbooks from 1874 to 1895." Pittsburgh, Pa.: University of Pittsburgh, 1951. (Unpublished doctoral dissertation)

699 WOOD, VIRGINIA N. "Spiritual and Moral Education in the Public Schools Curriculum." Stanford, Calif.: Stanford University, 1950. (Unpublished doctoral dissertation)

E. STATE MATERIAL (With cases)

Alabama:

700 KENNEDY, ROBERT T. "An Analysis of Three Representative Proposals for Teaching Moral Values and a Proposed Program for Teaching Moral Values at Grayton Junior High-School, Okatchee, Alabama." Montgomery, Alabama: Alabama State College, 1957. (Unpublished master's dissertation)

California:

701 IMBLER, RAY MALCOLM. "The Teaching of Moral and Spiritual Values in California Public Schools." Stanford, Calif.: Stanford University, 1954. 236pp. (Unpublished doctoral dissertation)

> Abstract. *Dissertation Abstracts*, 14 no. 12:2294-95 (1954). Microfilm. Ann Arbor, Mich.: University Microfilms, publication no. 10,354.

702 RUCH, THOMAS O. "Teaching Moral and Spiritual Values: A Study of Administrative Attitudes in the Public High Schools of California." Fresno, Calif.: Fresno State College, 1956. (Unpublished master's dissertation)

Illinois:

703 SHAVER, ERWIN L. "Significant Aspects of the River Forest Plan," *Religious Education*, 35:231-35 (Oct.-Dec., 1940).

704 WASSON, ISABEL B. "The River Forest Plan of Week-Day Religious Education," *Religious Education*, 35:227-31 (Oct.-Dec., 1940).

> N.B.: Material about the Champaign Plan is entered in Unit V, "Released Time."

Indiana:

705 LIGGETT, ROBERT L. "An Investigation of Certain Aspects of Religious Education in the Public Schools of Indiana." Bloomington, Ind.: Indiana University, 1950. (Unpublished doctoral dissertation)

706 "Religion in Public Education" (Indianapolis Plan), *Christian Century*, 72:102-04 (Jan. 26, 1954). Reply. Stanley Lichtenstein, 72:177 (Feb. 9, 1955). Developments. 72:196 (Feb. 16, 1955). 72:214, 216 (Feb. 16, 1955).

Iowa:

707 LEWISTON, JAMES. "Religious Education in Some Selected High Schools of Iowa." Des Moines, Iowa: Drake University, 1956. (Unpublished master's dissertation)

Kentucky:

(1. Case Material)

-- 1956 --

708 *Wooley v. Spalding*, 293 S.W.2d 563 (Kentucky, 1956)

Decision forbidding various religious influences in schools maintained as part of the public school system. (Difficulties had been caused by the adjustment of schedules for religious activities, and other practices.)

Some issues considered in this case were related to issues in *Rawlings v. Butler*, 290 S.W.2d 801 (Kentucky, 1956).

Summary. *Yearbook of School Law*, 1958, pp.121-22, 124-25.

(2. Other Literature)

709 BOWER, WILLIAM CLAYTON. *Moral and Spiritual Values in Education*. Lexington, Ky.: University of Kentucky Press, 1952. 214pp.

710 EARLY, JACK JONES. "Religious Practices in the Public Schools in Selected Communities in Kentucky." Lexington, Ky.: University of Kentucky, 1956. 224pp. (Unpublished doctoral dissertation) Abstract. *Religious Education*, 52:184-85 (May-June, 1957).

711 HARTFORD, ELLIS FORD. *Emphasizing Moral and Spiritual Values in a Kentucky High School* (Bulletin of the Bureau of School Service, College of Education, University of Kentucky, Vol. 25, no. 1). Lexington, Ky.: 1952. 92pp.

712 —————. *Emphasizing Values in Five Kentucky Schools* (Bulletin of the Bureau of School Service, College of Education, Univesity of Kentucky, Vol. 26, no. 4). Lexington, Ky.: 1954. 124pp.

713 —————. *Moral Values in Public Education; Lessons from the Kentucky Experience*. New York: Harper, 1958. 338pp.

714 ───────. *The Public Schools, Religion and Values;
A series of Addresses on the Teaching of Moral and
Spiritual Values in Public Schools* (Bulletin of the
Bureau of School Service, College of Education, University of Kentucky, Vol. 28, no. 4). Lexington, Ky.:
1956. 51pp.

> REVIEW:
> *School and Society*, 85:126 (Apr. 13, 1957).

715 TREVITT, VIRGINIA S. "A Study of the Program of Moral
and Spiritual Values in Education in the State of
Kentucky." Claremont, Calif.: Claremont College,
1956. (Unpublished master's dissertation)

716 TYDINGS, J. MANSIR. "Kentucky Pioneers," *Religious
Education*, 51:246-49 (July-Aug., 1956).

Massachusetts:

717 CULVER, RAYMOND BENJAMIN. *Horace Mann and Religion in the Massachusetts Public Schools (Yale
studies in the history and theory of religious education, 3)*. New Haven, Conn.: Yale University Press,
1929. 301pp. Bibliography: 291-96.

Michigan:

718 ANDERSON, ROBERT T. "Religion in the Michigan Public
Schools," *School and Society*, 87:227-229 (May 9,
1959).

Missouri:

719 STEWART, JOHN T. "Religion in the Schools," *Christian
Century*, 76:980 (Aug. 26, 1959).

> Appeal of the metropolitan Church federation (St. Louis,
> Mo.) in a "Religion and Public Education Statement" suggesting more non-sectarian religious teaching in the public
> schools.

Nebraska:

720 SJORGREN, DOUGLASS D. "The Teaching of Moral and
Spiritual Values in Ninety-six Nebraska High
Schools." Kearney, Nebraska: Nebraska State Teachers College, 1958. (Unpublished master's dissertation)

New Mexico:
(Case Material)

-- 1952 --

721   *Miller v. Cooper*, 56 N.M. 355; 244 P.2d 520 (N.M., 1952)

> Decision forbidding various religious influences in public schools. (Objections had been raised against the circulation of religious literature and against other practices.)

New York:
(1. Case Material)

-- 1956 --

722   *Lewis v. Allen*, 5 Misc.2d 68; 159 N.Y.S.2d 807 (N.Y., 1956). Affirmed. 207 N.Y.S.2d 862 (Dec. 2, 1960).

> Decision affirming the constitutionality of school regulation recommending the recitation of the "Pledge of Allegiance" to the flag with the words "under God." (The recitation was voluntary and no penalties were imposed on those who might not wish to participate.)

> The text was used in *U. S. Code*, title 36, Section 172, amended June 14, 1954. (Ch. 297, 68 Stat. 249.) The amendment to the statute added the words "under God" to the pledge.

723   GARBER, LEE ORVILLE. "Court Defends 'Under God' in Pledge of Allegiance," *Nation's Schools*, 60:50-53 (Aug., 1957).

724   "Phrase 'Under God' and the First Amendment," *Catholic Lawyer*, 3:366-67 (Autumn, 1957).

-- 1958 --

725   *Baer v. Kolmorgen et al.*, 181 N.Y.S.2d 230 (N.Y., 1958)

> Decision permitting groups to set up Nativity scene on public school property during the Christmas season.

726   GARBER, LEE ORVILLE. "Christmas Creche May be placed on School Grounds," *Nation's Schools*, 64:82-84 (Dec., 1959).

-- 1959 --

727   *Engel v. Vitale,* 191 N.Y.S.2d 453 (N.Y., 1959) Affirmed,
       Appellate Div., 206 N.Y.S.2d 183. Affirmed, Court of
       Appeals, 218 N.Y.S.2d 659; 176 N.E.2d 183.

> Decision permitting the noncompulsory recitation of a non-
> denominational prayer approved for use in schools by the New
> York State Board of Regents.
>
> REVIEWS:
> *New York Forum,* 6:321 (July, 1960)
> *Syracuse Law Review,* 11:285-887 (Spring, 1960)
>
> This decision was reversed by the United States Supreme
> Court which held that neither a state, nor the federal govern-
> ment had the power to prescribe by law any particular form
> of prayer to be used as an official prayer in carrying on any
> program of government sponsored religious activity. ——
> U.S. ——; 82 S.Ct. ——; 8 L. Ed.2d 601 (1962)

728   DRINAN, ROBERT F., S.J. "Prayer in the Public Schools,"
       America, 102: 70-71 (Oct. 17, 1959).

(2. Other Literature)

729   GILBERT, ARTHUR G. *Should there be Religion in the
       Schools?* New York, N.Y.: Anti-Defamation League
       of B'Nai B'rith, 1957. 8pp.

> Reprinted from the *National Jewish Monthly,* December,
> 1956 and January, 1957.

730   NEW YORK CITY. BOARD OF EDUCATION. *The Develop-
       ment of Moral and Spiritual Ideals in the Public
       Schools.* New York, N.Y.: Board of Education, 1956.
       16pp.

731   SHEERIN, JOHN B. "Religion in the Public Schools,"
       Homiletic and Pastoral Review, 56:723-27 (June,
       1956).

732   VOIGHT, JOHN J. "Moral and Spiritual Values in Public
       Education," *Catholic Theological Society of America,
       Proceedings,* XII:92-114 (1956).

> Case history of the "Guiding Statement on Moral and
> Spiritual Values and the Schools" in New York City, 1952-
> 1956.

News reports about the statement and reactions to it may be located in the *New York Times* through the *New York Times Index,* under the heading "Religious Education—U.S.— N.Y.C." (Search especially the volumes for 1955 and 1956.)

Rhode Island:

733 CAMPBELL, PAUL E. "Religion Classes Constitutional (editorial)," *Catholic Educator,* 28:440, 442 (March, 1958).

Comment on a ruling by the Department of the Attorney General of Rhode Island according to which religion classes held in public school buildings outside regular school hours are not unconstitutional.

Tennessee:

734 FALCONER, DAVID E. "A Study of the Teaching of Moral and Spiritual Values in Selected Public Schools of East Tennessee." Knoxville, Tenn.: University of Tennessee, 1955. (Unpublished master's dissertation)

735 HYDER, MYRA A. "Identification by the Citizens of Elizabethton of the Student Behaviors which Typify Desirable Moral and Spiritual Values." Johnson City, Tenn.: East Tennessee State College, 1954. (Unpublished master's dissertation)

736 "Scopes v. State; A Commemorative Case Note," *University of Chicago Law Review,* 27:505-534 (Spring, 1960).

A study of the case of *Scopes v. State,* 154 Tenn. 105; 289 S.W. 363 (Tennessee, 1927). The decision upheld a state law forbidding the teaching of evolution in the public schools.

Contents. "Scopes v. State," by Harry Kalven, Jr., 505-521. "The Scopes Case in Modern Dress," by Thomas I. Emerson and David Haber, 522-528. "Religion, Science and the Scopes Case," by Malcolm P. Sharp, 529-534.

Texas:

737 BUTLER, HARRIS D., JR. "Religious Education in the Public Schools of Texas." Austin, Texas: University of Texas, 1952. (Unpublished master's dissertation)

738　FLASHMEIER, WILLIAM A. "Religious Education in the
Public Schools of Texas." Austin, Texas: University
of Texas, 1955. (Unpublished doctoral dissertation.)
Abstract. *Religious Education,* 51:184 (May-June,
1956).

> A study of cooperation in religious education between public
> schools and churches through the last hundred years to the
> present.

739　WHITESIDE, THOMAS R. "Moral and Spiritual Values in
the High Schools of Shelby County, Texas." Nacog-
doches, Texas: Stephen F. Austin State College, 1953.
(Unpublished master's dissertation)

Virginia:

740　FLYNN, LUTHER. "A Study of Moral, Spiritual and Religious Values in the Public Schools of Virginia."
Charlottesville, Va.: University of Virginia, 1956.
(Unpublished doctoral dissertation) Abstract. *Dissertation Abstracts,* 16 no.9:1617 (1956). Microfilm.
Ann Arbor, Mich.: University Microfilms, publication
no.17,631.

> Covers the history of religious education from colonial times
> to the present.

Wisconsin:

741　BOYER, WILLIAM W. "Baccalaureate in Broadhead: A
Study in Interfaith Tension," *School and Society,* 88:
183-186 (April 9, 1960).

742　"Religious Education of Public School Pupils in Wisconsin," *Wisconsin Law Review,* 1953:181-225
(March, 1953).

IV

Religion In Public Education:
The Holy Bible

Note. In a number of colonies, as instanced by the "Old deluder law" of Massachusetts (1647), the ability to read the Bible was an objective and a standard of efficiency. Bible reading in the public schools is a longstanding American practice with a long history of court favor. Participation was at times required. For nearly forty years, the precedent of *Donahoe v. Richards et al.*, 38 Me. 379 (1854) held in court allowing school authorities to compel the reading of the King James version of the Bible until the case of *State (Wis.) ex rel. Weiss and others v. District Board of School District No. 8, of Edgerton*, 76 Wis. 177; 44 N.W. 967 (1890), helped to direct school administrators and courts away from the policy of compulsory participation.

Intergroup difficulties have brought about a decline of the practice. Catholics could not participate because of the characteristically Protestant teaching and worship which accompanied it. Jews naturally found the New Testament incompatible. Nonbelievers fought the practice altogether. Objections were raised against the version used, the commentaries given, the accompanying devotional exercises and, more recently, against Bible distribution.

Some of the material listed in I, II and III provides additional coverage of this issue.

A. BACKGROUND MATERIAL

SUMMARY MATERIAL AND LEGAL BACKGROUND:

743   HOOD, WILLIAM ROSS. *The Bible in the Public Schools, Legal Status and Current Practice* (U. S. Bureau of Education, Bulletin, 1923, No. 15). Washington, D.C.: U. S. Government Printing Office, 1923. 13pp.

744   KEESECKER, WARD W. *Legal Status of Bible Reading and Religious Instruction in the Public Schools* (U. S. Office of Education, Bulletin, 1930, No. 13). Washington, D.C.: U. S. Government Printing Office, 1930. 29pp.

745   MONROE, PAUL (ed.). *A Cyclopedia of Education.* New York: Macmillan, 1919. 5 Vols.

   See "Bible in the Schools—United States," Vol. I, pp.373-377, and "Colonial Period in American Education," Vol. II, pp.114-122.

746   PUNKE, HAROLD HERMAN. "Bible Reading and Kindred Exercises in Public Schools," in *Community Uses of Public School Facilities.* New York: King's Crown Press, Columbia University, 1951. Pp.47-63.

747   TORPEY, WILLIAM GEORGE. "Reading the Bible in Public Schools," in *Judicial Doctrines of Religious Rights in America.* Chapel Hill, N.C.: University of North Carolina Press, 1948. pp.244-49.

B. PERIODICAL ARTICLES

748 ABBOTT, WALTER M., S.J., and DRINAN, ROBERT F., S.J. "A Bible Reader for Public Schools," *America,* 104: 117-119 (Oct. 22, 1960).

749 "Bible Reading Becomes a National Issue" (Editorial), *Nation's Schools,* 66:71-72 (Oct., 1960). Also. 67: 56-57, 88, 90 (June, 1961).

750 BLACK, HAROLD GARNET. "The Bible in American Schools," *Christian Education,* 30:314-22 (Dec., 1947).

751 ————. "Shall We Break Another American Tradition?" *Christian Education,* 28:56-66 (Sept., 1944).

752 COAN, ROBERT J. "Bible Reading in the Public Schools," *Albany Law Review,* 22:156-173 (Jan., 1958).

753 "The Courts and Bible Reading in the Public Schools (student note)," *West Virginia Law Review,* 62:353-359 (June, 1960).

754 CONSALVO, GENNARO J. "Bibles, Wall of Separation and Rationality," *Catholic University Law Review,* 4: 118-27 (May, 1954).

755 CUSHMAN, ROBERT FAIRCHILD. "The Holy Bible and the Public Schools," *Cornell Law Quarterly,* 40:475-99 (Spring, 1955).

756 HUNT, MATE GRAYE. "Bible Study and the Public Schools," *Peabody Journal of Education,* 23:156-59 (Nov., 1945).

757 JOHNSON, ALVIN WALTER. "Bible Reading in the Public School," *Education,* 59:274-80 (Jan., 1939).

758 "Most Administrators Defend Bible Reading in Public Schools," *Nation's Schools,* 66:75 (Nov., 1960).

759 PETRIE, JOHN CLARENCE, and BACKUS, E. BURDETTE. "Shall We Teach the Bible in the Public Schools?" *Teachers College Journal*, 15:50, 51, 65 (Jan., 1944). Also. Joseph Lewis, "More Objections to Religion and the Bible in the Public Schools," pp.52-53.

760 RYAN, ZELDA JEANNE. "The Use of the Bible in Public Schools," *Religion in Life*, 21:603-12 (Autumn, 1952).

761 SANTEE, JOSEPH FREDERICK. "The Legal Status of Public School Bible Reading," *Social Studies*, 43:291-93 (Nov., 1952).

762 SHEFFEY, E. SUMMERS. "The First Amendment and Distribution of Religious Literature in the Public Schools," *Virginia Law Review*, 41:789-807 (Oct., 1955).

763 TRIMBLE, THOMAS J. "Bible Reading in the Public Schools," *Vanderbilt Law Review*, 9:849-60 (June, 1956).

C. STATE MATERIAL (With cases)

Alabama:

764 CREEL, E. M. "Is it Legal for the Public Schools of Alabama to Provide an Elective Course in Non-Sectarian Bible Instruction?" *The Alabama Lawyer*, 10:86-97 (Jan., 1949).

Colorado:

(Case Material)

-- 1927 --

765 VOLLMAR, EDWARD R., S.J. "The Colorado Bible Case," *American Ecclesiastical Review*, 138:190-195 (March, 1958).

History of the case of *People ex rel. Vollmar v. Stanley,* 81 Colo. 276; 255 P. 276 (Colorado, 1927). In this case, the court decided that the "Bible may be read without comment in the public schools" but that "children whose parents or guardians so desired may absent themselves" from such reading.

Florida:

766 GARBER, LEE ORVILLE. "Bible Reading Upheld in Miami Public Schools," *Nation's Schools,* 67:56-57, 88, 90 (June 1961) and 66:71-72 (Oct., 1960).

767 "What's at Stake in Florida?" *America,* 103:510-511 (August 6, 1960).

Maine:

(Case Material)

-- 1854 --

768 KOLMAN, LEONARD, S.J. "Out of the Dusk," in John P. Leary (ed.), *I Lift My Lamp; Jesuits in America.* Westminster, Md.: Newman, 1955. Pp.194-214.

The story behind the case of *Donahoe v. Richards* (38 Me. 379 (1854)) is given in this biographical sketch of Father John Bapst, S.J. (1815-1887) which relates his experiences in Ellsworth, Maine. Court action here validated expulsion of students who refused to attend Bible reading exercises and made attendance compulsory even for those who objected to the version used, for reason of conscience.

Other accounts are available in the following histories.

Robert H. Lord, and others, *History of the Archdiocese of Boston in the Various Stages of its Development, 1604-1943.* New York: Sheed and Ward, 1944. 3v. See Vol. II, pp.672-678.

William Leo Lucey, S.J., *The Catholic Church in Maine.* Francetown, N.H.: Marshall Jones Co., 1957. Pp.118-134. Notes, pp.352-353.

New Jersey:

(Case Material)

-- 1950 --

769 *Doremus v. Board of Education of Borough of Hawthorne (N.J.),* 5 N.J. 435; 71 A.2d 732 (N.J., 1950).

Appeal. 7 N.J. Super. 442; 75 A.2d 880 (Oct. 16, 1950)
Appeal to the U.S. Supreme Court dismissed. 342 U.S. 429;
72 S.Ct 395 (1952).

Decision affirming that reading verses from the Old Testament and permitting the recitation of the Lord's Prayer in public schools did not contravene the First and Fourteenth Amendments of the federal Constitution.

REVIEWS:

Alabama Law Review, 4:284-86 (Spring, 1952)
American Bar Association Journal, 38:496 (June, 1952)
Arkansas Law Review, 5:431-34 (Fall, 1951)
Baylor Law Review, 3:456-460 (Spring, 1951)
Columbia Law Review, 52:539-41 (Apr., 1952)
George Washington Law Review, 19:435-38 (Jan., 1951)
Georgetown Law Journal, 40:619-22 (May, 1952)
Georgia Bar Journal, 13:360-61 (Feb., 1951)
Harvard Law Review, 64:666-68 (Feb., 1951), 66:119-21 (Nov., 1952)
Marquette Law Review, 34:297-300 (Spring, 1951)
Michigan Law Review, 50:1100-02 (May, 1952)
Rutgers Law Review, 5:553-56 (Spring, 1951)
Syracuse Law Review, 2:371-73 (Spring, 1951)
Temple Law Quarterly, 25:89-91 (July, 1951)

770 GARBER, LEE ORVILLE. "What the New Jersey Courts Say About Bible Reading in the Public Schools," *Nation's Schools*, 50:61-62 (July, 1952).

771 REED, GEORGE E. "Another Tradition at Stake," *Catholic Action*, 32:4-5 (Feb., 1950).

-- 1953 --

772 *Tudor v. Board of Education of Borough of Rutherford (N.J.) et al.*, 14 N.J. 31; 100 A.2d 857 (N.J., 1953). Petition to the U. S. Supreme Court denied, 348 U. S. 816; 75 S.Ct. 25 (1954).

Decision declaring the distribution of Gideon Bibles in the public schools to be a violation of the federal and state constitutions.

REVIEWS:

Boston University Law Review, 34:375-80 (June, 1954)
DePaul Law Review, 3:277-80 (Spring-Summer, 1954)
Georgetown Law Journal, 42:455-58 (March, 1954)
Michigan Law Review, 52:1057-59 (May, 1954)
Minnesota Law Review, 38:663-67 (May, 1954)
Mississippi Law Journal, 25:271-73 (May, 1954)
New York University Law Review, 29:1290-92 (June, 1954)
Notre Dame Lawyer, 29:478-82 (Spring, 1954)

St. Louis University Law Journal, 3:269 (Spring, 1955)
Temple Law Quarterly, 27:339-42 (Winter, 1954)
Virginia Law Review, 40:487-89 (May, 1954)

773 CONSALVO, GENNARO J. "Bibles, Wall of Separation and Rationality," *Catholic University of America Law Review*, 4:118-27 (May, 1954).

774 CUSHMAN, ROBERT FAIRCHILD. "The Holy Bible and the Public Schools," *Cornell Law Quarterly*, 40:475-99 (Spring, 1955).

775 ROACH, STEPHEN F. "Board Participation in Distribution of Bible," *American School Board Journal*, 128:37-38 (Apr., 1954).

North Carolina:

776 GWYNN, P. H., JR. "Week-day Religious Education in North Carolina," *Religious Education*, 39:169-74 (May-June, 1944).

Pennsylvania:

(Case Material)

-- 1959 --

777 *Schempp v. School District of Abington Township, Pa.*, 177 F.Supp. 398 (Pennsylvania, 1959). Motion denied, 184 F.Supp. 381 (1960). Judgement vacated, remanded to lower court for rehearing, *School District of Abington Township, Pa., v. Schempp*, 81 S.Ct. 268 (Oct. 24, 1960). Motion granted, 195 F.Supp. 518 (June 22, 1961). Appeal pending.

Decision affirming that a statute which required Bible reading in public schools was a violation of the First Amendment of the federal Constitution. The law was subsequently modified. Action on the new statute is pending.

Tennessee:

(Case Material)

-- 1956 --

778 *Carden et al. v. Bland et al.*, 199 Tenn. 665; 288 S.W.2d 718 (Tenn., 1956)

In this decision, reading a selection from the Bible, repeating the Lord's Prayer and singing some inspiring songs in public schools were not found to be violations of the constitutional rights to freedom of worship.

REVIEWS:

American University Law Review, 6:51 (Jan., 1957)
Georgia Bar Journal, 19:227 (Nov., 1956)
Michigan Law Review, 55:715-17 (March, 1957)
Nebraska Law Review, 36:357-59 (March, 1957)
Tennessee Law Review, 24:883-86 (Winter, 1957)
Yearbook of School Law, 1957, pp.109-111.

Wisconsin:

779   BOYER, WILLIAM WALTER. "Bible in Wisconsin Public Schools: A Forbidden Book," *Religious Education,* 55:403-409 (Nov., 1960).

V

Religion In Public Education:
Released Time

Note. Religion classes during school hours have been organized to supplement the secular work of the public schools. In this attempt to bring religion back to the curriculum, children are released from school by parental request to attend religion classes taught by qualified instructors of participating religious groups. The practice is sometimes referred to as week-day religious instruction.

An early released time program organized in Gary, Indiana, (1913) gained widespread attention. Variations of this "Gary Plan," as it has been called, were tried in many cities and their application has been favorably treated by the courts.

The United States Supreme Court enjoined against released time classes held in public school buildings during school hours, in the McCollum decision (1948), but affirmed the constitutionality of released time programs when public school classrooms were not used during school time in the Zorach case (1952).

In some localities, all public school students are dismissed during the time set aside for religious instruction. The practice is referred to as "dismissed time." Recently, some attention has been given to the study of "shared time" programs which would make it possible for children to do part of their school work in the public schools while still receiving instruction in Church-related schools part of the time.

The following list should be used with I, II and III.

A. BACKGROUND MATERIAL

1. BIBLIOGRAPHIES:

780   COHEN, IVA. "Released Time," in *Church, State and Education; a Selected Bibliography*, 2d. rev. ed. New York: Library of Jewish Information, American Jewish Committee, 1954. Pp.21-24. (Mimeographed)

781   POPE, JAMES D. "The Released Time Program," in *Moral, Spiritual and Religious Values in Public Education (Bibliography, No. 31)*. Gainesville, Fla.: University of Florida Education Library, 1958. Pp. 33-35. (Mimeographed)

2. SUMMARY MATERIAL AND LEGAL BACKGROUND:

782   DAVIS, MARY DABNEY. *Weekday Religious Instruction: Classes for Public-School Pupils Conducted on Released School Time* (U. S. Office of Education, 1933, Pamphlet No. 36). Washington, D.C.: U. S. Government Printing Office, 1933. 34pp.

> Also: *Weekday Classes in Religious Education Conducted on Released School Time for Public School Pupils* (U.S. Office of Education, Bulletin, 1941, No. 3). Washington, D.C.: U. S. Government Printing Office, 1941. 66pp. Summary. *School Life*, 26:299-301, 306 (July, 1941).

783   EMERSON, THOMAS IRWIN, and HABER, DAVID (eds.). "Released Time," in *Political and Civil Rights in the United States; A Collection of Legal and Related Material*. Second Edition. Buffalo, N.Y.: Dennis & Co., 1958. Vol. II, pp.1157-1170.

784   KEESECKER, WARD W. *Laws Relating to the Releasing of Pupils from Public Schools for Religious Instruction* (U. S. Office of Education, 1933, Pamphlet No. 39). Washington, D.C.: U. S. Government Printing Office, 1933. 17pp.

785 SHAVER, ERWIN L. "The Weekday Church School," in Philip Henry Lotz (ed.), *Orientation in Religious Education.* New York: Abingdon-Cokesbury, 1950. Pp.274-286.

For an earlier summary see Philip Henry Lotz, "The Weekday Church School," in Philip Henry Lotz and L. W. Crawford (eds.), *Studies in Religious Education.* Nashville, Tenn.: Cokesbury Press, 1931. Pp.265-295.

786 TORPEY, WILLIAM GEORGE. "Excusing Students for Religious Instruction," in *Judicial Doctrines of Religious Rights in America.* Chapel Hill, N.C.: University of North Carolina Press, 1948. Pp.264-67.

3. EARLIER STUDIES:

787 ARCHDEACON, JOHN PHILIP. *The Weekday Religious School.* Washington, D.C.: Catholic University of America, 1927. 99pp. (Doctoral dissertation)

788 GORHAM, DONALD REX. *A Study of the Status of Weekday Church Schools in the United States* (Contributions to Christian Education, No. 1). Philadelphia, Pa.: School of Religious Education, Eastern Baptist Theological Seminary, 1934. 96pp.

789 GOVE, FLOYD SHERMAN. *Religious Education on Public School Time (Harvard Bulletins in Education, No. XI).* Cambridge, Mass.: Harvard University, 1926. 143pp. Bibliography: 133-143.

Material from a doctoral dissertation (1924).

790 THOMPSON, KENNETH L. *Weekday Religious Education in the High Schools of the United States (Contributions to Christian Education, No. 4.).* Philadelphia, Pa.: Eastern Baptist Theological Seminary, 1938. 40pp.

B. BOOKS AND PAMPHLETS

791 ALLRED, VINCENT C. *Legal Aspects of Released Time.*
Washington, D.C.: National Catholic Welfare Conference, 1946. 63pp.

> Gives statutory provisions for the states which had then
> legislated the practice.

792 BOWER, WILLIAM CLAYTON, and HAYWARD, PERCY ROY.
"Vacation and Weekday Religious Education," in
Protestantism Faces Its Educational Task Together.
Appleton, Wisconsin: C. C. Nelson Co., 1949. Pp.
166-84.

793 FINE, MORRIS. *The Released Time Plan of Religious
Education.* New York: American Jewish Committee,
1941. 24pp. Reprinted from *Contemporary Jewish
Record*, February, 1941.

794 INTERNATIONAL COUNCIL OF RELIGIOUS EDUCATION. *The
Weekday Church School* (Its Bulletin, No.601).
Chicago: The Council, 1940. 50pp.

795 SHAVER, ERWIN L. "The Weekday Church School," in
Philip Henry Lotz (ed.), *Orientation in Religious
Education.* Nashville, Tenn.: Abingdon Cokesbury,
1950. Pp.274-86.

796 WEARY, GERALD FABRIQUE. *Democracy's Case Against
Religious Education on School Time (Beacon Refer-
ence Series).* Boston: Beacon Press, 1947. 22pp.
"Reprinted from the *Journal of Liberal Religion.*"

C. PERIODICAL ARTICLES

797 BOROWSKI, MARIA C. R. "Released Time for Religious Instruction: A Reappraisal," *Education*, 68:205-07 (Dec., 1947).

798 BOWER, WILLIAM CLAYTON. "Religion on Released Time," *Christian Century*, 58:980-81 (Aug. 6, 1941). Comment. "Ethical Teaching Holds Promise," 58:1056 (Aug. 27, 1941).

799 COLLINS, JOSEPH B. "Released Time for Religious Education," *American Ecclesiastical Review*, 115:11-23 (July), 121-37 (August, 1946).

   Reprinted, 1946, n.p. (pagination as in original articles).

800 FOX, GEORGE G. "An Old Issue in a New Guise," *Christian Century*, 58:1027-30 (Aug. 20, 1941).

801 GREENBAUM, EDWARD S. and THAYER, VIVIAN TROW. "Released Time: The Parents' Right to Choose.— Released Time, a Crutch for the Churches," *The Nation*, 174:128-32 (Feb. 9, 1952).

802 HILL, HORATIO SEYMOUR. "A Case for the Released Time School," *Religious Education*, 40:172-73 (May-June, 1945).

803 HOLLAND, DEWITTE T. "Shared Time and Juvenile Delinquency," *Vital Speeches*, 23:405-408 (Apr. 15, 1957).

804 HOWLETT, WALTER M. "The Case For Released Time," *Education*, 71:370-74 (Feb., 1951).

805 LARSON, JORDAN L., and TAPP, ROBERT B. "Released Time for Religious Education?—Yes, says Jordan L. Larson; No, says Robert B. Tapp," *National Education Association Journal*, 47:572-574 (Nov., 1958).

806 MCKIBBEN, FRANK M. "Trends in Weekday Religious Education," *Education*, 64:525-27 (May, 1944).

807 MEYER, AGNES ELIZABETH. "The School, the State and the Church," *Atlantic Monthly*, 182:45-50 (Nov., 1948), and p.35 (Feb., 1949).

> Replies. M. W. Hess. "Devil Newly Invented! Released Time Case; Reply to A. E. Meyer," *Catholic World*, 168:295-301 (Jan., 1949).
>
> J. M. O'Neill. "The Supreme Court on the Separation of Church and State," *Commonweal*, 49:466-69 (Feb. 18, 1949).
>
> "One-Woman Crusade Against Religion" (editorial), *America*, 80:198-99 (Nov. 27, 1948).

808 —————. "Clerical Challenge to the Schools," *Atlantic Monthly*, 189:42-46 (March, 1952). Same in Ernest O. Melby and Morton Puner (eds.), *Freedom and Public Education*. New York: Praeger, 1953. Pp.76-88.

> Discussion. *Atlantic Monthly*, 189:22-23 (May), 21-3 (June, 1952).

809 MONES, LEON. "Religious Education and the Public Schools," *Clearing House*, 15:395-96 (March, 1941).

810 "Progress in Weekday Religious Education—A Symposium," *Religious Education*, 41:6-25 (Jan.-Feb., 1946).

> Contents. "The Movement for Weekday Religious Education," Erwin L. Shaver, 6-15; "Released Time in the Jewish Community," Ben M. Edidin, 16-19; "Released Time for Catholic Children," Joseph B. Collins, 20-21; "Adequate Religious Education in a Free Society," J. Paul Williams, 22-25.

811 SHAVER, ERWIN L. "The Legal Situation in Weekday Religious Education," *Religious Education*, 43:65-67 (March-Apr., 1948).

812 —————. "Weekday Religious Education, a Significant Addition to the Churches' Teaching Program," *Education*, 71:365-69 (Feb., 1951).

813 WATERHOUSE, HOWARD A. "Is Released Time Worth While?" *Christian Century,* 74:1164-66 (Oct. 2, 1957). Discussion. 1290-92 (Oct. 30), 1440-45 (Dec. 4).

814 "Weekday Religious Education in Your Future," *International Journal of Religious Education,* 36:5-11 (June, 1960).

> Contents. "Why I am Concerned," Velma I. Frasher, 5. "A Denominational Executive Answers Questions," Franklin I. Sheeder, 6-7. "Purpose of Religious Education," 7. "Weekday Religious Education Can be Ecumenical," Helene M. Suiter, 8-9. "Weekday Classes Open Doors," Burtis M. Dougherty, 10-11.

D. UNPUBLISHED DISSERTATIONS

815 BECKES, ISAAC K. "Interfaith Attitudes in Weekday Religious Education." New Haven, Conn.: Yale University, 1946. (Unpublished doctoral dissertation).

> Abstract. *Religious Education,* 42:105 (March-Apr., 1947).
>
> Summary published by the National Conference of Christians and Jews, N.Y., 1946. 28pp.

816 BODDEN, ROSALIND V. "Released Time." Newark, N.J.: State Teachers College, 1954. (Unpublished master's dissertation)

817 CORBETT, WILLIAM D. "The Status of Public Knowledge Concerning the Program of Released Time for Religious Education: a Case Study." Chestnut Hill, Mass.: Boston College, 1954. (Unpublished master's dissertation)

818 CORCORAN, GERTRUDE B. "Release-Time Religious Education in the Elementary School," San Jose, Cal.: San Jose State College, 1953. (Unpublished master's dissertation)

819   FRANER, WILLIAM A. "Religious Instruction on Re-
       leased School Time." Washington, D.C.: Catholic
       University of America, 1942. (Unpublished master's
       dissertation)

820   MCCLURE, LOIS V. "Weekday Religious Education at the
       High School Level." Evanston, Ill.: Northwestern
       University (1951?). (Unpublished master's disser-
       tation)

       Summary. *Religious Education*, 46:345-63 (Nov.-Dec., 1951).

821   YERDEN, ELSIE M. "Released Time for Religion in Pub-
       lic Schools." Kalamazoo, Mich.: Western Michigan
       College, 1955. (Unpublished master's dissertation)

E. CASE MATERIAL (U.S. Supreme Court)

1948—The McCollum Decision

822   *People of State of Illinois ex rel. McCollum v. Board of*
       Education of School District No. 71, Champaign
       County, Ill., 333 U.S. 203; 68 S.Ct. 461 (1948).
       Reversing 396 Ill. 14; 71 N.E.2d 161 (1947).

       Decision declaring a released time plan which made it
       possible for students to attend religion classes on school time
       in public school buildings to be a violation of the First Amend-
       ment of the federal Constitution.

       N.B.: For lower court decision see No. 888.

       REVIEWS:
       Alabama Lawyer, 10:86-97 (Jan., 1949)
       Baylor Law Review, 1:79-81 (Summer, 1948)
       Detroit Law Review, 9:119-26 (June, 1948)
       Fordham Law Review, 17:173-99 (Nov., 1948)
       George Washington Law Review, 16:556-61 (June, 1948)
       Harvard Law Review, 61:1248-49 (July, 1948), 62:1306-44
       (June, 1949)

Illinois Bar Journal, 35:361-64 (Apr., 1947)
Illinois Law Review, 43:374-88 (July-Aug., 1948)
Intramural Law Review (St. Louis University), 1:26-36 (May, 1949)
Kentucky Law Journal, 37:229-39 (March, 1949)
Louisiana Law Review, 9:409-13 (March, 1949)
Law and Contemporary Problems, 14:1-159 (Winter, 1949)
Lawyer's Guild Review, 8:387-99 (May-June, 1948)
Loyola Law Review, 4:186-88 (June, 1948)
Michigan Law Review, 46:828-30 (Apr., 1948)
Minnesota Law Review, 33:494-516 (Apr., 1949)
National Bar Journal, 6:166-69 (June, 1948)
New York University Law Quarterly Review, 23:523-26 (July, 1948)
Rutgers University Law Review, 3:115-27 (Feb., 1949)
St. John's Law Review, 22:253-56 (Apr., 1948)
Southern California Law Review, 22:56-59 (Dec., 1948);
26:186-95 (Feb., 1953)
Texas University Law Review, 27:256-59 (Dec., 1948)
University of Pennsylvania Law Review, 96:230-41 (Dec., 1947).
Yale Law Journal, 57:1114-22 (Apr., 1948)

(Books, Pamphlets)

823 DUGGAN, JOSEPH CHARLES. *Religious Teaching in Public Schools: a Critique of the Champaign School Decision.* Boston: Department of Education of the Boston Archdiocese (49 Franklin St., Boston 10, Mass.), 1948. 18pp.

A reprint of three articles which appeared in the *Boston Pilot,* March 27, Apr. 3, Apr. 10, 1948.

824 KUCERA, DANIEL WILLIAM, O.S.B. *Church-State Relationships in Education in Illinois.* Washington, D. C.: Catholic University of America Press, 1955. 252pp. Bibliography: pp.234-247. (Doctoral dissertation)

The McCollum decision is discussed in this history.

825 McCOLLUM, VASHTI CROMWELL. *One Woman's Fight.* Rev. ed. with a Postulate by Paul Blanshard and the Text of the Supreme Court Decision; Preface by George Axtelle. Boston: Beacon Press, 1961. 257pp.

Originally issued in 1951.

REVIEWS (1951 edition):
America, 85:422-43 (Aug. 4, 1951) J. M. O'Neill
Best Sellers, 11:19-20 (Apr. 15, 1951)
Books on Trial, 10:23 (June, 1951) J. G. Noth

Chicago Sunday Tribune, p.8 (Apr. 29, 1951) A. C. Ames
Christian Science Monitor, p.9 (May 17, 1951) D. Witt John
Churchman, 165:14 (June, 1951) E. R. Johnson
Bulletin from Virginia Kirkus' Book Shop Service, 19:143
   (March 1, 1951)
Library Journal, 76:775 (May 1, 1951) R. W. Henderson
Nation, 172:450 (May 12, 1951)
New York Herald Tribune Book Review, p.8 (March 25, 1951)
   Marcus Duffield
New York Times Book Review, p.31 (Apr. 22, 1951) N. K.
   Burger
New Yorker, 27:119 (May 3, 1951)
Saturday Review of Literature, 34:32 (June 30, 1951) V. T.
   Thayer
School and Society, 85:125 (Apr. 13, 1957) W. W. Brickman
Sign, 30:5-6 (May, 1951).

826   MANION, CLARENCE. *The Church, the State, and Mrs.
      McCollum.* Notre Dame, Indiana: Ave Maria Press,
      1950. 38pp.

      From: *Notre Dame Lawyer*, 23:456-80 (May, 1948).

827   MARTIN, RENWICK HARPER. *The U. S. Supreme Court's
      Tragedy of Errors in the Atheist School Case.* n.d.,
      n.p. (The Author. Dr. R. H. Martin, Grant Building,
      Pittsburgh 19, Pa.)

828   REED, GEORGE E. *The McCollum Case and Your Child:
      Lecture Delivered at the 1948 Convention of the Na-
      tional Council of Catholic Women.* Washington, D.C.:
      National Welfare Conference, 1949. 15pp.

829   SWANCARA, FRANK. *The Separation of Religion and
      Government: The First Amendment, Madison's In-
      tent, and the McCollum Decision; A Study of Separa-
      tionism in America.* New York: Truth Seeker Co.,
      1950. viii, 246pp. Bibliographical footnotes.

      Endorsed by the National Liberal League.

(Articles)

830   ASHLEY, HARMON, JR. "Church-State: Some Overlooked
      History," *Commonweal*, 52:625-27 (Oct. 6, 1950).
      Reply. Robert McWilliams, 63:118 (Nov. 10, 1950).

      Facts and comments concerning the exchange of opinion in
      Congress, Aug. 15, 1789, about the proposed First Amend-
      ment.

831 BENNETT, JOHN C. "Implication of the New Conception of 'Separation' ", *Christianity and Crisis,* 8 no. 12: 89-90 (July 5, 1948) followed by: "Statement on Church and State," p.90.

832 BLAKELY, STEPHEN L. "Judge-Made Law," *America,* 79: iii (June 12, 1948).

833 CARPENTER, WILLIAM WESTON. "Education Without Religion," *Phi Delta Kappan,* 29:368-70 (May, 1948).

834 "The Champaign Case," *Christian Century,* 65:308-09 (Apr. 7, 1948). Discussion. 65:449-50 (March 12, 1948), 65:576 (June 9, 1948).

835 "Church and State in American Education," *Illinois Law Review,* 43:374-88 (July-Aug., 1948).

836 DRINAN, ROBERT F., S.J. "The Lawyers and Religion," *America,* 80:593-95 (March 5, 1949).

837 ——————. "McCollum Decision: Three Years After," *America,* 84:611-13 (Feb. 24, 1951).

838 ——————. "Novel 'Liberty' Created by the McCollum Decision," *Georgetown Law Journal,* 39:216-241 (Jan., 1951).

839 FEY, HAROLD E. "Test Legality of Released Time," *Christian Century,* 62:1099-1100 (Sept. 26, 1945).

840 FRANKLIN, JOHN L. "Education and Religion," *Phi Delta Kappan,* 29:365-68 (May, 1948).

841 GAUSS, CHRISTIAN. "Should Religion Be Taught in Our Schools?" *Ladies' Home Journal,* 65:40, 266, 268, 270 (Sept., 1948).

842 HARTNETT, ROBERT CLINTON, S.J. "The McCollum Case," *America,* 79:49-52 (Apr. 24, 1948). Comment. 79:236 (June 5, 1948).

843 ——————. "Aftermath of the McCollum Decision," *America,* 79:561-63 (Sept. 25, 1948). See: "Is the 'Wall of Separation' an Iron Curtain?" *America,* 83: 75 (Apr. 22, 1950).

844 JOHNSON, F. ERNEST. "Protestant-Catholic Controversy," *Christianity and Crisis,* 8 no. 8:61-2 (May 10, 1948).

845 LASSITER, JAMES M. "The McCollum Decision and the Public School," *Kentucky Law Journal,* 37:402-11 (May, 1949).

846 MOEHLMAN, CONRAD HENRY. "The Wall of Separation: the Law and the Facts," *American Bar Association Journal,* 38:281-84, 343-48 (Apr., 1952).

> For a different view, see pp.277-80, 335-42 of the same issue, and June, 1948, pp.482-85.

847 MORRISSON, CHARLES CLAYTON. "What Did the Supreme Court Say?" *Christian Century,* 66:707-09 (June 8, 1949). "The Concurring Opinions," 66:734-37 (June 15, 1949). "The Dissent of Mr. Justice Reed," 66: 760-63 (June 22, 1949). Discussion. 66:894 (July 27, 1949).

848 MULFORD, HERBERT B. "The Illinois 'Atheist' Case," *School and Society,* 65:461-62 (June 21, 1947).

849 ——————. "The Supreme Court Sets Hurdles in Religion for the American School Board," *American School Board Journal,* 116:37-39 (Apr., 1948).

850 NATIONAL CATHOLIC WELFARE CONFERENCE. "The Christian in Action," statement issued by the Catholic Bishops of the United States, Nov. 21, 1948, in Raphael M. Huber (ed.), *Our Bishops Speak, National Pastorals and Annual Statements of the Hierarchy of the United States.* Milwaukee, Wis.: Bruce, 1952. Pp.145-54. Same. *Catholic Mind,* 47:58-64 (Jan., 1949), *New York Times,* Nov. 21, 1948, p.63, col. 1.

> N.B.: In discussions of the McCollum decision the preceding statement is often referred to with the one issued Nov. 14, 1947, on "Secularism." (Text: Huber (above), pp.137-45. Same. *Catholic Mind,* 46:1-8 (Jan., 1948)).

> Comments. "The State Schools and the Sects" (editorial), *Life,* 33:36 (Dec. 1, 1952). Discussion. 33:7 (Dec. 22, 1952).

> G. Bromley Oxnam, *Nation,* 168:67-70 (Jan. 15, 1949). Reply. Robert C. Hartnett, *America,* 80:516 (Feb. 12, 1949).

> Simeon Stylites, "Out in the Open," *Christian Century,* 65:1327-29 (Dec. 8, 1948).

851 NATIONAL EDUCATION ASSOCIATION OF THE UNITED STATES, RESEARCH DIVISION. "The Released-Time Decision," *National Education Association Journal*, 37: 209-10 (Apr., 1948).

852 NIEBUHR, REINHOLD. "Editorial Note," *Christianity and Crisis*, 8 no. 5:34 (March 29, 1948).

853 "No Law But Our Own Prepossessions," *American Bar Association Journal*, 34:482-85 (June, 1948).

854 O'BYRNE, JOHN P. "God and Our Government," *St. John's Law Review*, 23:292-6 (Apr., 1949).

855 OWEN, RALPH DORNFIELD. "The McCollum Case," *Temple Law Quarterly*, 22:159-73 (Oct., 1948).

856 PARSONS, WILFRID, S.J. "No Religion in the Schools?" *Sign*, 27:12-14 (May, 1948).

857 PATRICK, GORDON. "The Impact of a Court Decision: Aftermath of the McCollum Case," *Journal of Public Law*, 6:455-464 (Fall, 1957).

858 "Protestants: Come Clean!" *Christian Century*, 65: 591-92 (June 16, 1948). Discussion. 65:675-76 (July 7, 1948), 778-80 (Aug. 4, 1948), 798-800 (Aug. 11, 1948).

859 "Releasing the Time," *Commonweal*, 47:581-82 (March 26, 1948).

860 "Religious Education and the Public Schools," *High School Journal*, 31:99-111 (May, 1948).

861 "Religious Instruction in the Public School System," *Columbia Law Review*, 47:1346-55 (Dec., 1947).

862 REMMLEIN, MADALINE KINTER. "The Legal Situation Resulting from the Recent Supreme Court Decision," *Religious Education*, 43:211-216 (July-August, 1948).

863 "Salvaging Released Time," *Christian Century*, 65:405-06 (May 5, 1948).

864 SHAVER, ERWIN L. "Three Years After the Champaign Case," *Religious Education,* 46:33-38 (Jan., 1951).

865 "Supreme Court Bans Released Time," *Christian Century,* 65:294 (March 17, 1948). Discussion. 65:352-53 (Apr. 21, 1948).

866 SUTHERLAND, ARTHUR E., JR. "Due Process and Disestablishment," *Harvard Law Review,* 62:1306-1344 (June, 1949).

867 TAYLOR, T. RABER. "Equal Protection of Religion: Today's Public School Problem," *American Bar Association Journal,* 38:277-80, 335-42 (Apr., 1952). See other pages in the same issue.

868 VAN VLEET, W. B., JR. "Constitutional Law—Result of the 'Everson Amendment'—The McCollum Case," *Marquette Law Review,* 32:138-45 (Sept., 1948).

869 WALKER, HARVEY, SR. "Church and State, 1948," *Ohio State Law Journal,* 9:336-42 (Spring, 1948).

870 WEIGLE, LUTHER ALLAN. "Freedom of Religion and Education," *Christianity and Crisis,* 10 no. 13:98:103 (July 24, 1950).

871 WETZEL, WILLIAM A. "Religious Education—a Layman's Analysis," *National Association of Secondary-School Principals, Bulletin,* 33:66-74 (Oct., 1949).

1952—The Zorach Decision

872 *Zorach v. Clauson,* 343 U.S. 306; 72 S.Ct. 679 (1952). Affirming 303 N.Y. 161; 102 N.Y. Supp.2d 27; 100 N.E.2d 463 (1951).

In this decision, the court declared a statute permitting students to leave public school buildings to attend religious classes not to be a violation of the religion clauses of the First Amendment of the federal Constitution.

N.B.: For lower court decision see No. 894.

REVIEWS:

American Bar Association Journal, 38:760-61 (Sept., 1952)
Brooklyn Law Review, 19:134-37 (Dec., 1952)
California Law Review, 26:186-95 (Feb., 1953)
DePaul Law Review, 2:116-19 (Autumn-Winter, 1952)
Georgia Bar Journal, 15:363-66 (Feb., 1953)
Harvard Law Review, 66:118-19 (Nov., 1952)
Marquette Law Review, 35:385-90 (Spring, 1952)
Michigan Law Review, 50:1359-67 (June, 1952)
North Dakota Law Review, 28:222-24 (July, 1952)
Rocky Mountain Law Review, 25:104-06 (Dec., 1952)
Southern California Law Review, 26:186-195 (Feb., 1953)
Syracuse Law Review, 4:157-58 (Fall, 1952)
Texas Law Review, 31:327-30 (Feb., 1953)
University of Cincinnati Law Review, 21:481-83 (Nov., 1952)
Washington Law Review, 28:156-57 (May, 1953)
Washington & Lee Law Review, 9:213-22 (1952)

(Articles)

873 DRINAN, ROBERT F., S.J. "The Supreme Court and Religion," *Commonweal,* 41:554-56 (Sept. 12, 1952).

874 ELBIN, PAUL N. "Religion in State Schools," *Christian Century,* 69:1061-63 (Sept. 17, 1952).

875 HARTNETT, ROBERT CLINTON, S.J. "Religious Education and the Constitution," *America,* 87:195-97 (May 17), 223-26 (May 24, 1952).

876 JOHNSON, F. ERNEST. "An Issue that Needs Rethinking," *Christianity and Crisis,* 12 n.14:105-06 (Aug. 4, 1952).

877 POWERS, FRANCIS JOSEPH. "The Supreme Court and the Constitutional Prohibition Against 'an establishment of religion' ", *The Jurist,* 12:282-314 (July, 1952).

878 REED, GEORGE E. "Church-State and the Zorach Case," *Notre Dame Lawyer,* 27:529-551 (Summer, 1952).

879 "Released Time Considered: The New York Plan is Tested," *Yale Law Journal,* 61:405-16 (March, 1952).

880 SHAVER, ERWIN L. "Weekday Religious Education Secures Its Charter and Faces a Challenge," *Religious Education,* 48:38-43 (Jan.-Feb., 1953).

881   SMITH, THOMAS L., JR. "Separation of Church and State
       in Public Schools," *Alabama Law Review,* 7:99-107
       (Fall, 1954).

882   SORAUF, FRANK J. "Zorach v. Clauson: The Impact of a
       Supreme Court Decision," *American Political Science
       Review,* 53:777-79 (Sept., 1959).

883   "Supreme Court Validates New York's Released Time
       Plan," National Council of the Churches of Christ in
       the United States, *Information Service,* 31, no. 20
       (May 17, 1952) 4pp.

F. STATE MATERIAL (With cases)

California:
(1. Case Material)

-- 1947 --

884   *Gordon v. Board of Education of City of Los Angeles
       (Cal.),* 178 P.2d 488 (California, 1947).

   Decision upholding a statute which allowed students to be
   excused from class at the request of parents to attend religion
   classes.

   REVIEW:
   Oregon Law Review, 27:150-56 (Feb., 1948)

(2. Other Literature)

885   WINTERS, MARGUERITE. "The Weekday Church School
       in California," *Religious Education,* 40:43-71 (Jan.-
       Feb., 1945).

Illinois:
(Case Material)

-- 1946 --

886 *People ex rel. Latimer et al. v. Board of Education of the City of Chicago,* 394 Ill. 228; 68 N.E.2d 305 (Ill., 1946).

Decision affirming the constitutionality of a statute permitting school authorities to release students to attend religion classes at the request of parents.

887 BRODEN, THOMAS F. "Church and State—Excusing of Public School Pupils for Religious Instruction," *Notre Dame Lawyer,* 22:360-62 (March, 1947).

-- 1947 --

888 *People ex rel McCollum v. Board of Education of School District No. 71, Champaign County, Ill.,* 396 Ill. 14; 71 N.E.2d 161 (Ill., 1947). Reversed. 333 U.S. 203; 68 S.Ct. 461 (1948).

Decision (later reversed) affirming the constitutionality of a released time plan making it possible for students to attend religion classes in public school buildings during school time.

N.B.: For U.S. Supreme Court decision see No. 822.

Massachusetts:

889 GILLIS, FREDERICK J. "Weekday Religious Education— Boston Public Schools," *Education,* 71:375-81 (Feb., 1951).

890 HARRIS, ELIZABETH. "Protestant Weekday Religious Education in Boston," *Education,* 71:382-84 (Feb., 1951).

Michigan:

891 GODDARD, ALICE L. "Week-day Religious Education in Detroit," *Religious Education,* 37:294-98 (Sept.-Oct., 1942).

892 MACGRATH, (Sister) MARY. "Brady Plan in a Detroit School," *America,* 74:510-11 (Feb. 9, 1946).

New York:

(1. Case Material)

-- 1949 --

893   *People ex rel. Lewis v. Spalding*, 193 Misc. 66; 85
N.Y.S.2d 682 (Sup. Ct., Albany Co., 1948). Dismissed.
299 N.Y. 564; 85 N.E.2d 791 (Court of Appeals, New
York, N. Y. 1949).

Decision affirming the constitutionality of a statute permitting school authorities to release students from classes at
the request of parents to attend religion classes.

REVIEWS:

University of Pittsburgh Law Review, 10:409-10 (March,
1949)
George Washington Law Review, 17:516-29 (June, 1949)
Columbia Law Review, 49:836-45 (June, 1949)

-- 1951 --

894   *Zorach v. Clauson*, 303 N.Y. 161; 102 N.Y.Supp.2d
27; 100 N.E.2d 463 (N.Y., 1951). Affirmed. 343 U.S.
306; 72 S. Ct. 679 (1952).

Decision affirming the constitutionality of a released time
plan in which religious instruction was received outside public
school buildings. The court declared that the McCollum decision was not controlling in this case.

N.B.: For U.S. Supreme Court material see Nos. 872-883.

REVIEWS:

Albany Law Review, 116:85-80 (Jan., 1952)
Buffalo Law Review, 1:198-201 (Winter, 1951)
Fordham Law Review, 20:328-32 (Dec., 1951)
George Washington Law Review, 19:716-19 (June, 1951)
Georgetown Law Journal, 39:148-50 (Nov., 1950)
Iowa Law Review, 37:286-91 (Winter, 1952)
Journal of Public Law, 1:212-17 (Spring, 1952)
Notre Dame Lawyer, 27:120-24 (Fall, 1951)
St. John's Law Review, 25:91-94 (Dec., 1950)
Syracuse Law Review, 3:204-06 (Fall, 1951)
Temple Law Quarterly, 25:371-76 (Jan., 1952)
University of Cincinnati Law Review, 20:297-99 (March,
1951)
University of Detroit Law Journal, 14:216-17 (May, 1951)
Virginia Law Review, 37:1146-51 (Dec., 1951)
Yale Law Journal, 61:405-16 (March, 1952)

(2. Other Literature)

895 FINE, BENJAMIN. "Religion and the Public Schools," *Menorah Journal*, 32:93-101 (Apr., 1944).

896 FULCHER, BEATRICE CARD. "Weekday Religious Education on Released Time in New York City," *Education*, 71:385-88 (Feb., 1951).

897 HOWLETT, WALTER M. "Released Time for Religious Education in New York City," *Education*, 64:523-25 (May, 1944).

898 ————. "Released Time for Religious Education in New York City," *Religious Education*, 37:104-08 (March-Apr., 1942).

899 MCPHERSON, IMOGENE M., EDIDIN, BEN M., RYAN, THOMAS A. "Released Time in New York City, A Symposium," *Religious Education*, 38:15-24 (Jan.-Feb., 1943).

900 WHITESIDE, ROBERT J. "The Released Time Program of the Diocese of Buffalo." Chestnut Hill, Mass.: Boston College, 1952. (Unpublished master's dissertation).

Oregon:
(Case Material)

901 *Dilger v. School District 24,* 352 P.2d 564 (Oregon, 1960).

Decision stating that a released time statute was not unconstitutional even if it failed to designate the official or board in the school system to whom applications made by parents were to be referred. A punishment clause was declared separable from the released time statute.

Utah:

902 JORGENSEN, LEROY I. "Weekday Religious Education on Released Time and the History of South Cache Seminary." Logan, Utah: Utah State Agricultural College, 1957. (Unpublished master's dissertation).

903 WILKINS, RUTH W. "Constitutionality of the Utah Released Time Program," *Utah Law Review*, 3:329-39 (Spring, 1953).

Virginia:

904 GOSNELL, JOHN W. "Released Time Religious Education in Virginia." Chicago, Ill.: DePaul University, 1935. (Unpublished master's dissertation).

Washington:
(Case Material)

-- 1959 --

905 *Perry v. School District No. 81, Spokane, Wash.*, 154 Wash. Dec. 920; 344 P.2d 1036 (1959).

Decision affirming that a released time program did not contravene the constitution if practiced in a manner not inconsistent with constitutional limitations. In so far as this plan involved the distribution of cards and the making of announcements in public schools, the plan was declared to be a violation of the constitution.

Wisconsin:

906 BOYER, W. W., JR. "Religious Education of Public School Pupils in Wisconsin: Sectarian Instruction of Public School Pupils; Release of Public School Pupils for Religious Instruction," *Wisconsin Law Review*, 1953: 181-255 (March, 1953).

VI

Religion In Public Education:
The Religious Garb

Note. This unit includes material about problems arising when public school boards a) conclude various types of agreements by which Church-related schools are incorporated into the public school system, or b) hire teachers who are members of religious societies (usually members of Catholic religious orders) wearing a distinctive garb. Practices of that order are not generally favored, but decisions rendered in several state courts show that there is disagreement about the various aspects of the issue. An interesting example occurred in North Dakota where the court ruled the wearing of the religious garb by public school teachers to be constitutional in 1936 (*Gerhardt v. Heid,* 66 N.D. 444; 267 N.W. 127) but subsequent legislation proscribed the practice (1948).

The following list should be used along with units I, II, III and VIII.

A. BACKGROUND MATERIAL

SUMMARY MATERIAL AND LEGAL BACKGROUND:

907　CRONIN, JAMES THOMAS, and DONOHUE, FRANCIS J. "Catholic Public Schools in the United States." New York: Fordham University, Institute of Catholic Educational Research, 1937. 3pp. (Mimeographed).

Summary. *School and Society*, 45:756-758 (May 27, 1937).

908　PUNKE, HAROLD HERMAN. "Parochial Schools Taken into the Public School System," in *Community Uses of Public School Facilities*. New York: King's Crown Press, Columbia University, 1951. Pp.67-72.

909　――――. "Taking Over by Churches of Public Schools and Revenues," in "Religious Issues in American Public Education," *Law and Contemporary Problems*, 20:158-168 (Winter, 1955). Pp.158-165.

910　TORPEY, WILLIAM GEORGE. "Wearing Distinctive Garb," and "Use of Religious Property for Public School," in *Judicial Doctrines of Religious Rights in America*. Chapel Hill, N. C.: University of North Carolina Press, 1948. Pp.258-260, 262-264.

B. PERIODICAL ARTICLES

911　BLUM, VIRGIL CLARENCE, S.J. "Religious Liberty and the Religious Garb," *University of Chicago Law Review*, 22:875-88 (Summer, 1955).

912　CHAMBERS, MERRITT MADISON. "When is a School Sectarian?" *Nation's Schools*, 29:53-54 (Feb., 1942).

913 ————. "Public and Parochial Cooperation," *Nation's Schools*, 26:61-62 (Dec., 1940).

914 "Religious Garb in the Public Schools: a Study in Conflicting Liberties," *University of Chicago Law Review*, 22:888-95 (Summer, 1955).

C. STATE MATERIAL (With cases)

Connecticut:
(Case Material)

-- 1940 --

915 *New Haven v. Torrington,* 132 Conn. 194; 43 A.2d 455 (Conn., 1945).

> Decision stating that a town board of education had authority to establish and control a school in the building of a Catholic orphanage.

Indiana:
(Case Material)

-- 1945 --

916 *State (Ind.) ex rel. Johnson et al. v. Boyd et al.,* 217 Ind. 348; 28 N.E.2d 256 (Ind., 1940).

> Under conditions of economic depression, parochial schools were discontinued. The buildings and facilities were made available to the city and the schools were incorporated into the public school system for a few years. The court upheld the validity of the arrangement.

917 "Catholic Schools and Public Money," *Yale Law Journal*, 50:917-27 (March, 1941).

918 PAWLOWSKI, JOSEPH T. "Validity of Salary Payments to Teachers Wearing Religious Garb While Teaching," *Notre Dame Lawyer*, 16:148-50 (Jan., 1941).

919 ROSENFIELD, HARRY N. "Cooperation Between Local Public and Parochial Schools," *Nation's Schools*, 31: 23-24 (Feb., 1943).

Kansas:
(Case Material)

-- 1940 --

920 *Wright v. School District No. 27 of Woodson County (Kansas)*, 151 Kan. 485; 99 P.2d 737 (Kansas, 1940).

Decision prohibiting the use of public school funds to support a Church-related school.

Kentucky:
(Case Material)

-- 1956 --

921 *Rawlings v. Butler*, 290 S.W.2d 801 (Kentucky, 1956).

Decision declaring that the use of public funds for the payment of salaries to members of a religious society hired as public school teachers and for rent of school buildings from a church was not a violation of the constitution.

Summary. *Yearbook of School Law*, 1958, pp.135-138. Some issues raised in this case were decided in *Wooley v. Spalding*, 293 S.W.2d 563.

922 BLUM, VIRGIL CLARENCE, S.J. "Liberty Under Attack," *Columbia*, 35:24,25,33,40 (July, 1955).

923 GARBER, LEE ORVILLE. "If Nuns Teach in Public School, Kentucky Court Ruling Permits Them to Wear Religious Garb," *Nation's Schools*, 59:81-82 (March, 1957).

924 GORMAN, ASHLEY. ". . . Teachers Wearing Religious Garb," *Wayne Law Review*, 3:57-62 (Winter, 1956). Notes.

925 HALL, DONALD M. ". . . Members of Religious Orders as Teachers in Public Schools," *Tulane Law Review*, 31:676-79 (June, 1957).

Missouri:
(Case Material)

-- 1923 --

926 HERRON, (Sister) MARY RUTH, O.S.F. "An Unsuccessful Attempt to Use Legal Action to Prevent State Support for a School Conducted by Religious." Washington, D. C.: Catholic University of America, 1948. 79pp. (Unpublished master's dissertation).

Action taken against the authorities of St. Patrick, Clark County, Missouri, from 1910 to 1923. History of the case of *Kircher v. Evers et al.*, 238 S.W. 1086 (Mo., 1922). Affirmed in the St. Louis Court of Appeals, Jan. 2, 1923, with mention "Not to be officially published."

-- 1942 --

927 *Harfst v. Hoegen et al.*, 39 Mo. 808; 163 S.W.2d 609 (Mo., 1942). Rehearing denied, July 2, 1942.

Decision prohibiting the incorporation of Church-related schools into the public school system and the wearing of religious garbs in class by public school teachers.

REVIEWS:

Minnesota Law Review, 27:311-13 (Feb., 1943)
Notre Dame Lawyer, 18:170-72 (Dec., 1942)
University of Detroit Law Journal, 6:174-78 (May, 1943)
Nation's Schools, 31:23-24 (Feb., 1943)

-- 1954 --

928 *Berghorn et al. v. Reorganized School District No. 8, Franklin County (Mo.)*, 364 Mo. 121; 260 S.W.2d 537 (Mo., 1954).

Decision prohibiting the support from public funds of Church-related schools incorporated into the public school system.

929 GARBER, LEE ORVILLE. "May Public and Parochial School Authorities Maintain a Single School System?" *Nation's Schools*, 53:61-62 (June, 1954).

New Mexico:
(Case Material)

-- 1951 --

930 *Zellers v. Huff*, 55 N.M. 501; 236 P.2d 949 (New Mexico, 1951).

Decision against the use of denominational books, the wearing of a religious garb by public school teachers and the incorporation of Church-related schools into the public school system.

The following case involving religious influence in the public schools followed the Zellers case and was decided on the same basis. *Miller v. Cooper,* 56 N.M. 355; 244 P.2d 520 (1952).

931 "Catholicism and Public Schools in New Mexico," *Utah Law Review,* 3:467-80 (Fall, 1953).

932 DAWSON, JOSEPH MARTIN. "Public Schools, Catholic Model," *Christian Century,* 65:627-29 (June 23, 1948).

933 GARBER, LEE ORVILLE. "Supreme Court Defines Church-State Separation for Public Schools in New Mexico," *Nation's Schools,* 49:69-71 (Feb., 1952).

934 McGEE, (Sister) CLARE MARY. "The Causes and Effects of the 'Dixon Case'." Washington: Catholic University of America, 1955. (Unpublished master's dissertation.)

935 PHILIBERT, (Sister) MARY, S.L. "Nuns in New Mexico's Public Schools," *America,* 80:207-08 (Nov. 27, 1948).

North Dakota:

936 McEACHERN, MARGARET. "Nuns Carry on in North Dakota," *Catholic Digest,* 13:93-96 (March, 1949).

937 "Protestant Ministers in Public Schools" (Note about North Dakota's anti-garb bill), *America,* 79:47 (Apr. 24, 1948).

938 REED, GEORGE E. "Legal Developments Affecting the Church," *Catholic Action,* 30:11 (Sept., 1948).

939 "Unusual but Not Unprecedented, Bishop Muench Says of Secular Dress Used by Nun-Teachers," *Catholic Educational Review,* 47:132-33 (Feb., 1949). See *Time,* 52:37 (July 12), 58 (July 26, 1948), *Newsweek,* 31:84 (May 17, 1948).

940 "What Happened in North Dakota," *Christian Century,* 65:754-55 (July 28, 1948). Also *Christian Century,* 65:699 (July 14, 1948).

Ohio:

941 SEITZ, W. C. "Religious Education in Homogeneous School Districts," *Religious Education,* 37:49-51 (Jan.-Feb., 1942).

VII

Religion In Public Education:

Compulsory Flag Salute

Note. The courts frowned upon the first refusals of the Jehovah's Witnesses to salute the American flag. A cycle of state decisions adverse to the Witnesses culminated in appeals to the United States Supreme Court which upheld state compulsory flag salute regulations in 1940 but ruled against any coercion where objection was raised for reasons of conscience when it reversed itself in 1943.

A. BACKGROUND MATERIAL

1. SUMMARY MATERIAL AND LEGAL BACKGROUND:

942 KEESECKER, WARD W. "State Laws Relating to the Flag in American Education," *School Life*, 25:74-75 (Dec., 1939).

Includes a table of state legislation.

943 TORPEY, WILLIAM GEORGE. "Compulsory Flag Salute," in *Judicial Doctrines of Religious Rights in America*. Chapel Hill, N. C.: University of North Carolina Press, 1948. Pp.249-256.

944 STOKES, ANSON PHELPS. "Compulsory Salute to the Flag in the Schools," in *Church and State in the United States*. New York: Harper, 1950. Vol. II, pp.600-616.

2. EARLIER STUDY:

945 FENNELL, WILLIAM GEORGE. *Compulsory Flag Salute in the Schools: A Survey of the Statutes and an Examination of their Constitutionality*. 2d ed. New York: American Civil Liberties Union, Committee on Academic Freedom, 1938. 29pp. (Mimeographed).

B. PERIODICAL ARTICLES

946 BOOTH, THOMAS. "Compulsory Flag Salute," *Law Notes*, 43:9-10 (Apr., 1939).

947 GRINNELL, FRANK W. "Children, the Bill of Rights and the American Flag," *Massachusetts Law Quarterly*, 24:1-7 (Apr.-June, 1939).

948 HODGDON, DANIEL R. "Flag Salute Issue Setteld," *Clearing House*, 19:192-93 (Nov., 1944). Also, "Patriotism and Compulsion," 20:430 (March, 1946), "No More Compulsory Flag Salute Allowed," 21:499-50 (Apr., 1947).

949 PUNKE, HAROLD HERMAN. "The Flag and the Courts in Free Public Education," *Journal of Religion*, 24:119-30 (Apr., 1944).

An excellent summary review.

950 SCOTT, R. FOSTER. "Saluting the Flag and Civil Liberties," *World Education*, 6:233-35 (May, 1941).

C. CASE MATERIAL (U.S. Supreme Court)

1940—The Gobitis Decision

951 *Minersville School District v. Gobitis*, 310 U.S. 586; 60 S.Ct. 1010 (1940). Reversing 108 F.2d 683 (1939). Reversed. *West Virginia State Board of Education v. Barnette*, 319 U.S. 624; 63 S.Ct. 1178 (1943).

Decision stating that school regulations requiring public school students to salute the national flag, in spite of sincere religious convictions forbidding this act, are not violations of the federal Constitution. The decision was reversed by the court in 1943. (See No.962)

N.B.: For lower court decision see No.970.

REVIEWS:
Bill of Rights Review, Vol. 1, No. 1 (Supp.)
California State Bar Journal, 15:161-65 (June, 1940)
Cornell Law Quarterly, 26:127-30 (Dec., 1940)
Georgetown Law Journal, 29:112-14 (Oct., 1940)
Georgia Bar Journal, 2:74-76 (May, 1940)
International Juridical Assn. Bulletin, 9:1, 10-12 (July, 1940)
The Journal. Bar Association of Kansas, 9:276-80 (Feb., 1941)
Michigan Law Review, 39:149-52 (Nov., 1940)

Missouri Law Review, 6:106-111 (Jan., 1941)
New York University Law Quarterly Review, 18:124-27 (Nov., 1940)
St. John's Law Review, 15:95-97 (Nov., 1940)
South California Law Review, 14:57-58, 73-76 (Nov., 1940)
Temple University Law Quarterly, 14:545-47 (July, 1940)
University of Cincinnati Law Review, 14:444-47, 570-71 (May, Nov., 1940)
University of Detroit Law Journal, 4:38-41 (Nov., 1940)
Washington Law Review, 15:265-66 (Nov., 1940)

(Articles)

952　BALTER, HARRY GRAHAM. "Freedom of Religion Interpreted in Two Supreme Court Decisions," *The State Bar Journal of the State of California,* 15:161-65 (June, 1940).

953　BLAKELY, PAUL L. "Flag Salute vs. Oregon Case," *America,* 63:259-60 (June 15, 1940). Discussion. 63:353-54 (July 6, 1940).

954　―――――. "Omnipotent Schoolboards," *America,* 63: 286-87 (June 22, 1940).

955　"Court Abdicates; Flag Salute Case," *Christian Century,* 57:845-46 (July 3, 1940).

956　FENNELL, WILLIAM G. "The 'Reconstructed Court' and Religious Freedom: the Gobitis Case in Retrospect," *New York University Law Quarterly Review,* 19:31-48 (Nov., 1941). Bibliographic notes.

957　"Flag Salute Case," *Christian Century,* 57:791-92 (June 19, 1940).

958　FULLER, EDGAR. "Constitutional Liberties of Pupils and Teachers," *Harvard Educational Review,* 11:76-87 (Jan., 1941).

959　"The Gobitis Case in Retrospect," *Bill of Rights Review,* 1:267-68 (Summer, 1941).

960　KEARNEY, JAMES J. "Supreme Court Abdicates as National School Board," *Catholic Educational Review,* 38:457-60 (Oct., 1940).

961   "Religious Freedom: A Debate," *New Republic,* 102:
       843, 852-5 (June 24, 1940).

    Text of decision and dissent, with editorial comment.

1943—The Barnette Decision

962   *West Virginia State Board of Education v. Barnette,*
       319 U.S. 624; 63 Sup.Ct. 1178 (1943). Affirming
       Barnette v. West Virginia State Board of Education,
       47 F.Supp. 251 (1942). Reversing Minersville School
       District v. Gobitis, 310 U.S. 586; 60 Sup.Ct. 1010
       (1940).

    Decision stating that establishing salute to the national
    flag and recitation of the pledge of allegiance as a requisite
    for continued attendance at public schools is a violation of
    the First and Fourteenth Amendments of the federal Constitu-
    tion in the case of students who object to the practice for
    reasons of conscience. This is a reversal of the 1940 Gobitis
    decision. (See No.951.)

    N.B.: For lower court decision see No.972.

    REVIEWS:
    Georgetown Law Journal, 32:93-99 (Nov., 1943)
    George Washington Law Review, 12:70-80 (Dec., 1943)
    Georgia Bar Journal, 6:249-50 (Feb., 1944)
    Michigan Law Review, 42:186-87 (Aug.), 319-21 (Oct., 1943)
    Minnesota Law Review, 28:133 (Jan., 1944)
    Temple University Law Quarterly, 17:465-66 (Aug., 1943)
    University of Pennsylvania Law Review, 92:103-05 (Sept.,
       1943)

(Articles)

963   BAGLEY, WILLIAM CHANDLER. "The Supreme Court
       Hands an Educationally Significant Decision," *School*
       and Society, 57:696-97 (June 26, 1943).

964   "Court Upholds Freedom of Conscience," *Christian*
       Century, 60:731 (June 23, 1943).

965   "Education and the Flag," *Education for Victory,* 2:29-
       30 (Nov. 15, 1943).

966 POWELL, THOMAS REED. "The Flag Salute Case," *New Republic*, 109:16-18 (July 5, 1943).

967 ROSENFIELD, HARRY N. "Nobody Has to Salute the Flag," *Nation's Schools*, 32:45-46 (Aug., 1943).

D. STATE MATERIAL (With cases)

Arizona:
(Case Material)

-- 1942 --

968 *State v. Davis et al.*, 58 Ariz. 444; 120 P.2d 808 (Ariz., 1942).

Decision stating that school flag-salute regulations may be made compulsory.

Massachusetts:
(Case Material)

-- 1941 --

969 *Commonwealth (Mass.) v. Johnson*, 309 Mass. 476; 35 N.E.2d 801 (Mass., 1941).

Decision stating that a child who had been excluded from school for refusing to salute the flag and had been readmitted could not be declared an "habitual school offender" liable to be committed to a training school.

Pennsylvania:
(Case Material)

-- 1937 --

970 *Gobitis v. Minersville School District (Pa.)*, 21 F.Supp. 581 (1937). Plaintiff's rights affirmed, 23 F.Supp. 271 (1938). Affirmed. *Minersville School District v. Gobitis*, 108 F.2d 683 (1939). Reversed. 310 U.S. 586; 60 S.Ct. 1010 (1940).

This decision originally affirmed a student's constitutional right to refuse to salute the national flag for reasons of conscience. The decision was reversed by the United States Supreme Court in 1940. The court reversed its stand on the issue in 1943. (See Nos.951 and 962 in this unit.)

REVIEWS:

Cornell Law Quarterly, 23:582-86 (June, 1938)
Georgetown Law Journal, 27:231-33 (Dec., 1938)
Iowa Law Review, 23:424-25 (March, 1938)
Kansas City Law Review, 6:217-19 (Apr., 1938)
Minnesota Law Review, 23:247-49 (Jan., 1939)
Temple Law Quarterly, 12:513-14 (July, 1938)
University of Pennsylvania Law Review, 86:431-32 (Feb., 1938)
University of Pittsburgh Law Review, 3:243-44 (March, 1938)

-- 1944 --

971 *Commonwealth (Pennsylvania) v. Crowley*, 154 Pa. Super. 116; 35 A.2d 744 (1944).

Decision stating that school authorities are not authorized to require students to participate in flag-salute ceremonies when refusal is based on reasons of conscience.

West Virginia:
(Case Material)

-- 1942 --

972 *Barnette v. West Virginia State Board of Education*, 47 F.Supp. 251 (1942). Affirmed. *West Virginia State Board of Education v. Barnette*, 319 U.S. 624; 63 S.Ct. 1178 (1943).

N.B.: For U.S. Supreme Court decision see No.962

Decision stating that under the constitutional guaranty of "religious freedom," members of the sect of Jehovah's Witnesses who refused to salute the national flag for reasons of conscience could not be required to do so as a prerequisite to continued attendance at public schools. The decision was upheld by the United States Supreme Court.

REVIEWS:

Columbia Law Review, 43:134-35 (Jan., 1943)
George Washington Law Review, 11:113-14 (Dec., 1942)
Georgetown Law Journal, 31:85-88 (Nov., 1942)
Harvard Law Review, 56:652-54 (Jan., 1943)
Minnesota Law Review, 27:471-72 (Apr., 1943)
Oregon Law Review, 22:198-202 (Feb., 1943)
Tulane Law Review, 17:497-500 (Feb., 1943)

VIII

Public Aid
To Church-Related Schools

Note. Various plans of direct aid to Church-related schools were applied in New York City, Lowell, Mass., Poughkeepsie, N.Y., Faribault, Minn. and a number of other localities during the nineteenth century. State constitutional provisions, court action and legislation generally caused arrangements of that nature to discontinue.

Contemporary opinions favor a variety of positions ranging from the policy of total exclusion to proposals of fair-share tax credit certificate plans by which subsidies could be granted directly to students. There is more sympathy for the provision of civic benefits in the way of health and welfare services than for plans of assistance which would contribute directly to finance the cost of education.

Special aspects of aid are covered in units VI, IX, X and XI. Additional material will be found in I and II.

Working arrangements and solutions achieved in foreign countries are beyond the scope of this bibliography but some readings in this closely related field are suggested in the background material which follows.

A. BACKGROUND MATERIAL

1. BIBLIOGRAPHY:

973   COHEN, IVA. "Federal Aid to Parochial Schools," in
Church, State and Education; A Selected Bibliography 2d. rev. ed., New York City: Library of
Jewish Information, American Jewish Committee,
1954. Pp.24-28. (Mimeographed)

2. SUMMARY MATERIAL AND LEGAL BACKGROUND:

974   BEACH, FRED FRANCIS, and WILL, ROBERT F. *The State
and Nonpublic Schools (U. S. Office of Education,
Misc., No. 28, 1958).* Washington: U. S. Government
Printing Office, 1958. 152pp.

See Table 7, "State constitutional provisions regulating
public aid to nonpublic schools, by state, 1957," pp.16-17.

975   EMERSON, THOMAS IRWIN, and HABER DAVID (eds.).
"Aid to Education," in *Political and Civil Rights in
the United States; A Collection of Legal and Related
Materials.* Second Edition. Buffalo, N.Y.: Dennis &
Co., 1958. Vol. II, pp.1137-1157.

976   TORPEY, WILLIAM GEORGE. "Public Aid," in *Judicial
Doctrines of Religious Rights in America.* Chapel
Hill, N.C.: University of North Carolina Press, 1948.
Pp.234-244.

3. EARLIER STUDIES:

977   GABEL, RICHARD JAMES. *Public Funds for Church and
Private Schools.* Washington, D.C.: Catholic University of America, 1937. xiv, 858pp. (Doctoral dissertation) Bibliography: pp.783-837.

Privately printed, Toledo, Ohio, 1937. Copyrighted by the
author.

978   PIZOR, RAYMOND. *The Use of Public Funds and Public
School Property for Other than Public School Purposes.* Philadelphia, Pa.: Temple University, Sullivan
Memorial Library, 1938. 175pp. (Published doctoral
dissertation) Bibliography: pp.169-174.

4. PUBLIC AID IN OTHER COUNTRIES:
(Suggested Readings)

979   BENABARRE, BENIGNO, O.S.B. *Public Funds for Private
Schools in a Democracy; Theory and Practice in
Fifty-one Countries.* Manila, Philippine Islands:
M.C.S. Enterprises (Tiaoqui Building, Plaza Sta.
Cruz), 1958. 325pp.

980   DRINAN, ROBERT F., S.J. "Ten Nations Discuss Freedom
of Education," *America*, 93:526-528, 530 (Sept. 3,
1955).

981   HARTNETT, ROBERT CLINTON, S.J. (ed.). *The Right to
Educate; Democracy and Religious Education—A
Symposium.* New York: America Press, 1949. 48pp.

Contents. "The Dutch Show the Way," E. F. Schroeder,
5-13. "Canada Lets Parents Choose," D. J. Pierce, 14-22.
"Australia: a Study in Courage," W. K. Keane, 23-33.
"Britain Revamps Her System," T. Quirk, 33-42. "Is Religious Education Divisive?" R. C. Hartnett, 43-48.

B. BOOKS AND PAMPHLETS

982   BLUM, VIRGIL CLARENCE, S.J. *Freedom of Choice in
Education.* New York: Macmillan, 1958. 230pp.
Notes: pp.205-224.

REVIEWS:
Sign, 38:70-71 (March, 1959) Francis X. Gallagher
Social Justice Review, 51:310 (Jan., 1959)

983   DALY, ANTHONY W. *Inalienable Civil Rights in Education.* St. Louis, Mo.: Citizens for Educational Freedom, 1959. (12 pages, not numbered.)

984   FEDERAL COUNCIL OF THE CHURCHES OF CHRIST IN AMERICA. *Federal Aid to Sectarian Education?* New York: the Council, 1947. 22pp.

985   HARTNETT, ROBERT CLINTON, S.J. *Equal Rights for Children.* New York: America Press, 1948. 40pp. Bibliography.

986   ——————. *Federal Aid to Education, the Rights of Children Attending Nonpublic Schools, A sequel to "Equal Rights for Children."* New York: America Press, 1950. 48pp. Bibliography.

987   HARVARD LAW SCHOOL FORUM. *Public Aid to Parochial Education; a transcript of a Discussion on a Vital Issue, Presented by the Harvard Law School Forum Held at Rindge Technical School, Cambridge, Mass.* Harvard Law School Forum, Hastings Hall, Cambridge 28, Mass., 1951. 56pp.

   Speakers: Dr. George H. Williams (Harvard Divinity School), Dr. Vincent A. McGrossen (Boston College), Bishop G. Bromley Oxnam (Methodist Church), James M. O'Neill (Professor, Brooklyn College). Moderator: George C. Homens (Professor, Harvard University).

988   JORDAN, EDWARD B. *Federal Aid for Education.* Washington, D.C.: National Catholic Welfare Conference, 1944. 14pp.

989   McCLUSKEY, NEIL GERARD, S.J. *Federal Aid to Private Schools.* St. Louis, Missouri: The Queen's Work, 1950. 40pp.

990   McMANUS, WILLIAM E. *Question of State Aid for Parochial Schools.* Washington, D.C.: National Catholic Welfare Conference, 1948. 21pp.

   Address delivered at the national convention of the Catholic Press Association, Cleveland, Ohio, May 21, 1948.

991   McNICHOLAS, JOHN TIMOTHY, O.P. *Federal Aid for American Education.* Washington, D.C.: National Catholic Educational Association, 1946. 12pp.

   General discussion followed by detailed comment on the Thomas-Hill-Taft Bill, (S. 181).

992 MEYER, AGNES E. "The Battle to Improve Public Schools," in *Out of These Roots, the Autobiography of an American Woman.* Boston: Little, Brown, 1953. Pp.284-312.

> Replies. William E. McManus. "Agnes Meyer on Parochial Schools," *Catholic World,* 178:346-51 (Feb., 1954). John B. Sheerin, "Mrs. Meyer 'warns' the American Hierarchy," *Homiletic and Pastoral Review,* 56: 547-51 (Apr., 1958).

993 NATIONAL EDUCATION ASSOCIATION OF THE UNITED STATES. RESEARCH DIVISION. *State Aid to Private Schools: Constitutional Provisions, Statutes, Court Decisions.* Washington, D.C.: the Association, May, 1943. 34pp. (Mimeographed)

> Earlier report: *State Aid to Private and Sectarian Schools,* 1937. 36pp. (Mimeographed)

994 O'BRIEN, JOHN ANTHONY. *What! Public Funds for a Catholic School?* Huntington, Indiana: Our Sunday Visitor Press, n.d. 35pp.

> Same. "Public Funds for Catholic Schools?", *Ave Maria,* 65:679-83, 718-22, 747-52, 778-84 (May 31-June 21, 1947).

C. PERIODICAL ARTICLES

995 "ABC's of Fight Over Aid to Parochial Schools," *United States News and World Report,* 50:52-54 (April 3, 1961).

996 "Aid to Parochial Schools—Why Kennedy Says it's Illegal," and "U.S. Funds Already Given to Church-run Schools," *United States News and World Report,* 50:100-101 (April 10, 1961).

> Summary of a legal brief prepared by the U. S. Department of Health, Education and Welfare, and presented to Congress by Abraham Ribicoff, Secretary of the department. The full text was printed in the *Congressional Record* (Daily ed.), 87th Congress, First Session, Vol. 107, No. 56, pp.5054-5070 (March 30, 1961).

A legal analysis representing another viewpoint was submitted by Senator Kenneth B. Keating. See the *Congressional Record* (Daily ed.), 87th Congress, First Session, Vol. 107, No. 68, pp. 6195-6198 (April 24, 1961).

997 BENNETT, JOHN COLEMAN. "Aid to Parochial Schools: Two Considerations," *Christianity and Crisis*, 21:61-62 (May 1, 1961).

998 BLAKELY, PAUL L. "School Taxes Penalize Catholics," *America*, 62:233 (Dec. 9, 1939).

999 BLUM, VIRGIL CLARENCE, S.J. "Educational Benefits Without Enforced Conformity," *Homiletic and Pastoral Review*, 58:27-33 (Oct., 1957). Excerpts, with title "Freedom of Choice in Schools," *U. S. News and World Report*, 43:109-112 (Oct. 25, 1957). Reply. 43:134 (Nov. 8, 1957), G. L. Archer.

1000 ————. "Freedom of Choice in Education," *Catholic Educator*, 28:529-534 (April, 1958).

1001 ————. "The Right to Choose Your Own School," *Catholic World*, 190:15-23 (Oct., 1959).

1002 BODE, BOYD HENRY. "Federal Funds for Non-Public Schools? Warning," *Virginia Journal of Education*, 41:331-32+ (Apr., 1948).

1003 BOHN, WILLIAM E. "American Unity and the Problem of Federal Aid to Education (editorial)," *New Leader*, 44:10 (March 20, 1961).

1004 BRADY, WILLIAM A. "The 'Luxury' of a Catholic Education," *America*, 104:821-22 (March 25, 1961).

1005 BRICKMAN, WILLIAM WOLFGANG. "Federal Funds and Parochial Schools," *The Young Israel Viewpoint*, Sept.-Oct., 1950.

1006 ————. "Public Aid to Religious Schools?" *Religious Education*, 55:279-288 (July-Aug., 1960).

1007 BROWNE, HENRY J. "Public Support of Catholic Education in New York, 1825-1842: Some New Aspects," *Catholic Historical Review*, 39:1-27 (Apr., 1953).

1008 BURTON, PHILIP. "Public Funds for Public Schools Only," *Christian Century,* 78:415-417 (April 5, 1961).

1009 BUTLER, PAUL. "Government Aid to the Private School," *Catholic Mind,* 59:205-215 (May-June, 1961).

Address to the Holy Name Society of St. Jane Frances de Chantal Parish, Bethesda, Maryland, March 9, 1961.

1010 BUTTS, ROBERT FREEMAN, and MCCLUSKEY, NEIL G., S.J. "Public Funds for Parochial Schools?" *Teachers College Record,* 62:49-62 (Oct., 1960).

1011 CANAVAN, FRANCIS P., S.J. "Politics and Constitutional Law," *America,* 104:804-805 (March 25, 1961).

1012 "Church Schools Get Public Aid," *U.S. News and World Report,* 27:17-19 (Aug. 5, 1949).

1013 "The Churches Kill Aid for Schools," *New Republic,* 122:5-6 (March 27, 1950).

About federal aid.

1014 "Congress and the Modern Move for Federal Aid to Education: Pro and Con," *Congressional Digest,* 28:261-88 (Nov., 1949).

1015 CONNELL, EDWARD A. "Federal Aid: the Forgotten Family," *America,* 83:169-71 (May 13, 1950).

1016 "Constitutionality of Tax Benefits Accorded Religion," *Columbia Law Review,* 49:968-992 (Nov., 1949).

Follows the Everson-McCollum argument.

1017 CORNELL, FRANCIS GRIFFITH. "Federal Aid Is a Religious Issue," *School Executive,* 72:47-49 (June, 1953). Bibliography. Comment. R. H. Schenk, S.J., 72:13 (Aug., 1953).

1018 COSTANZO, JOSEPH F. "Federal Aid to Education and Religious Liberty," *University of Detroit Law Journal,* 36:1-46 (Oct., 1958).

1019 CREEGAN, ROBERT T. "Subsidized Pluralism," *School and Society,* 86:32-34 (January 18, 1958).

1020   CUSHMAN, ROBERT FAIRCHILD. "Public Support of Religious Education in American Constitutional Law," *Illinois Law Review,* 45:333-56 (July-Aug., 1950).

1021   DRINAN, ROBERT F., S.J. "Should the State Aid Private Schools?" *Vital Speeches of the Day,* 27:397-401 (April 15, 1961). Same. *Social Order,* 11:241-250 (June, 1961).

Address delivered at the Regional Convention of the American Association of School Administrators, Philadelphia, Pa., March 28, 1961.

1022   "Establishment of Religion by State Aid," *Rutgers Law Review,* 3:115-27 (Feb., 1949).

1023   EVANS, JOHN WHITNEY. "Catholics and the Blair Education Bill," *Catholic Historical Review,* 46:273-298 (Oct., 1960).

A historical study of the Blair Bill for federal support of education, 1880-1890.

1024   FALLON, JOHN J. "Appropriations of Public Funds Beneficial to Sectarian Schools—Validity Under State Constitutions," *University of Detroit Law Journal,* 6:174-78 (May, 1943).

1025   "Federal Aid and Catholic Schools," *Nation,* 164:618-19 (May 24, 1947).

1026   "Federal Aid for Schools," *Christian Century,* 63:710-11 (June 5, 1946).

1027   "Federal Aid in the National School Lunch Act," and "Federal Aid for School Lunches," *Catholic School Journal,* 46:226-227, 231-232 (Sept., 1946).

1028   "Federal Aid Minus Jokers," *Christian Century,* 66:782-84 (June 29, 1949). Other comments in the *Christian Century:* "Federal Aid and the Catholic Veto," 66:813 (July 6, 1949), "Why is the Federal Council Silent?" 66:1003 (Aug. 31, 1949), 1123, 1139-40 (Sept. 28, 1949), "Federal Aid is Shelved," 67:389 (March 29, 1950).

About the Barden Bill.

1029 "Federal Aid: Round Two," *Commonweal,* 51:548-49 (March 3, 1950).

1030 "Federal Aid to Education," *The Jurist,* 9:438-41 (Oct., 1949).

Statements on the Barden Bill.

1031 FLANNERY, HARRY W. "The Barden Bill: a Possible Threat to both Church and States," *Commonweal,* 50:430-31 (Aug. 12, 1949).

1032 FLEEGE, URBAN H. "Catholic Schools and Government Aid," *America,* 72:385-86 (Feb. 17, 1945).

1033 "Freedom of Conscience in the U. S. A." (Editorial), *Catholic Educational Review,* 47:363-64 (June, 1949).

1034 FREEMAN, HARROP A. "Exemptions from Civil Responsibilities," *Ohio State Law Journal,* 20:437-460 (Summer, 1959).

See: "Use of State Funds—Bus, Textbooks and Similar Cases," and "Use of Public Educational Facilities for Religious Purposes—Religious Instruction," 439-443.

1035 GILBERT, HUGH W. "State Aid to Sectarian Institutions," *Georgia Bar Journal,* 19:354-58 (Feb., 1957).

1036 GUSTIN, ARNO, and HYNES, EMERSON. "Federal Aid, a Time for Decision," *Commonweal,* 39:638-40 (Apr. 14, 1944). Comment. Joseph G. Grundle, 40:109-10 (May 19, 1944).

1037 HAGAN, JOHN R. "A Plea for Conciliation," *National Catholic Educational Association, Bulletin* (Proceedings issue), 36: 56-75 (Aug., 1939).

1038 HANNAN, JEROME D. "Not One Cent for Religion," *The Jurist,* 7:45-59 (Jan., 1947).

1039 HARDIMAN, EDWARD J. "Federal Aid to Education— For Some or For All?" *Temple Law Quarterly,* 23: 227-31 (Jan., 1950).

1040 HARTNETT, ROBERT CLINTON. "Central Issue in Federal Aid," *America*, 81:497-98 (Aug. 6, 1949).

1041 ————. "The Courts and Aid to Schools," *America*, 77:683-86 (Sept. 20, 1947).

1042 ————. "Is the NEA in Good Faith? *America*, 85: 395-96 (July 21, 1951).

1043 ————. "Who's Blocking Federal Aid? *America*, 81:417-18 (July 9, 1949).

1044 HEFFRON, EDWARD J. "The Protestant, the Catholic, and School Taxes," *Catholic Digest*, 13:6-9 (April, 1949).

1045 HERBERG, WILL. "Justice for Religious Schools," *America*, 98:190-193 (Nov. 16, 1957). Discussion. 98:188 (Nov. 16, 1957), Nathan A. Perilman and Will Herberg, 98:426-28 (Jan. 11, 1958). Summary. *Newsweek*, 50:93 (Nov. 25, 1957).

Reprinted by the America Press.

1046 HOCHWALT, FREDERICK G. "Pattern for Federal Aid: 1945," *Catholic School Journal*, 45:205-07 (Oct., 1945).

1047 JOHNSON, FREDERICK ERNEST. "Federal Aid to Education," *Christianity and Crisis*, 21:46, 47 (April 3, 1961).

1048 KATZ, WILBER G. "Freedom of Religion and State Neutrality," *University of Chicago Law Review*, 20: 426-440 (Spring, 1953).

See also Paul G. Kauper, "Church and State: Cooperative Separation," *Michigan Law Review*, 60:1-40 (Nov. 1961).

1049 KEARNEY, JAMES J. "Public Aid for Private and Sectarian Schools," *The Yearbook of School Law*, pp. 144-51 (1940).

On state and local aid.

1050 KELLEY, JOSEPH A. "Toward Equalizing Citizens' Shares in Supporting American Education," *Catholic Educational Review*, 55:240-49 (Apr., 1957).

1051   KERWIN, JEROME G. "A Political Scientist Looks at the Relationship of Government and Religious Education," *National Catholic Educational Association, Bulletin*, 45:6-14 (May, 1949).

1052   KLINKHAMER, (Sister) MARIA CAROLYN. "The Blaine Amendment of 1875: Private Motives for Political Action," *Catholic Historical Review*, 42:15-49 (Apr., 1956).

1053   KNIGHTS OF COLUMBUS. "On Church and State." *Columbia*, 29:11 (Oct., 1949).

> Text of a resolution adopted at a national convention in Portland, Oregon, August 18, 1949.

1054   LEWIS, EDWARD R. "The Threat in the School Aid Bills," *Christian Century*, 64:652-53 (May 21, 1947).

1055   LIEBSON, BERNARD, AND SHUSTER, GEORGE NAUMAN. "Public and Private Education," *The American Scholar*, 19:217-26 (Apr., 1950).

> Contents: "Public Funds and the Public Schools," B. Liebson. "A Plea for Cooperation," G. N. Shuster.

1056   MCCLUSKEY, NEIL GERARD, S.J. "How Much State Support?" *America*, 101:722-728 (Sept. 19, 1959).

1057   MCGIFFERT, ARTHUR CUSHMAN, JR. "Horace Bushnell on Parochial Schools," *Christian Century*, 66:1385-87 (Nov. 23, 1949).

1058   MCKEOUGH, MICHAEL J., O. Praem. "Freedom of Conscience in the U.S.A. (Editorial)," *Catholic Educational Review*, 47:363-364 (June, 1949).

> Remarks following the vote on the Thomas Bill in the Senate.

1059   MCMAHON, PAUL B. "State Aid to Education and the Doctrine of Separation of Church and State," *Georgetown Law Journal*, 36:631-47 (May, 1948).

1060   MCMANUS, WILLIAM E. "The Federal Aid Controversy," *America*, 77: (Section two) xiv, xv (Apr. 12, 1947).

1061 ————. "Federal Aid for All School Children," *Catholic Educational Review,* 43:193-202 (Apr., 1945).

1062 ————. "Federal Aid in Education; Statement before a Subcommittee of the House Committee on Education and Labor, June 3, 1949," *Catholic Mind,* 47:630-640 (Oct., 1949).

> Statement made for the National Catholic Welfare Conference, Department of Education.

1063 ————. "Federal Legislation," *National Catholic Educational Association, Bulletin,* 44:303-22 (Aug., 1947).

> Remarks. "NEA Technique," *America,* 77:86-87 (Apr. 26, 1947), "Mr. Givens and the NEA," *America,* 78:172 (Nov. 15, 1947).

1064 ————. "Proposed Changes in the 'G.I. Bill of Rights'", *Catholic Educational Review,* 43:513-19 (Nov., 1945).

1065 ————. "School Lunches, a New Law," *Catholic Action,* 27:10-11 (July, 1945).

1066 ————. "School Lunch Legislation," *Catholic Educational Review,* 44:200-205 (April, 1946).

1067 MARLING, (Bishop) JOSEPH M. "Government Aid to Parochial Schools," *Social Justice Review,* 52:16-17 (April, 1959).

> Reprinted from *The Catholic Missourian* of February 15, 1959.

1068 MITCHELL, WILLIAM A. "Religion and Federal Aid to Education," *Law and Contemporary Problems,* 14:113-43 (Winter, 1949).

1069 MOEHLMAN, CONRAD HENRY. "Federal Aid to Education?" *Christian Century,* 64:106-08 (Jan. 22, 1947).

1070 MURRAY, JAMES J. "What is the Real Issue?" *America,* 104:818-820 (March 25, 1961). Comment. "Aid to Education," 105:137 (April 15, 1961).

1071   NELSON, CLAUD D. "Proposal on the School Aid Impasse," *Christian Century*, 78:448-450 (April 12, 1961).

1072   "The New Education Bill," *Christian Century*, 78:291-92 (March 8, 1961).

Other editorial remarks as follows: "Hierarchy Opposes Education Bill," 78:317 (March 15, 1961). "Catholics Demand Patronage," 78:381-82 (March 22, 1961). "Church Flexes Muscles," 78:411-412 (April 5, 1961). "Study Supports Kennedy in School-Aid Dispute," 78:446 (April 12, 1961). "Roman Catholic Church 'Goes for Broke'," 78:476-77 (April 19, 1961). "Long Range Catholic Strategy," 78:508-509 (April 26, 1961).

1073   NIEBUHR, REINHOLD. "School Aid, the President and the Hierarchy," *New Leader*, 44:8-9 (March 20, 1961).

1074   "No Federal Aid to Churches," *Christian Century*, 66: 166-67 (Feb. 9, 1949).

1075   O'GARA, JAMES. "The School Question," *Commonweal*, 73:602 (March 10, 1961).

1076   PITT, FELIX NEWTON. "Federal Aid for Catholic Schools?" *Catholic Educational Review*, 43:65-82 (Feb., 1945). Same. *Catholic Mind*, 43:461-75 (Aug., 1945).

1077   "Public Aid for Private Schools? Catholic and Protestant Views," *U. S. News and World Report*, 39:102-105 (Dec. 2, 1955), "More on Aid to Schools," 39: 121-22 (Dec. 16, 1955), "State Aid to Build Schools?" 39:67 (Dec. 23, 1955).

1078   "Public Money for Nonpublic Schools?" *Nation's Schools*, 39:32 (March, 1947).

1079   PUNKE, HAROLD HERMAN. "Public Funds for Private and Sectarian Schools," *Yearbook of School Law*, pp.108-20 (1942).

1080   "Roadblock to Federal Aid," *National Education Association Journal* 38:494-95 (Oct., 1949). Reply. William E. McManus, "Roadblock to Federal Aid," *America*, 82:95-97 (Oct. 29, 1949).

1081 ROOSEVELT, ANNA ELEANOR (ROOSEVELT) (Mrs. Franklin Delano Roosevelt).

> Her statements about federal aid to education after the introduction of the 'Barden Bill' occasioned an exchange of correspondence with Cardinal Spellman.
>
> The first statements appeared in "My Day," her column in the *World Telegram*, June 23, July 8 and July 15, 1949.
>
> For column texts and texts of letters from both Cardinal Spellman and Mrs. Roosevelt see the *New York Times* (1949), July 23, p.1, col. 4 and p.26, cols. 2 and 7; July 28, p.1, col. 2 and p.16, col. 3; Aug. 6, p.1, col 2; Aug. 25, col 5.
>
> For representative reactions, see: *Christian Century*, 66: 907, 955-56, 981-83 (Aug. 3, 17, 24, Sept. 7, 1949); *Nation*, 169:163-64 (Aug. 13, 1949); *Catholic World*, 169:401-05 (Sept., 1949); *Social Justice Review*, 42:231-32, 268-69 (Nov., Dec., 1949).

1082 "School Aid and Religion" (Editorial), *Life*, 50, no. 11:46 (March 17, 1961).

> Reprinted in the *Congressional Record* (Daily ed.), 87th Congress, First Session, Vol. 107, No. 53, p.A2150 (March 27, 1961).

1083 SHEERIN, JOHN B. "Eisenhower and Parochial Schools," *Catholic World*, 181:1-3 (April, 1955).

1084 SHERRILL, LEWIS J. "Federal Aid in Education," *Christianity and Crisis*, 8:50-53 (April 26, 1948).

> Comment. F. Ernest Johnson, p.53.

1085 "Should Taxpayers Support Non-Public Schools?" *U.S. News and World Report*, 39:35, 36, 38, 40, 41 (Dec. 2, 1955).

1086 SMITH, RICHARD JOYCE. "Aid to Private and Parochial Schools," *America*, 46:152-57 (Nov. 10, 1956).

> General discussion with special references to Connecticut.

1087 STANLEY, CHARLES J. "Organized Interests and Federal Aid to Education," *School and Society*, 73:1-4 (Jan. 6, 1951). Reply. 73:116 (Feb. 24, 1951).

1088 SUTHERLAND, ARTHUR E. "Does the Constitution Really Ban U. S. Aid to Parochial Schools? A Harvard Law Professor Gives Congress an Answer," *United States News and World Report*, 50:109-112 (April 3, 1961).

> Excerpts from a letter written to Representative John W. McCormack. For the complete text see the *Congressional Record* (Daily ed.), 87th Congress, First Session, Vol. 107, No. 50, pp.A2026-A2029 (March 22, 1961).

1089 "Validity of Appropriation of Public Funds that Inure to the Benefit of Sectarian Schools," *Minnesota Law Review*, 27:311-13 (Feb., 1943).

1090 WALSH, J. HARTT. "Wall of Separation," *National Education Association Journal*, 39:99-101 (Feb., 1950).

> About federal aid.

1091 WANAMAKER, PEARL A. "Things are in the Saddle, and Ride Mankind," *National Education Association Journal*, 36:433-34 (Sept., 1947). Same. *National Education Association of the United States, Proceedings*, 1947, pp.9-19.

> About federal aid.

1092 WHELAN, CHARLES M., S.J. "Only Higher Education, Mr. President?" *America*, 104:758-760 (March 11, 1961).

> See also "School Question: Stage Two," *America*, 105:17-19 (April 1, 1961). "The President's Brief on Federal Aid," *America*, 105:140-41 (April 15, 1961).

1093 WIDEN, IRWIN. "Federal Aid and the Church School Issue," *Phi Delta Kappan*, 36:271-76 (Apr., 1955).

1094 WILLIAMS, JOSEPH C., and CARR, JAMES. "Forum: Should the Federal Government Aid Parochial Schools?" *Forum*, 111:100-06 (Feb., 1949).

1095 WISE, JOHN E., S.J. "Federal Aid for Religious Schools," *School and Society*, 62:363-65 (Dec. 8, 1945). Discussion. 63:170-72 (March 9, 1946).

D. UNPUBLISHED DISSERTATIONS

1096   ABRAMS, ALBERTINA ADELHEIT. "The Policy of the National Education Association Toward Federal Aid to Education (1857-1953)," Ann Arbor, Mich.: University of Michigan, 1955. (Unpublished doctoral dissertation)

> Abstract. *Dissertation Abstracts*, 15 no. 5:744. Microfilm. Ann Arbor, Mich.: University Microfilms, Publication no. 11,235.

1097   ACKERLUND, GEORGE C. "Federal Attitude Toward Public Support of Sectarian Education," Ann Arbor, Mich.: University of Michigan, 1950. (Unpublished doctoral dissertation)

> Abstract. *Dissertation Abstracts*, 10 no. 4:72-73 (1950). Microfilm. Ann Arbor, Mich.: University Microfilms, publication no. 1940.

1098   BOKSANSKY, (Sister) MARY E. "Catholic Opinion on Federal Aid to Education Since 1918," Detroit, Michigan: University of Detroit, 1954. (Unpublished master's dissertation)

1099   CALDWELL, CLEON ARTHUR. "The Development of Concepts Regarding the Use of Tax Funds for Public and Parochial Schools," Minneapolis, Minn.: University of Minnesota, 1956. (Unpublished doctoral dissertation)

> Abstract. *Religious Education*, 52:181-82 (May-June, 1957) and *Dissertation Abstracts*, 16, No. 10:1822-1823 (1956). Microfilm. Ann Arbor, Michigan: University Microfilms, publication no. 17,841.

1100   CLYNE, JAMES BARTLEY. "The Catholic Attitude Toward Federal Aid to Education in the United States, 1870-1892," Washington, D.C.: Catholic University of America, 1952. (Unpublished master's dissertation)

1101   CUSHMAN, ROBERT FAIRCHILD. "Public Support of Religious Education in American Constitutional Law,"

Ithaca, N.Y.: Cornell University, 1949. (Unpublished doctoral dissertation)

See: "Public Support of Religious Education in American Constitutional Law," *Illinois Law Review*, 45:333-56 (July-Aug., 1950).

1102 DONOHUE, FRANCIS JOSEPH. "The Development of American Catholic Theory, Attitudes, and Practices with Regard to Public Support for Parochial Schools," Ann Arbor, Mich.: University of Michigan, 1944. (Unpublished doctoral dissertation)

1103 FARNAND, (Rev.) EVARSIT, O.F.M. "An Investigation of the Social Philosophies of Three Major Groups Opposing Federal Aid to Education." Saint Louis, Mo.: St. Louis University, 1957. (Unpublished doctoral dissertation)

1104 GARDNER, LAURENCE R. "The Blaine Amendment of 1876: a Proposal to Extend the Constitution to Prohibit Indirect Aid to Sectarian Institutions," Washington, D.C.: Catholic University of America, 1947. (Unpublished master's dissertation)

1105 HAMILTON, LORNE D. "The Issue of Public Aid to Catholic Parochial Schools in the United States with Reference to Education in Quebec," Cambridge, Mass.: Harvard University, 1953. (Unpublished doctoral dissertation)

1106 JONES, ROBERT DANA. "An Analysis of Public Support of Private Schools." Los Angeles, California: University of Southern California, 1958. (Unpublished doctoral dissertation)

1107 KINDRED, LESLIE W., JR. "Public Funds for Private and Parochial Schools: a Legal Study," Ann Arbor, Mich.: University of Michigan, 1938. (Unpublished doctoral dissertation)

1108 KRASH, OTTO. "Power-Group Strategy in the Development of a National Educational Policy: a Study of the Congressional Committee Hearings on Federal Aid to Education; 1945-49," New York.: Columbia University, Teachers College, 1951. (Unpublished doctoral dissertation)

1109   McLAUGHLIN, HELEN G. "A Survey of Periodical Liter-
       ature on the Federal Aid to Education Controversy,
       January, 1946-December, 1949," Newark, N.J.: New
       Jersey State Teachers College, 1952. (Unpublished
       master's dissertation)

1110   McMANUS, WILLIAM E. "Current Educational Policy
       Toward Public Service for Nonpublic School Pupils
       in Particular Reference to Free Transportation and
       Textbooks," Washington, D.C.: Catholic University
       of America, 1942. (Unpublished master's disserta-
       tion)

1111   MONTIEL, HILDA D. "A Study of the Relationship Be-
       tween Church-State Separation and Public Tax Fund
       Aid to Catholic Parochial Education," Chico, Cal.:
       Chico State College, 1954. (Unpublished master's
       dissertation)

1112   OTTE, (Sister) MARY AQUINATA. "Catholic Opinion Re-
       garding Federal Aid to Education from 1919 to 1950."
       Washington, D.C.: Catholic University of America,
       1951. (Unpublished master's dissertation)

1113   STEPHENS, MARY A. "A Comparative Study of State
       Aid to Catholic Education in the United States and
       Selected Countries," Cleveland, Ohio: St. John Col-
       lege, 1953. (Uupublished master's dissertation)

1114   SWEENEY, JOHN J. "The Position of the National Edu-
       cation Association with Regard to Federal Aid to
       Education," Washington, D.C.: Catholic University
       of America, 1951. (Unpublished master's disserta-
       tion)

1115   THOMPSON, JOHN CHARLES. "Legal Aspects of Federal
       Aid to Sectarian Schools," Nashville, Tenn.: George
       Peabody College for Teachers, 1955. (Unpublished
       doctoral dissertation)

           Abstract. *Yearbook of School Law,* p.159 (1957), and *Dis-
           sertation Abstracts,* 16 no. 1:57-58. Microfilm. Ann Arbor,
           Mich.: University Microfilms, publication no. 15,476.

1116   WEAVER, CHARLES T. "The Child Benefit Theory and the
       Separation of Church and State," Emory University,
       Georgia, 1958. (Unpublished master's dissertation)

1117 WIDEN, IRWIN. "The Issue of Public Support for Sectarian Schools," Berkeley, Cal.: University of California of Berkeley, 1950. (Unpublished doctoral dissertation)

E. STATE MATERIAL (With cases)

New York:

1118 COSTANZO, JOSEPH F., S.J. "New York's Aid to Education Program," *Catholic World*, 193:154-161 (June, 1961).

Ohio:
(Case Material)

-- 1943 --

1119 *Findley v. City of Conneaut*, 12 Ohio Supp. 161 (1943) (N.B.: Bound with the Ohio Edition of 51 N.E.2d). Modified. 145 Ohio St. 480; 62 N.E.2d 318 (1945) Affirmed. 76 Ohio App. 153; 63 N.E.2d 449 (1945)

Under a will bequeathing an estate to a village for the purpose of establishing a private Protestant religious technical school, support from public funds could not be allowed without violating the constitution.

Vermont:
(Case Material)

-- 1956 --

1120 *Donoghue v. Smith*, 126 A.2d 93 (Vermont, 1956).

Summary. *Yearbook of School Law*, 1958, p.125.

The tuition of students attending classes in the school district of another town may be paid with public funds only if the school attended is a public school. (The court declined to state whether the religion clauses of the state and federal Constitutions prohibited such payments made to Church-related schools.)

-- 1961 --

1121　*Swarth v. South Burlington Town School District,* 167 A.2d 514 (Vermont, Jan. 3, 1961).

In this case, the payment of tuition for students attending Church-related schools was declared to be a violation of the religion clauses of the federal Constitution.

Comment. Paul Butler, "Government Aid to the Private School," *Catholic Mind,* 59:205-215 (May-June, 1961).—Robert F. Drinan, S.J., "Should the State Aid Private Schools?" *Vital Speeches,* 27:397-401 (April 15, 1961).—William S. Bach, *Michigan Law Review,* 59:1254-1256 (June, 1961).

Virginia:
(Case Material)

-- 1955 --

1122　*Almond v. Day,* 197 Va. 419; 89 S.E.2d 851 (Virginia, 1955).

Decision stating that money appropriated for the education of service men could not be used for tuition payments to non-public institutions without violating state constitutional provisions limiting the use of public funds to public institutions. In this instance, the institution was Church-related.

REVIEW:

Virginia Law Review, 42:437-439 (Apr., 1956).

IX

Public Aid To Church-Related Schools:
The School Bus Problem

Note. The first initiatives to transport private and parochial school children on public school buses met the disfavor of the courts. A negative precedent was set in the case of *State (Wisconsin) ex rel. Straten v. Milquet,* 180 Wis. 109; 192 N.W. 392 (1923). A marked change of attitude in the matter showed in the legislation and litigation of some states in the late thirties. In the case of *Judd v. Board of Education of Hempstead, Nassau County (N.Y.), et al.,* 278 N.Y. 200; 15 N.E.2d 576 (1938), the New York Court forbade the practice as unconstitutional but the New York constitutional convention of 1938 preferred the minority argument in the decision when it amended the basic education law and enabled the legislature to provide transportation to and from any school. The same year, the Maryland court sanctioned the transportation of parochial school children in *Board of Education of Baltimore County (Md.) v. Wheat,* 174 Md. 314; 199 A. 628 (1938). The New Jersey bus law which led to the *Everson* decision was enacted in 1941.

The judicial doctrines expressed in the *Everson* case (1947) have been developed in the *McCollum* decision (1948) and modified in the *Zorach* case (1952). In many respects, the items listed with these decisions (in this unit and in V) should be considered as a unit of continuing material. The relevance of any case study and discussion will be fully understood only if chronological perspectives are kept in mind.

Units I, II and VIII should be checked for additional material.

A. BACKGROUND MATERIAL

SUMMARY MATERIAL AND LEGAL BACKGROUND:

1123 BEACH, FRED F., and WILL, ROBERT F. *The State and Nonpublic Schools* . . . (U.S. Office of Education, Misc. No. 28, 1958). Washington, D.C.: U.S. Government Printing Office, 1958. 152pp.

See "Pupil Transportation" under the name of each state, pp.32-152. A convenient summary is given on pp.26-27.

1124 McCLUSKEY, NEIL GERARD, S.J. "How Much State Support?" *America*, 101:722-728 (Sept. 19, 1959).

See "The Bus Issue," pp.723-728.

1125 PUNKE, HAROLD HERMAN. "Public Funds for Transporting Pupils to Parochial Schools," in *Community Uses of Public School Facilities*. New York, N.Y.: Kings Crown Press, Columbia University, 1951. Pp. 72-83.

B. BOOKS

1126 NATIONAL CATHOLIC WELFARE CONFERENCE. *School Bus Transportation Laws in the United States*, a survey by the National Catholic Welfare Conference, Legal Department, Washington, D.C., 1946. 257pp.

1127 PUNKE, HAROLD HERMAN. *Law and Liability in Pupil Transportation*. Chicago: University of Chicago Press, 1943. 291pp.

See the following units: "Transportation to Private or Parochial Schools," pp.34-45, and "Meaning of Public School Pupil Within Common Carrier Laws on Transportation," pp. 45-48.

C. PERIODICAL ARTICLES

1128 "And Now, School Buses; Transportation to Parochial Schools," *Commonweal*, 65:651-53 (March 29, 1957). Discussion. 66:129 (May 3, 1957), 66:233-5 (May 31, 1957).

1129 BENNETT, JOHN C. "The School Bus Issue," *Christianity and Crisis*, 17, no.7:49-50 (Apr. 29, 1957).

> Comment. "Helpful Controversy (Editorial)," *Catholic Mind*, 55:356-357 (July-August, 1957). Reprinted from *The Pilot*, Boston, Mass.

1130 BLUM, VIRGIL CLARENCE, S.J. "Religious Liberty and Bus Transportation," *Notre Dame Lawyer*, 30:384-437 (May, 1955).

1131 BRENNAN, EUSTACE F. "School Bus Transportation and Religious Liberty," *Catholic Mind*, 39:9-19 (Sept. 22, 1941). Reprinted from *The Salesianum*, July, 1941.

1132 COSGROVE, JOHN E., and FLATTERY, EDWARD J. "Constitutional Law—Transportation of Parochial-School Pupils," *Notre Dame Lawyer*, 22:192-200 (Jan., 1947).

1133 DORZWEILLER, EDWIN. "Taxation Without Transportation," *Catholic Home Journal*, 50:16-18 (Feb., 1950).

1134 DUGGAN, MAY, and DUGGAN, MARTIN. "Must We Miss the Bus?" *Ave Maria*, 86:8-11 (Sept. 14, 1957).

1135 FARRELL, ALLAN P. "Bus Transportation, a Public Service," *America*, 76:67-68 (Oct. 19, 1946). Reply. J. A. Davis, 76:140 (Nov. 2, 1946).

1136 HARTNETT, ROBERT CLINTON, S.J. "Why the Furor About Buses?" *America*, 82:466-68 (Jan. 21, 1950).

1137 MCMANUS, WILLIAM E. "Non-Sectarian Bus," *Columbia*, 26:5, 17, 18 (Apr., 1947). Also printed separately. Washington, D.C., National Catholic Welfare Conference, 1947. 13pp.

1138 O'BRIEN, JOHN ANTHONY. "Equal Rights for All Children," *Christian Century* 65:473-76 (May 19, 1948). Discussion. 65:655 (June 30, 1948). Condensed. *Catholic Digest*, 12:52-56 (Aug., 1948).

1139 O'NEILL, F. J. "School Bus Problem," *Catholic Digest*, 11:19-23 (Jan., 1947). Condensed from the *Liguorian*, Nov., 1946.

1140 OXNAM, GARFIELD BROMLEY. "Federal Funds and Parochial Education," *Nation's Schools*, 39:24-25 (March, 1947). Same, with subtitle "The Camel's Nose is under the Tent." *Churchman*, 166:13-14 (March 1, 1947).

1141 REED, GEORGE E. "The School Bus Challenge," *The Catholic Lawyer*, 5:99-105 (Spring, 1959).

1142 REED, GEORGE E., and BARRY, E. R. "Public Benefit and School Bus Transportation," *The Jurist*, 6:425-32 (June, 1946).

D. UNPUBLISHED DISSERTATIONS

1143 KELLY, THOMAS J. "Legal Issues Involved in the Transportation of School Children," Pittsburgh, Pa.: University of Pittsburgh, 1951. (Unpublished doctoral dissertation.) Abstract. *Yearbook of School Law*, 1953. P.110.

One chapter discusses issues arising out of the transportation of children to parochial schools.

1144 McMANUS, WILLIAM E. "Current Educational Policy Toward Public Services for Nonpublic School Pupils in Particular Reference to Free Transportation and Textbooks," Washington, D.C.: Catholic University of America, 1942. (Unpublished master's dissertation)

1145 SHANAHAN, PATRICK E. "State Laws Providing for the Transportation of Nonpublic School Children; Their Nature, Interpretation and Execution," Washington, D.C.: Catholic University of America, 1960. (Unpublished doctoral dissertation)

> Abstract published under the same title by the Catholic University of America Press. 25pp.

1146 STALZER, JOSEPH A. "A Survey of Provisions for Transportation of Nonpublic School Pupils at Public Expense," Washington, D.C.: Catholic University of America, 1959. (Unpublished master's dissertation)

1147 WILSON, (Sister) M. LAWRENCE, O.S.U. "Public Transportation of Private School Pupils," New York, N.Y.: Fordham University, 1944 (?). (Unpublished master's dissertation). Summary. *Catholic School Journal,* 45:5-7 (Jan.), 62-4 (March), 92-97 (Apr.), 153-54 (June, 1945).

E. CASE MATERIAL (U.S. Supreme Court)

1947—The Everson Decision

1148 *Everson v. Board of Education of Ewing Township (N.J.),* 330 U.S. 1; 67 S.Ct. 504 (Feb. 10, 1947). Rehearing denied. 330 U.S. 855; 67 S.Ct. 962 (March 10, 1947). Affirming. 133 N.J.L. 350; 44 A.2d 333 (1945).

> Decision affirming the constitutionality of a statute which authorized school district boards of education to provide transportation for parochial school students.

> N.B.: For lower court decision see No.1195.

> REVIEWS, COMMENT:
> *Boston University Law Review,* 27:281-85 (June, 1947)

Columbia Law Review, 49:836-45 (June), 968-92 (Nov., 1949)
Cornell Law Quarterly, 33:122-29 (Sept., 1947)
George Washington Law Review, 15:361-64 (Apr., 1947)
Georgetown Law Journal, 36:631-34 (May, 1948)
Georgia Bar Journal, 9:461-62, 471-73 (May, 1947)
Harvard Law Journal, 60:793-800 (May, 1947)
Iowa Law Review, 32:769-74 (May, 1947)
The Jurist, 7:259-80 (July, 1947)
Kentucky Law Journal, 36:324-31 (March, 1948), 37:220-39
   (March, 1949)
Louisiana Law Review, 8:136-41 (Nov., 1947)
Law and Contemporary Problems, 14:1-159 (Winter, 1949)
Lawyers' Guild Review, 8:387-99 (May-June, 1948)
Minnesota Law Review, 31:739-42 (June, 1947), 33:494-516
   (Apr., 1949)
Missouri Law Review, 12:465-68 (Nov., 1947)
Nation, 164:198-99 (Feb. 22, 1947)
Nebraska Law Review, 27:468-71 (March, 1948)
New York University Law Quarterly Review, 22:331-34 (Apr.,
   1947)
North Carolina Law Review, 25:330-34 (Apr., 1947)
Oklahoma Bar Association. Journal, 18:1309-13 (Sept. 27,
   1947)
Oregon Law Review, 27:150-56 (Feb., 1948)
Saint John's Law Review, 21:176-84 (Apr., 1947)
South California Law Review, 21:61-76 (Dec., 1947)
Time, 49:25-26 (Feb. 24, 1947), "Church and State."
U.S. News and World Report, 22:18-19 (Feb. 21, 1947)
Virginia Law Review, 33:349-51 (May, 1947)

(Articles)

1149   BARRETT, EDWARD F., JR. "Wayward School Bus,"
   Columbia, 27:7, 19-21 (Sept., 1947).

1150   "Bishops Denounce Roman Political Activities," *Church-man*, 61:6 (May 15, 1947).

   Statement of the Council of Bishops of the Methodist
   Church. Text and comment.

1151   BRYSON, JOSEPH R. "Mending the Breach," *Christian
   Century*, 65:649-51 (June 30, 1948).

1152   "Church and State," *National Education Association
   Journal*, 36:380 (May, 1947).

1153   DRINAN, ROBERT F., S.J. "Everson Case: Ten Years
   After," *America*, 96: 524-26 (Feb. 9, 1957).

1154 HANNAN, JEROME D. "The New Jersey Statute and the Supreme Court Minority," *American Ecclesiastical Review*, 116:321-38 (May, 1947).

1155 HEFFRON, EDWARD J. "Supreme Court Oversight," *Commonweal*, 46:9-11 (Apr. 18, 1947).

1156 McCARTHY, (Sister) MARY BARBARA, S.S.J. "The Application of the First Amendment to the States by the Fourteenth Amendment of the Constitution," *Notre Dame Lawyer*, 22:400-11 (May, 1947).

1157 McMAHON, PAUL B. "State Aid to Education and the Doctrine of Separation of Church and State," *Georgetown Law Journal*, 36:631-647 (May, 1948).

1158 McMANUS, WILLIAM E. "No Breach in the Wall," *Catholic Educational Review*, 45:195-203 (Apr., 1947).

1159 ——————. "The Supreme Court's School Bus Decision," *Catholic Action*, 29:9, 17, 18 (March, 1947).

1160 MURRAY, JOHN COURTNEY, S.J. "Court Upholds Religious Freedom," *America*, 76:628-30 (March 8, 1947).

1161 "Now Will Protestants Awake?" *Christian Century*, 64:262-64 (Feb. 26, 1947). Same. Abridged. *Time*, 49:94 (March 3, 1947).

1162 O'BRIEN, KENNETH, and O'BRIEN, DAVID E. "Separation of Church and State in Restatement of Inter-Church-and-State Common Law," *The Jurist*, 7:259-80 (July, 1947).

1163 POWELL, THOMAS REED. "Public Rides to Private Schools," *Harvard Educational Review*, 7:73-84 (Spring, 1947).

1164 "Public Aid to Establishments of Religion," *University of Pennsylvania Law Review*, 96:230-41 (Dec., 1947).

1165 "Public Funds for Sectarian Schools," *Harvard Law Review*, 40:793-800 (May, 1947).

1166 REED, GEORGE E. "Let's Look at the Record," *Catholic Action,* 27:8, 17 (May, 1947). Remarks on the Rutledge dissent.

> See remarks in *The Jurist,* 6:425-32 (June, 1946).

1167 ROSENFIELD, HARRY N. "The Supreme Court Decides the Parochial School Bus Case," *Nation's Schools,* 39:41-43 (Apr., 1947).

> See also: Digest of dissenting opinions, 40:25-26 (July), 40:28-30 (Aug., 1947).

1168 STOUT, WILLIAM DAVID. "The Establishment of Religion Under the Constitution," *Kentucky Law Review,* 37: 220-39 (March, 1949).

1169 "Supreme Court Hears Argument on Busses," *Christian Century,* 63:1459-60 (Dec. 4, 1946).

1170 WESTBROOK, P. F., JR. "Constitutional Law—Establishment of Religion—Due Process—Equal Protection— Public Aid to Parochial Schools," *Michigan Law Review,* 45:1001-21 (June, 1947).

F. STATE MATERIAL (With cases)

California:
(Case Material)

-- 1946 --

1171 *Bowker v. Baker,* 73 Cal.App.2d 653; 167 P.2 256 (Cal., 1946)

> Decision upholding a section of the education code which permitted the transportation of children to Church-related schools.

Connecticut:
(Case Material)

-- **1960** --

1172 *Snyder v. Town of Newton (Conn.)*, 147 Conn. 374; 161 A.2d 770 (Conn., 1960).

> Permissive legislation empowering municipalities to transport children to parochial schools was tested in this case. The court upheld the constitutionality of the practice but decided that public school funds could not be spent for the purpose.

1173 BLUM, VIRGIL CLARENCE, S.J. "Are Catholics Second-Class Citizens?" *Catholic World*, 186:418-424 (March, 1958).

1174 KENNEDY, JOHN S. "Opposition to a Bus Bill," *America*, 97:570-74 (Sept. 7, 1957). See news item "Bumps and Buses; Transportation for Private and Parochial School Students," *Newsweek*, 49:75 (June 10, 1957).

1175 POWELL, THEODORE. *The School Bus Law; A Case Study in Education, Religion, and Politics.* Middletown, Conn.: Wesleyan University Press, 1960. xi, 334pp. Bibliography: pp.318-322.

> REVIEW:
>
> Robert F. Drinan, S.J., "School Bus Law and Lobbying," *America*, 103:640-642 (Sept. 17, 1960).

1176 SHEERIN, JOHN B. "Connecticut and Free Bus Service" (Editorial), *Catholic World*, 185:244-45 (July, 1957).

1177 "Though they go to the Same School Building. . ." (Editorial), *Catholic Educational Review*, 54:561-62 (Nov., 1956).

Iowa:
(Case Material)

-- **1947** --

1178 *Silver Lake Consolidated School District v. Parker*, 29 N.W.2d 214 (Iowa, 1947).

> Decision limiting bus transportation to children attending public schools.

Kentucky:
(Case Material)

-- **1942** --

1179 *Sherrard v. Jefferson County (Ky.) Board of Education et al.*, 294 Ky. 469; 171 S.W.2d 963 (Court of Appeals, Ky., 1942).

Decision stating that public school funds could not be used to provide transportation for children attending Church-related schools.

1180 BLAKELY, PAUL L. "The School Bus for the Privileged," *America*, 68:372-73 (Jan. 9, 1943). Same. Abridged. *Catholic Digest*, 7:49-51 (March, 1943).

1181 ————. "Legal Penalties for Being Catholic," *America*, 68:517 (Feb. 13, 1943).

-- **1945** --

1182 *Nichols v. Henry*, 301 Ky. 434; 191 S.W.2d 930 (Court of Appeals, Ky., 1945).

Decision upholding a welfare statute providing transportation for children attending Church-related schools.

Maine:
(Case Material)

-- **1959** --

1183 *Squires v. City of Augusta*, 155 Me. 151; 153 A.2d 80 (Me., 1959)

Decision overruling a city ordinance permitting the transportation of children to parochial schools. The court noted the absence of permissive legislation and declared that an enabling act would meet constitutional requirements. Permissive legislation was later enacted.

1184 "Buses for Catholic Students—Who Should Pay for Them: Community or Family?" *U.S. News and World Report*, 42:40, 43 (March 22, 1957). Also 42:16 (March 15, 1957).

1185 "Confusing the Maine Bus Issue (Editorial)," *America*, 102:575-76 (Feb. 13, 1960).

1186 DRINAN, ROBERT F., S.J. "School Bus Rides in Maine," *America,* 101:424 (June 13, 1959).

1187 REED, GEORGE E. "The School Bus Challenge," *The Catholic Lawyer,* 5:99-105 (Spring, 1959).

Remarks about the Maine case, pp.101-102.

Maryland:
(Case Material)

-- 1942 --

1188 *Adams et al. v. County Commissioners of St. Mary's County (Md.),* 180 Md. 550; 26 A.2d 337 (Court of Appeals, Md., 1942).

Decision upholding a statute which permitted the expenditure of public funds for the transportation of children to Church-related schools.

REVIEWS:
Minnesota Law Review, 27:311-13 (Feb., 1943)
University of Detroit Law Journal, 6:174-78 (May, 1943)

Massachusetts:
(Case Material)

-- 1955 --

1189 *Quinn and others v. School Committee of Plymouth (Mass.),* 125 N.E.2d 410 (Mass., 1955).

Decision declaring that a town school committee was required to provide transportation for pupils attending Church-related elementary schools to the same extent that transportation was provided for elementary public school pupils.

Michigan:

1190 HASENBERG, ALOYSIUS J. "School Bus Transportation for Parochial Schools in the State of Michigan," Washington, D.C.: Catholic University of America, 1955. (Unpublished master's dissertation)

1191 McLEAN, W. MAURICE. "Public School Buses for Private and Parochial School Pupils?" *School and Society,* 74:181-82 (Sept. 22, 1951).

Missouri:
(Case Material)

-- 1953 --

1192   *McVey v. Hawkins,* 258 S.W.2d 927 (Missouri, 1953).

Decision declaring that the transportation of parochial school pupils on public school buses was contrary to the state constitution and to statutory provisions.

COMMENTS:

Ave Maria, 86:8-11 (Sept. 14, 1957) May and Martin Duggan. *St. Louis University Law Journal,* 3:273-82 (Spring, 1955) Marianne J. Cegas.

1193   "Discriminating Against Parochial School Children in Missouri," *Social Justice Review,* 48:50-51 (May, 1955).

1194   "Missouri Branch Promotes Justice in Transportation of Pupils," *Social Justice Review,* 51:360 (Feb., 1959).

New Jersey:
(Case Material)

-- 1944 --

1195   *Everson v. Board of Education of Ewing Township (N.J.),* 113 N.J.L. 350; 44 A.2d 333 (New Jersey, 1945). Affirmed. 330 U.S. 1; 67 S.Ct. 504 (1947).

Decision affirming the constitutionality of a statute which authorized school district boards of education to provide transportation for parochial school students. The decision was upheld by the United States Supreme Court in 1947. (See No.1148)

-- 1958 --

1196   *Board of Education of the Central Regional High School District of Ocean County v. State Board of Education (N.J.),* 27 N.J. 76; 141 A.2d 542 (New Jersey, May 19, 1958).

Decision stating that a high school district had statutory power to transport resident parochial school children who were in grades below those for which the district had been established.

New York:
(Case Material)

-- 1959 --

1197   *Board of Education of Central School District No. 1 of the Towns of Ballston, Clifton Park and Charlton and Town of Glennville v. Allen, 192 N.Y.S.2d 186 (N.Y., 1959).*

    Decision stating that under an amendment to the state constitution permitting the expenditure of public funds for the transportation of children to and from any school, the transportation of students to nonpublic schools was a constitutional expenditure.

Oklahoma:
(Case Material)

-- 1941 --

1198   *Gurney v. Ferguson, 190 Okla. 254; 122 P.2d 1002 (Okla., 1941).*

    Decision declaring a legislative act which permitted the transportation of children to Church-related schools to be a violation of the state constitution.

Pennsylvania:
(Case Material)

-- 1947 --

1199   *Connell v. Board of School Directors of Kennett Township (Pa.), 356 Pa. 585; 52 A.2d 645 (Pa., 1947).*

    Decision stating that under statutory provisions for public schools, school boards have no statutory authority and no obligation to transport children to other than public schools.

-- 1956 --

1200   *School District of Robinson Township (Pa.) v. Houghton, 387 Pa. 236; 128 A.2d 58 (Pa., 1956).*

    Decision declaring that the board of directors of a school district had no discretionary powers to provide transportation for children attending Church-related schools.

Washington:
(Case Material)

-- 1943 --

1201 *Mitchell v. Consolidated School District No. 201 (Wash.),* 17 Wash.2d 61; 135 P.2d 79 (Washington, 1943).

A statute which required directors of school districts (where public school buses were operated) to transport children attending Church-related schools, was declared to be a violation of the state constitution in this decision.

-- 1949 --

1202 *Visser v. Nooksack Valley School District No. 506, Whatcom County (Wash.),* 33 Wash.2d 699; 207 P.2d 198 (1949).

Decision declaring that a transportation statute which entitled "all children attending school" to use transportation facilities was a violation of the state constitution because it included service to children attending Church-related schools.

Wisconsin:
(Case Material)

-- 1946 --

1203 *Costigan v. Hall,* 249 Wis. 94; 23 N.W.2d 495 (Wis., 1946). Rehearing denied. 249 Wis. 94; 24 N.W.2d 408.

Decision declaring that a school district board had no authority to pay for the transportation of children to Church-related schools under a statute requiring a board, whose school district was suspended, to pay tuition for children attending another district's school and to transport students so attending.

1204 BOYER, WILLIAM W. "Public Transportation of Parochial-School Pupils," *Wisconsin Law Review,* 1952: 64-90 (Jan., 1952).

1205 PURTELL, JOSEPHINE. "Where to—On Bus Transportation?" *Extension,* 42:12-14 (June, 1947).

1206 "Wisconsin Bus Bill," *Christian Century*, 63:1302-03 (Oct. 30, 1947). For developments and comments see the following in the *Christian Century*. 63:1395-96, 1410 (Nov. 20), 1441 (Nov. 27), 1493 and 1505 (Dec. 11, 1946), 64:265-67 (Feb. 26, 1947).

X

Public Aid To Church-Related Schools: Free Textbooks

Note. The courts impeded early attempts to supply text-books to students attending Church-related schools *(Smith v. Donahue,* 195 N.Y.S. 715 (1922)).

The issue came to the fore in two Louisiana cases *(Borden v. Louisiana State Board of Education,* 168 La. 1005; 123 So. 655 (1929) and *Cochran v. Louisiana State Board of Education,* 168 La. 1030; 123 So. 664 (1929)). They were appealed to the United States Supreme Court which affirmed the constitutionality of the practice on the basis of the pupil benefit doctrine *(Cochran v. Louisiana State Board of Education,* 281 U.S. 370; 50 S.Ct. 335 (1930)).

A. BACKGROUND MATERIAL

SUMMARY MATERIAL:

1207 BEACH, FRED FRANCIS, and WILL, ROBERT F. *The State and Nonpublic Schools . . . (U.S. Office of Education, Misc., No. 28)*. Washington, D.C., U.S. Government Printing Office, 1958. 152pp.

> See "Textbooks," p.27.
>
> For background information on the free textbook movement in general, see the following.

1208 KEESECKER, WARD W. *Textbooks for Public School Children (U.S. Office of Education, Circular, No.60, 1932)*. Washington, D.C.: the Office of Education. 15 pp. (Mimeographed)

1209 ——————. *Legislation Concerning Free Textbooks (U.S. Office of Education, Pamphlet No.59, 1935)*. Washington, D.C.: U.S. Government Printing Office, 1935. 16pp.

1210 PROFFITT, MARIS MARION. *State Provisions for Free Textbooks and Instructional Materials (U.S. Office of Education, Bulletin, 1944, No.1)*. Washington, D.C.: U.S. Government Printing Office, 1944. 42pp.

B. PERIODICAL ARTICLES

1211 CHAMBERS, MERRITT MADISON. "Textbooks in Nonpublic Schools," *Nation's Schools*, 29:53-54 (Jan., 1942).

1212 PUNKE, HAROLD HERMAN. "Public Funds for Private and Sectarian Schools," *Yearbook of School Law*, pp.108-20 (1942). See: "Textbooks," pp.112-17.

C. UNPUBLISHED DISSERTATION

1213   ALLEN, (Sister) MARY COLUMBA, R.S.M. "A Study of the Legal Aspect and the Administration of Free Textbooks for Parochial Schools," Washington, D.C.: Catholic University of America, 1954. (Unpublished master's dissertation)

      Abstract. *Catholic Educational Review*, 54:618-19 (Dec., 1956).

D. STATE MATERIAL (With cases)

Mississippi:
(Case Material)

-- 1941 --

1214   *Chance et al. v. Mississippi State Textbook Rating and Purchasing Board*, 190 Miss. 453; 200 So. 706 (Mississippi, 1941).

      Decision affirming the validity of a state law which made textbooks available to children attending parochial schools.

1215   COOKE, DENNIS H. "Public Taxes for Private Schools," *American School Board Journal*, 104:26-27 (Feb., 1942).

1216   "Free Textbooks in Mississippi," *The Jurist*, 2:370-71 (Oct., 1942).

1217   "Relation of Freedom of Religion to Loan of Textbooks to Private Schools," *Bill of Rights Review*, 1:307-10 (Summer, 1941).

Oregon:

1218   "The Opposition to the Oregon Free Textbook Bill,"
       The Jurist, 2:363-70 (Oct., 1942).

XI

Tax Exemption

Note. The tax exemption of churches has been termed the most important government recognition of religion made in the United States. The privilege has almost universally been extended to Church-related and other private schools. California, long an exception among the states in this respect, was the last to extend it. Its citizens refused to let their state stand as the only one to deny tax exemption to nonpublic schools when they voted down "Proposition 16" in November, 1958.

A. BACKGROUND MATERIAL

SUMMARY MATERIAL AND LEGAL BACKGROUND:

1219 COOLEY, THOMAS M. *The Law of Taxation.* Chicago, Ill.: Callaghan & Co., 1924. 4v.

In volume 2, see "Specific Exemptions: Sectarian Schools," section 773; "Schools," sections 770-83; "Churches and Religious Societies," sections 742-747.

1220 KILLOUGH, LUCY WINSOR. "Exemptions to Educational, Philanthropic and Religious Organizations," in Tax Institute, *Tax Exemptions (Tax Policy League Symposium),* by James W. Martin, Lucy Winsor Killough, and others. New York City: Tax Policy League, Inc., 1939. Pp.23-38.

Symposium conducted by the Tax Policy League, Dec. 28-30, 1938, in Detroit, Michigan.

1221 "State Constitutional Provisions Regulating Tax Exemptions for Property of Nonpublic Schools, by State: Jan., 1957," in Fred F. Beach and Robert F. Will, *The State and Nonpublic Schools . . .* (U.S. Office of Education, Misc. No. 28, 1958). Washington, D.C.: U.S. Government Printing Office, 1958. Table 8, p.20.

1222 TORPEY, WILLIAM GEORGE. "The Exemption of Church Property from Taxation," in *Judicial Doctrines of Religious Rights in America.* Chapel Hill, N.C.: University of North Carolina Press, 1948. Pp.171-197.

B. PERIODICAL ARTICLES

1223 BRYANT, C. E. "Churches in a Tax-Grab," *Christian Century,* 69:1223-24 (Oct. 22, 1952).

1224 "Exemption of Educational, Philanthropic and Religious Institutions from State Real Property Taxes," *Harvard Law Review*, 64:288-99 (Dec., 1950).

1225 GARDINER, HAROLD CHARLES, S.J. "Danger to Schools in Tax Proposals," *America*, 67:150-51 (May 15, 1942).

1226 PAULSEN, MONRAD G. "Preferment of Religious Institutions in Tax and Labor Legislation," *Law and Contemporary Problems*, 14:144-59 (Winter, 1949).

1227 VAN ALSTYNE, ARVO. "Tax Exemption of Church Property," *Ohio State Law Journal*, 20:461-507 (Summer, 1959).

See "Church-affiliated Schools and Colleges," 490-496.

C. UNPUBLISHED DISSERTATION

1228 BRINDLE, PAUL L. "Tax Exemptions of Real Property of Religious, Educational and Charitable Institutions," Washington, D.C.: Southeastern University, 1941. Bibliography, pp. 53-63. (Unpublished master's dissertation)

N.B.: Copy at the Library of Congress.

D. STATE MATERIAL (With cases)

California:
(1. Case Material)

-- 1957 --

1229   *Lundberg v. County of Alameda (Cal.) et al.*, 46 Cal.2d 644; 298 P.2d 1 (California, June 6, 1956). Rehearing denied, July 5, 1956. Dismissed by the U. S. Supreme Court for want of a substantial federal question under the name of *Heisey v. County of Alameda (Cal.) et al.*, 352 U.S. 921; 77 S.Ct. 224 (Dec. 3, 1956).

> Decision upholding a statute which allowed exemption from property tax for Church-related and other nonprofit private schools of less than collegiate level.

REVIEW:
Stanford Law Review, 9:266 (March, 1957)

(2. Other Literature)

1230   ANTCZAK, AL. "This Makes it Forty-Eight," *America*, 88:206-08 (Nov. 22, 1952).

1231   ――――――. "California's Proposition 16," *America*, 100:233 (Nov. 22, 1958).

1232   BOUSCAREN, ANTHONY T. "Schools and Taxes in California," *America*, 87:306-08 (July 21, 1952).

1233   CARY, KENNETH WORTHINGTON. "Protestant Strategy in California," *Christianity Today*, 3:6-8 (Oct. 27, 1958).

1234   FITZPATRICK, EDWARD AUGUSTUS. "California Defeats a Proposal to Tax the Private Schools (Editorial)," *Catholic School Journal*, 59:32 (February, 1959).

1235   HURLEY, MARK JOSEPH. *Church-State Relationships in Education in California.* Washington, D.C.: Catholic University of America Press, 1948. 183pp. Bibliography: 168-180. (Doctoral dissertation)

For information about tax exemption in California, see "Tax Exemption," pp.110-132, and "Recent Church-State Relationships," pp.103-150.

1236   KING, LAWRENCE T. "Bigotry in California," *Commonweal*, 69:514-516 (Feb. 13, 1959).

1237   LE BERTON, TED. "Trouble in California," *Commonweal*, 68:299-301 (June 20, 1958).

   Discussion. 68:424-425 (July 25, 1958).

1238   OXTON, CHARLES. "School Crisis in California," *Catholic Digest*, 22:5-8 (Sept., 1958).

Nebraska:

1239   ZABEL, ORVILLE HERMANN. "Tax Exemption," in *God and Caesar in Nebraska (University of Nebraska Studies: new ser., no.14)*. Lincoln, Neb.: University of Nebraska Press, 1955. Pp.160-181.

XII

The Church-Related School and Municipal Zoning

Note. Zoning ordinances are predicated on the police power of the state. This delegated power to preserve the safety, health and morals of the public is of vast and undefined extent. The courts are divided in their interpretation of its relation to statutes and ordinances which zone out private schools from certain districts. To date, the weight of authority appears to be on the side of those who question the validity of statutes which exclude private Church-related schools from districts in which public schools are permitted.

A. BACKGROUND MATERIAL

LEGAL BACKGROUND:

1240 METZENBAUM, JAMES. *The Law of Zoning.* New York: Baker, Voorhis Co., 1955. 3v.

> See "Schools and Churches," chapter X-m(2), v.II, pp.1451-1454.

1241 RATHKOPF, CHARLES A., and RATHKOPF, ARDEN H. *The Law of Zoning and Planning.* New York: Clark Broadman & Co., and Albany: Banks & Co. 3d.ed., 1959. 2v. (with supplements).

> See "Churches, Convents, Schools Conducted by Churches, Camp Meetings," Vol. I, pp.259-267 and cumulative supplement to Vol. I, pp.54-67.

1242 YORKLEY, EMMETT CLINTON. *Zoning Law and Practice.* Charlottesville, Va.: Michie Co., 1953. 2v.

> See "Churches," Sec. 222, and "Schools," Sec. 247.

> N.B.: Both Metzenbaum and Yorkley have pocket supplements which should be checked through for recent material.

B. PERIODICAL ARTICLES

1243 BRINDEL, PAUL. "Building Permit—Denied!" *Catholic School Journal,* 58:47-50 (June, 1958).

1244 ————. "Zoning Out Religious Institutions," *Notre Dame Lawyer,* 32:627-41 (Aug., 1957).

1245 "Churches and Zoning," *Harvard Law Review,* 70:1428-38 (June, 1957).

1246   GARBER, LEE ORVILLE. "Courts Disagree on Validity of
        Zoning Ordinances to Prohibit Private Schools in
        Certain Areas," *Nation's Schools*, 59:79-81 (Jan.,
        1957).

1247   SHARFF, MICHAEL. "Religion and the Zoning Laws,"
        New York University Intramural Law Review, 15:
        194-207 (March, 1960).

1248   SEITZ, REYNOLDS C. "Constitutional and General Wel-
        fare Considerations in Efforts to Zone Out Private
        Schools," *Miami Law Quarterly*, 11:68-84 (Fall,
        1956).

1249   "Zoning Laws and the Church," *St. John's Law Review*,
        27:93-103 (Dec., 1952).

1250   "Zoning Litigation," *Catholic Lawyer*, 3:277 (July,
        1957).

1251   "Zoning Restrictions: Parochial Schools," *Catholic
        Lawyer*, 1:153-54 (Apr., 1955). Also, 3:277 (July,
        1957).

C. STATE MATERIAL (With cases)

California:
(Case Material)

-- 1955 --

1252   *Roman Catholic Welfare Corporation of San Francisco
        v. City of Piedmont (Cal.) et al.*, 278 P.2d 943 (Cal.,
        Oct. 27, 1955). Modified on denial of rehearing. 45
        Cal.2d 325; 289 P.2d 438 (Cal., Nov., 1955).

    Decision stating that a city zoning ordinance which pro-
    hibited the conduct of any but public schools in a district was
    unconstitutional.

REVIEWS:
California Law Review, 44:775-80 (Oct., 1956)
Minnesota Law Review, 40:863-65 (June, 1956)
Notre Dame Lawyer, 31:113 (Dec., 1955)
Stanford Law Review, 8:712-18 (July, 1956)
University of California Law Review, 3:387-90 (Apr., 1956)
University of Detroit Law Journal, 18:434-36 (May, 1955)
Yearbook of School Law, 1957. pp.116-118.

1253   BRINDEL, PAUL. "The Piedmont Case and Restrictive Zoning," *Catholic Lawyer*, 2:245-48 (July, 1956).

Illinois:
(Case Material)

-- 1939 --

1254   *Catholic Bishop of Chicago v. Kingery et al.*, 371 Ill. 257; 20 N.E.2d 583 (Illinois, 1939).

Decision invalidating a zoning ordinance which expressly permitted the maintainance of public schools in a given zone while implicitly prohibiting private or parochial schools in the same area.

Michigan:
(Case Material)

-- 1952 --

1255   *Mooney et al. v. Village of Orchard Lake (Mich.) et al.*, 333 Mich. 389; 53 N.W.2d 308 (Michigan, 1952).

Decision invalidating a zoning ordinance which, as a practical matter, excluded churches and schools from an entire village.

New Jersey:
(Case Material)

-- 1955 --

1256   *Ranney et al. v. Instituto Pontificio Delle Maestre Filippini*, 20 N.J. 189; 119 A.2d 142 (N.J., 1955).

Decision revoking a permit granted by a municipal zoning board to a Catholic teacher-training school. The permit would have allowed the expansion of facilities in spite of limitations prescribed for the district.

New York:
(Case Material)

-- 1956 --

1257 *Diocese of Rochester et al. v. Planning Board of Town
of Brighton (N.Y.),* 1 N.Y.2d 508; 136 N.E.2d 827
(New York, 1956).

Decision overruling the refusal of a municipal planning
board to grant a permit for the construction of a church and
a school.

REVIEWS:

Michigan Law Review, 55:601-03 (Feb., 1957)
St. John's Law Review, 31:318-21 (May, 1957)

1258 GOLDBLOOM, IRWIN. "Constitutional Limitations on the
Zoning Power," *Syracuse Law Review,* 8:230-37
(Spring, 1957).

Wisconsin:
(Case Material)

-- 1954 --

1259 *State of Wisconsin ex rel. Wisconsin Lutheran High
School Conference v. Sinar, Inspector of Buildings et
al.,* 267 Wis. 91; 65 N.W.2d 43 (Wisconsin, 1954).
Appeal dismissed. 75 S.Ct. 604; 349 U.S. 913 (U.S.
Supreme Court, Apr. 25, 1955).

Decision upholding the refusal of a building inspector to
issue a permit for the construction of a private Lutheran high
school.

REVIEWS:

America, 91:409-10 (July 24, 1954)
Marquette Law Review, 38:274-78 (Spring, 1955)
Michigan Law Review, 53:747-49 (March, 1955)
Nebraska Law Review, 34:139-41 (Nov., 1954)
Notre Dame Lawyer, 31:113-16 (Dec., 1955)
University of Cincinnati Law Review, 24:149-51 (Winter,
1955)

APPENDIX A

Notes on the *Nation* case

(New York City, 1948)

On November 1, 1947, *The Nation* began the publication of a series of articles (Nov. 1, 8, 15) written by Paul Blanshard about the Catholic Church. The nature of these articles led the Board of Education of Newark, N. J., to remove the periodical from the schools under its jurisdiction in January, 1948. A new series of similar articles appeared between April 10 and June 5, 1948. These moved the Board of Education of New York City to take action. It first authorized the school principals to remove from school libraries issues of periodicals containing religious material objectionable for school purposes. The Board of Superintendents further discussed the matter on June 1, and voted to exclude the periodical from school libraries on June 8. The decision was publicly confirmed on June 23, and reported in the *New York Times* on June 24. (N.B.: The *Christian Century* published similar articles by the same author on April 13, 20, 27, and on May 4, 1949).

A1   The controversy about this directive may be followed in the *New York Times* for 1948, as follows: (June 24) p.1, col.6—(June 25) p.25, col.8—(June 27) p.34, col.3—(July 20) p.1, col.6—(Oct. 11) p.25, col.5—(Oct. 12) p.23, col.5—(Oct. 29) p.22, col.5—(Oct. 31) p.74, col.5

A2   Mr. Blanchard's letter of protest appeared with a reply by Superintendent William Jansen on June 27, p.34, col.3.

      Mr. Jansen prepared the following summary statement on the case for the Board of Superintendents.

A3   JANSEN, WILLIAM. *Should Religious Beliefs Be Studied and Critized in an American Public High School?* A statement by William Jansen, Superintendent of

Schools, City of New York, and Chairman of the
Board of Superintendents, concerning the elimina-
tion of *The Nation* from the list of publications
authorized for use in the high schools. Brooklyn, New
York: Board of Education of the City of New York
(110 Livingston St.), Oct. 1, 1948. 12pp.

Reply. "Can the Ban be Justified?" *The Nation*, 167:569-71,
and back cover (Nov. 20, 1948).

Paul Blanshard and Archibald McLeish, *New York Times*,
Oct. 31, p.74, col.5 (1948).

REVIEW:
Archibald W. Anderson, "The Nation Case," *Progressive
Education*, 26:151-57 (March, 1949).

A4   *The Nation* pleads its case in its own pages.

"*The Nation* Banned," *The Nation*, 167:4-6 (July 3, 1948)
by Freda Kirchwey.

'Lift the Ban!" 167:29 (July 10, 1948).

"A Victory for Censorship," 167:89-90 (July 24, 1948).

"Will You Give a Dollar To Stop a Plague?" 167:154-55
(Aug. 17, 1948), and August 14 (back cover).

"For a Public Hearing," 167:248 (Sept. 4, 1948).

"The Fight to Lift the Ban" (Correspondence), 167:299-
301 (Sept. 11, 1948).

"An Appeal to Reason and Conscience; In Defense of the
Right of Freedom of Inquiry in the United States," 167:419-
20, 447-49 (Oct. 16, 1948).

"An Arbitrary Ruling," 168:627-28 (June 4, 1948).

"The 'Nation' Ban," 168:647-49 (June 11, 1948).

"Banned Again," 171:3-4 (July 1, 1950).

A5   Information related to the controversy may be located
through the *New York Times Index*

1948: p.326, cols.1,2... Under "Education and Schools
—N.Y.C.—General."

p.332, col.2... Under "U. S.—High Schools"

p.701, col.3... Under "Nation (Pub.) Association"

1949: p.614, cols.1,2... Under "Magazines—Censorship and bans."

Typical Catholic reactions may be read in the following articles.

A6   BURNHAM, PHILIP. "Outstretched Fist," *Commonweal,* 49:364-65 (Jan. 21, 1949). Discussion. 49:446 (Feb. 11), 469 (Feb. 18, 1949).

A7   DUNNE, GEORGE HAROLD, S.J. "Blanshard Charges in 'The Nation,'" *Commonweal,* 47:536-42 (March 12, 1948). See also: Joseph Stocker "Father Dunne: a Study in Faith," *The Nation,* 173:236-39 (Sept. 22, 1951).

A8   GARDINER, HAROLD CHARLES, S.J. "Analysis of a Smear Stunt: With Reply by Paul Blanshard," *The Nation,* 166:27-28 (Jan. 3, 1948).

A9   O'NEILL, JAMES MILTON. "Catholic Censorship," in *Catholicism and American Freedom.* New York: Harper, 1952. Pp.115-28 (Especially 119-25).

More related material may be located through the *Readers' Guide to Periodical Literature* and the *Catholic Periodical Index* in the volumes covering the years 1948-51. (Search under heading: *"Nation* (Periodical))"

APPENDIX B

Notes on the Blanshard Controversy

Paul Blanshard's accusations against the Catholic Church gained widespread attention in the *Nation* case (see Appendix A). The following chronological list relates reactions, reviews and replies to his better known writings about the Catholic Church.

1949

B1 BLANSHARD, PAUL. *American Freedom and Catholic Power* (Beacon Press Studies in Freedom and Power). Boston: Beacon Press, 1949. 350pp.

> Same with title *Freedom and Catholic Power*. London: Secker & Warburg. 320pp.

> *American Freedom and Catholic Power*, 2d ed., rev. and enl. Boston: Beacon Press, 1958. 420pp.

> Material previously published in *The Nation* and the *Christian Century* has been incorporated in this book.

REVIEWS (1949 edition):
America, 81:200 (May 7, 1949) E. R. Clinchy
American Ecclesiastical Review, 123:180-87 (Sept., 1950) Francis J. Connell
Atlantic Monthly, 185:74-77, 77-79 (Feb., 1950) T. R. Ingram and Paul Blanshard; p.18 (May, 1950) T. R. Ingram
Best Sellers, 9:17-18 (May 1, 1940) E. V. Stanford
Catholic World, 169:233-34 (June, 1949) J. C. Murray
Catholic World, 171:14-19 (Apr., 1950) J. L. Benevisti
Christian Century, 66: 709 (June 8, 1940) W. E. Garrison
Christian Century, 69:828-29 (July 16, 1952)
Christian Science Monitor, p.18 (Apr. 28, 1949) Tully Nettleton
Christianity and Crisis, 9, No. 7 (May 21, 1949) Henry Sloane Coffin
Columbia, 29:4- (March, 1950) E. Beyer
Commentary, 8:198-200 (Aug., 1949) Will Herberg
Commonweal, 50:250-53 (June 17, 1949) M. G. Ballantyne
Commonweal, 51:380-81 (Jan. 13, 1950)
Commonweal, 54:94-95 (May 4, 1951) J. C. Murray
Cornell Law Quarterly, 35:678-84 (Spring, 1951) F. J. Connell
Cornell Law Quarterly, 36:406-15 (Winter, 1951) P. Blanshard
Crozer Quarterly, 26:247 (July, 1949) M. S. Enslin
Journal of Pastoral Care, 4 nos. 1-2:73-74 (1950) G. Williams

Bulletin from Virginia Kirkus' Book Shop Service, 17:138 (March 15, 1949)
Library Journal, 74:736 (May 1, 1949) R. E. Kingery
Lutheran Quarterly, 4:109-10 (Feb., 1952) R. Iversen
The Nation, 168:560 (May 14, 1949) Norman Thomas
The Nation, 169:59-60 (July 16, 1949), 170:132-33 (Feb. 11, 1950)
New Republic, 121:20 (Oct. 10, 1949) Russell Rhodes
New Statesman and Nation, 38:236 (Sept. 3, 1949) Norman McKenzie. Also 38:267-68 (Sept. 10, 1949), 41:397 (Apr. 7, 1951) C. E. M. Joad. Discussion. 41:424, 450, 479, 507, 566, 654, 709, 748 (Apr. 14-May 5, May 19, June 9, 23-30, 1951)
New York Times, p.15 (May 15, 1949)
New Yorker, 25:66 (Aug. 27, 1949)
Religion in Life, 19:124-133 (Winter, 1949-50) W. E. Garrison
Saturday Review of Literature, 32:13-14 (July 30, 1949) H. M. Kallen and W. S. Lynch
School and Society, 70:95 (Aug. 6, 1949); 71:279-280 (May 6, 1950) W. W. Brickman
Social Forces, 28:226 (Dec., 1949) A. S. Foley
Studies, 40:158-66 (June, 1951) J. Crehan
Theology Today, 6:561-63 (Jan., 1950) G. A. Barrois

REVIEWS (1958 edition):

American Sociological Review, 23:455 (August, 1958) J. M. Yinger
Chicago Sunday Tribune, p.2 (March 30, 1958) Edmund Fuller
The Critic, 16:24 (May, 1958) J. O'Neill
Bulletin from Virginia Kirkus' Book Shop Service, 26:57 (Jan. 15, 1958)
Library Journal, 83:1211 (Apr. 15, 1958) M. L. Barrett
New York Times, p.42 (March 23, 1958) Stanley Rowland
Saturday Review, 41:37 (Apr. 19, 1958) G. N. Shuster
Sign, 37:10-11 (March, 1958)
Union Seminary Quarterly Review, 14:67-69 (March, 1959) T. G. Sanders

B2   DUNNE, GEORGE HAROLD, S.J. *Religion and American Democracy; a Reply to Paul Blanshard's American Freedom and Catholic Power.* New York: America Press, 1949. 48pp.

Material published in *America* from June 4 to July 30, 1949, was revised and incorporated in this pamphlet.

B3   ————. "Is Catholic Doctrine Changing?" by Father Dunne and Paul Blanshard, *Christian Century,* 66: 957-58 (Aug. 17, 1949).

Reply. M. Martinez, 66: 1014 (Aug. 31, 1949).
See: Joseph Stocker. "Father Dunne: a Study in Faith," *The Nation,* 173:236-39 (Sept. 22, 1951).

1950

B4   FRANCIS, DALE. *American Freedom and Paul Blanshard*. Notre Dame, Ind.: Ave Maria Press, 1950. 32pp. Same. Condensed. With title: "Who is Paul Blanshard?" *Catholic Digest*, 14:36-41 (May, 1950).

B5   HARTNETT, ROBERT CLINTON, S.J. "Debate with Blanshard," *Catholic Mind*, 48:262-70 (May, 1950). Text of Father Harnett's address before the Forum of the Yale Law School Student Association, Yale Law School, Feb. 21, 1950.—In delivering this address, Father Harnett departed somewhat from the text.

B6   ————. "My Debate With Mr. Blanshard," *America*, 82:689-91 (March 18, 1950).

B7   HARVARD LAW SCHOOL FORUM. *The Catholic Church and Politics; a transcript of a discussion on a vital issue, presented by the Harvard Law School Forum.* Speakers: Paul Blanshard and George H. Dunne; Moderator: Henry D. Aiken. Held at Cambridge High and Latin School, Cambridge, Mass., 1950. 4pp.

1951

B8   BLANSHARD, PAUL. *Communism, Democracy, and Catholic Power* (Beacon Studies in Freedom and Power). Boston: Beacon Press, 1951. 340pp.

REVIEWS:
America, 85:247-48 (June 2, 1951) W. Parsons
American Political Science Review, 45:1202 (Dec., 1951) Philip Selznick
Annals of the American Academy of Political and Social Science, 278:230 (Nov., 1951) B. E. Nelson
Atlantic Monthly, 188:74 (Aug., 1951) S. E. Johnson
Ave Maria, 73:683-91 (June 2, 1951) D. Francis
Blackfriars, 33:261-66 (June, 1952) A. C. F. Beales
Books on Trial, 10:8 (June, 1951) Sister M. Augustina
Catholic Library World, 24:5-10 (Oct., 1952) J. M. O'Neill
Catholic World, 173:478 (Sept., 1951)
Christian Century, 68:965 (Aug. 22, 1951) W. E. Garrison
Christian Science Monitor, p.9 (May 21, 1951) Tully Nettleton
Christianity and Crisis, 11 no. 11:86-87 (June 25, 1951) Henry Sloane Coffin
Churchman, 165:11 (July, 1951) J. P. Jones
Commonweal, 54:144-46 (May 18, 1951) John Cogley
Reply. 54:215 (June 8, 1951) F. J. Lally

Crozer Quarterly, 28:348-50 (Oct., 1951) M. S. Enslin
Integrity, 5:39-42 (June, 1951) C. Jackson
Bulletin from Virginia Kirkus' Book Shop Service, 19:219 (Apr. 15, 1951)
Library Journal, 76:1224 (Aug., 1951) A. D. Osborn
Lutheran Quarterly, 4:109-10 (Feb., 1952) R. Iversen
Manchester Guardian, p.4 (June 22, 1951)
Month, 8:305-07 (Nov., 1952) T. Corbishley
Nation, 172:590 (June 23, 1951) Norman Thomas
New Republic, 125:18 (July 2, 1951) M. R. Werper
New York Herald Tribune Book Review, p.5 (June 10, 1951) J. M. O'Neill and Perry Miller
New York Times, p.7 (May 20, 1951) F. E. Johnson
New Yorker, 27:120 (May 26, 1951)
Saturday Review of Literature, 34:26 (June 23, 1951) Herbert Brucker
School and Society, 74:335 (Nov. 24, 1951) M. J. Williams
Sign, 30:60-61 (July, 1951) M. Tansey
Social Forces, 30:243 (Dec., 1951) M. J. Williams
Theology Today, 9:275-77 (July, 1952) H. Gezork
Time, 57:126 (May 21, 1951)

B9 FLYNN, FREDERICK E. "Church, State and the Person. The Two Loyalties Are Rooted in One and the Same Human Being," *Commonweal*, 54:447-50 (Aug. 17, 1951).

B10 FRANCES, DALE. *Answering Paul Blanshard*. Notre Dame, Ind.: Ave Maria Press, 1951. 38pp.

B11 MURRAY, JOHN COURTNEY, S.J. "Paul Blanshard and the New Nativism," *The Month*, 5 (new series): 214-25 (Apr., 1951). Same. Abridged. *Commonweal*, 54:94-95 (May, 1951).

1952

B12 BLANSHARD, PAUL. *My Catholic Critics* (Beacon Reference Series). Boston, Mass.: Beacon Press, 1952. 53pp.

B13 O'NEILL, JAMES MILTON. *Catholicism and American Freedom*. New York: Harper, 1952. 287pp.

A reply to Paul Blanshard.

REVIEWS:

America, 87:16 (Apr. 5, 1952) R. C. Hartnett, 87:394 (July 19, 1952)
American Academy of Political and Social Science, Annals, 282:168 (July, 1952) A. G. Hayes

American Benedictine Review, 3:265 (Autumn, 1952) A. Graham
American Catholic Sociological Review, 13:185-86 (Oct., 1952) J. J. Kane
American Ecclesiastical Review, 126:476 (June, 1952) J. Fenton
Ave Maria, 75:762 (June 14, 1952) T. McAvoy
Books on Trial, 10:273 (Apr., 1952) V. J. Giese
Catholic Historical Review, 38:330-31 (Oct., 1952) G. H. Dunne
Catholic Home Journal, 52:31 (June, 1952) U. Adelman
Catholic Library World, 23:275 (May, 1952) E. Jordan
Catholic School Journal, 52:42A (May, 1952)
Catholic World, 175:235 (June, 1952) J. J. Maguire
Christian Century, 69:828 (July 16, 1952) W. E. Garrison
Christian Science Monitor, p.13 (Apr. 18, 1952) Tully Nettleton
Churchman, 166:2 (Sept., 1952) W. S. Rycroft
Columbia, 31:10- (June, 1952) J. Kennedy
Commonweal, 56:179-80 (May 23, 1952) B. I. Bell, 56:318-19 (July 4, 1952)
Dominicana, 37:338-39 (Sept., 1952)
Foreign Affairs, 30:676 (July, 1952)
Historical Bulletin, 31:253-54 (May, 1953) B. McGrath
Bulletin from Virginia Kirkus' Book Shop Service, 20:141 (Feb. 15, 1952)
Library Journal, 77:526 (March 15, 1952) F.E. Hirsch
Nation, 175:34 (July 12, 1952) W. H. Kilpatrick
New York Herald Tribune Book Review, p.6 (Apr. 6, 1952) F. E. Johnson
New York Times Book Review, p.6 (Apr. 13, 1952) Theodore Maynard
School and Society, 75:254 (Apr. 19, 1952)
Sign, 31:64 (May, 1952) H. Feldman
Springfield Republican, p.10D (June 22, 1952)
Thought, 27:443 (Autumn, 1952) V. Yanitelli
U. S. Quarterly Book Review, 8:143 (June, 1952)
Wilson Library Bulletin, 48:166 (July, 1952)

1954

B14   BLANSHARD, PAUL. "The State and Catholic Power in the United States," *Hibbert Journal*, 52:231-239 (April, 1954).

1958

B15   ROBINSON, ALLYN P. "A Protestant Looks at the Catholic 'Threat,' " *Catholic Mind*, 56:485-95 (Nov.-Dec., 1958).

Address delivered at the First Church and State Assembly of the New York East Methodist Conference, June, 1958.

1959

B16   BRICKMAN, WILLIAM WOLFGANG. "Paul Blanshard and Catholic Education," *School and Society,* **87:152-153** (March 28, 1959).

1960

B17   BLANSHARD, PAUL. *God and Man in Washington.* Boston: Beacon Press, 1960. 251pp. Notes, pp.223-239.

(See also No. 825 in this bibliography.)

REVIEWS:

America, 102:656-58 (Feb. 27, 1960) R. Graham
Atlantic Monthly, 205:70-72 (May, 1960) C. J. Rolo
Best Sellers, 19:417 (March 1, 1960) J. Snee
Booklist, 56:256 (Jan. 1), 286 (Jan. 15, 1960)
Catholic Historical Review, 47:50-51 (April, 1961) W. Kailer Dunn
Catholic Messenger, 78:11 (Feb. 18, 1960)
Catholic World, 191:190 (June, 1960) James Finn
Chicago Sunday Tribune, p.4 (Feb. 14, 1960) Walter Trohan
Christian Science Monitor, p.12 (Jan. 28, 1960) S. R. Davis
The Critic, 18:61 (May, 1960) J. O'Connor
Information, 74:56 (Sept., 1960)
Bulletin from Virginia Kirkus' Book Shop Service, 28:20 (Jan. 1, 1960)
Library Journal, 85:127 (Jan. 1, 1960) G. A. Beebe
New York Times Book Review, p.32 (Jan. 24, 1960) Anthony Lewis
New Yorker, 36:175 (Feb. 20, 1960)

B18   CLANCY, WILLIAM. "Paul Blanshard Returns to his Subject," *New Republic,* 142:16-18 (Feb. 22, 1960). Comment. "The Catholic Issue" (Editorial), *New Republic,* 142:3-4 (March 7, 1960).

Correspondence. "Catholics and Freedom," 142: 30-31 (March 7, 1960); 142:23 (March 14, 1960).

Note. More material on this subject is indexed under Paul Blanshard's name in the *New York Times Index,* the *Readers' Guide to Periodical Literature,* the *American Theological Library Association Index to Religious Periodical Literature* and the *Catholic Periodical Index.*

APPENDIX C

Notes on "Protestants and other Americans United for Separation of Church and State" (POAU)

"Protestants and Other Americans United for the Separation of Church and State," (POAU), was founded in the wake of the Everson decision for reasons and with objectives stated in its *Manifesto* (1948). The nature of the organization is revealed by its literature and its activities. The beginnings of the group may be followed in the *New York Times* and in a number of publications which have discussed POAU accusations. The society speaks for itself in *Church and State*, the official POAU newsletter. The following material is listed chronologically to help follow some of the activities of the group and to correlate original statements with replies.

C1 NEW YORK TIMES:

(Jan. 12, 1948) p.1, col.2: Foundation of POAU announced. Text of *Manifesto* released. RELATED MATERIAL: "Oppose Sectarian Domination," *Nation's Schools*, 41:28 (March, 1948). —The text of the *Manifesto* was released as a brochure by "Protestants and Other Americans United for the Separation of Church and State," Washington, D.C., 1958. It may also be read in the following sources: *Christian Century*, 65:79-82 (Jan. 21, 1948); Joseph Martin Dawson. *Separate Church and State Now*. New York: Richard R. Smith, 1948. Pp.199-211. (REVIEWS: *Christian Century*, 65:1240 (Nov. 17, 1948); *Nation*, 169:285 (Sept. 17, 1949); *School and Society*, 71:279 (May 6, 1950)).

(Jan. 13, 1948) p.1, col.3: Reply for the Knights of Columbus (J. E. Swift). RELATED MATERIAL: J. Donahue, "To Protestants and Other Americans," *Columbia*, 27:1 (Feb., 1948). —"Let Us Have Reason," *America*, 78:513-516 (Feb. 7, 1948).

(Jan. 26, 1948) p.17, col.1: Reply to POAU, The National Catholic Welfare Conference (John T. McNicholas).

(Feb. 16, 1948) p.15, col.1: Bishop Oxnam defends POAU claims and scores the charges of Archbishop Cushing.

223

(March 8, 1948) p.20, col.3: POAU reply to NCWC. Role of the Church in education scored. RELATED MATERIAL: "Second Protestant Manifesto," *America*, 78:676 (March 20, 1948).

C2 *Church and State*, Washington, D.C.; Protestants and Other Americans United for the Separation of Church and State. 1948- (Monthly).

> Official newsletter of POAU. Originally entitled *Church-State Newsletter*.

C3 MURRAY, JOHN COURTNEY, S.J. "Religious Liberty is the Concern of All," *America*, 78:513-16 (Feb. 7, 1948). See note: "Are Public Schools Protestant?" *America*, 82:627-28 (March 4, 1950).

C4 "Indecent Controversy," *Christian Century*, 65:198-200 (Feb. 18, 1948).

C5 DANA, ELLIS A. "Mounting Church-State Issues: Time for a Showdown," *Education*, 69:124-30 (Oct., 1948).

1949

C6 HEFFRON, EDWARD J. "Protestant-Catholic Tensions," *Catholic Digest*, 13:61-66 (Feb., 1949).

C7 MORRISSON, CHARLES CLAYTON. "Objectives of POAU," *Christian Century*, 66:236-39 (Feb. 23, 1949). For other references in the *Christian Century*, see: 65:84-86 (Aug., 1948). 66:190 (Feb. 9, 1949). 68:247-48 (Feb. 21, 1951). 72:901 (Aug. 3, 1955). Reply. 1027 (Sept. 7), 117 (Sept. 28, 1955). 73:190 (Feb. 8, 1956).

1951

C8 EBERSOLE, LUKE. "Protestants and Other Americans United for the Separation of Church and State," in *Church Lobbying in the Nation's Capital*, New York: Macmillan, 1951. Pp.67-73.

1954

C9 "Issues Between Catholics and Protestants at Mid-century," by George H. Williams, Waldo Beach, H. Richard Niebuhr, *Religion in Life*, 23:163-205 (Spring, 1954).

> See: remarks by Waldo Beach, pp.193-94.

1955

C10 FRANCIS, DALE. "Bigotry in Action," *Sign*, 34:17-19 (March, 1955).

> The author's observations about the seventh annual convention of P.O.A.U. in Washington, D.C.

1957

C11 BROWN, ROBERT MCAFEE. "A Step Forward in Catholic-Protestant Understanding," *Christianity and Crisis*, 17 no. 5:35-38 (Apr. 1, 1957). Comment. C. Stanley Lowell. "P.O.A.U. Replies," with reply by Robert McAfee Brown, 17 no. 8:63-64 (May 13, 1957).

C12 SANDERS, TOM G. "Protestantism, Catholicism and POAU," *Christianity and Crisis*, 17:115-118 (Sept. 16, 1957).

1958

C13 KRUMM, (Rev.) JOHN M. "Krumm Upbraids Religious Bigots," *New York Times*, 1958, Nov. 17, p.45, col. 6.

> Reply (letter). W. Stanley Roycroft, Dec. 3, p.36, col.5.

> Rejoinder (letter). Rev. John M. Krumm, Dec. 8, p.30, col.5. Letter reprinted in the *Catholic Mind*, 57:143-45 (March-April, 1959).

C14 LAWRENCE, WILLIAM. "POAU: An Expose," *Information*, 72:20-26 (Jan., 1958).

C15 LICHTENSTEIN, STANLEY L.

> Mr. Lichtenstein resigned from P.O.A.U. early in 1958. He released a letter from his home to explain his reasons.

> Newspaper reports. "Issue Separates Lichtenstein from Church and State." Feb. 4, 1958, *Washington Daily News*. "Hunting Trouble" (editorial). Feb. 5, 1958, *Washington Daily News*. "Church-State Aide Resigns. . ." Feb. 4, 1958, *Washington Post*.

> Text of letter: *NCWC News Service*, Feb. 1, 1958.

> See *United for Separation*, pp.143-151 (No. C18 in this unit).

C16 LOWELL, C. STANLEY. "Another View of Catholic Religious Liberty," *Christianity and Crisis*, 18, No. 17: 142, 144 (Oct. 13, 1958).

Remarks about "A Protestant View of Roman Catholic Power," by John C. Bennett, *Christianity and Crisis*, Aug. 4, and Sept. 15, 1958.

Reply. William Clancy. "A Catholic View of Mr. Blanshard and Mr. Lowell," *Christianity and Crisis*, 18, No. 18:151-52 (Oct. 27, 1958).

C17 "Your Witness, POAU" *Catholic Mind*, 56:249-250 (May-June, 1958).

Remarks about the *Ten-Year Balance Sheet of the Struggle for Church-State Separation* (POAU, 1958). Reprinted from *Columbia*, March, 1958 (Editorial).

Other remarks. *Columbia*, 38:16 (Feb., 1958). "Deserving Particular Scrutiny," *Commonweal*, 67:396 (Jan. 17, 1958).

1959

C18 CREEDON, LAWRENCE P., AND FALCON, WILLIAM D. *United for Separation; An Analysis of POAU Assaults on Catholicism.* Milwaukee, Wisconsin: Bruce, 1959. 259pp. Bibliographic footnotes.

1960

C19 MOORE, ARTHUR J., JR. "The Methodist Conference, 1960," *Christianity and Crisis*, 20:78-79 (May 30, 1960). Comment. C. Stanley Lowell, 20:95-96 (June 27), Arthur J. Brown, Jr., 20:96 (June 27, 1960).

Note. Related material and reports of POAU activities may be located through the *New York Times Index*, the *Readers' Guide to Periodical Literature*, *The American Theological Library Association Index to Religious Periodical Literature* and the *Catholic Periodical Index*.

APPENDIX D

Notes on President James Bryant Conant's Address on "Unity and Diversity in Secondary Education"

(AASA Convention, Boston, Mass., Apr. 7, 1952)

"Are private schools divisive? Is a dual system of education a threat to democratic unity? Affirmative answers to these questions as expressed by James B. Conant, President of Harvard University, and other speakers at the recent AASA meeting in Boston set up reverberations across the nation" (*Nation's Schools*, p.49, June, 1952).

Benjamin Fine reported this regional convention of the American Association of School Administrators and its pronouncements on the issue of private schools and divisiveness in the *New York Times*.

D1   NEW YORK TIMES, 1952:

(April 7) p.27, col.5: Address by Roy E. Larsen & John K. Norton.

(April 8) p.31, col.8: Address by James B. Conant.

(April 9) p.25, col.4: Statements made at a press conference by Dr. Kenneth E. Oberholtzer, Dr. Worth McClure, Dr. Edgar Fuller and Dr. James B. Conant.

(April 10) p.34, col.1: Resolutions of the convention.

(April 12) p.14, col.5: Remarks of Rev. James Pike (Dean of the Cathedral of St. John the Devine) in answer to Dr. Conant.

(April 13) Section IV, p.9, cols. 1&2: Summary

D2 CONANT, JAMES BRYANT. "Unity and Diversity in Secondary Education" ("A revised version"), *Harvard Alumni Bulletin,* 54:579-81 (April 19, 1952). Same text: *American Association of School Administrators, Official Report,* 1952: 235-43.—*Nation's Schools,* 49:48-50 (June, 1952).—*Saturday Review,* 35:11-14 (May 3, 1952).—*Vital Speeches,* 18:463-65 (May 15, 1952).

An adapted text was included in James B. Conant, *Education and Liberty,* Cambridge, Mass.: Harvard University Press, 1953. Pp.77-87. (N.B.: This text should be read with the notes on pages 140 to 152.)

(Articles)

D3 "Conant and Private Education," *Social Justice Review,* 45:39-40 (May, 1952).

D4 "Conant, in Science Pure, in Education Controversial," *Newsweek,* 40:72-74, Sept. 22, 1952). Also: 41:20-22 (Feb. 9, 1953).

D5 "Contra Conant!" *Catholic Education Review,* 50:419-20 (June, 1952).

D6 "Education and Liberty: a Look Ahead." *Virginia Quarterly Review,* 28:500-17 (Oct., 1952).

D7 FOLEY, ALBERT SIDNEY, S.J. "Who's Segregating Whom?" *America,* 87:375-76 (July 12, 1952).

This article contains references to the remarks of Edgar Fuller. See: *New York Times,* Apr. 9, p.25, col.4 (1952).

D8 GUPTILL, NATHANIEL M. "Clash on Public-Private Schools," *Christian Century,* 69:622-23 (May 21, 1952).

D9 HARTNETT, ROBERT C., S.J. "Don't be Afraid, Dr. Conant," *America,* 87:130-33 (May 3, 1952).

D10 HOCHWALT, FREDERICK G. "The Recent Attack on Catholic Schools," *Catholic School Journal,* 52:168-69 (May, 1952).

D11   KANDEL, ISAAC LEON. "Nation's Schools: Public and Private," *School and Society*, 75:268 (Apr. 26, 1952). Discussion. E. B. Chamberlain. "More on Public and Private Schools," 76:3, 4 (July 5, 1952).

D12   KRAMER, GEORGE N. "Open Letter to President Conant of Harvard," *Catholic Mind*, 50:577-84 (Oct., 1952).

D13   LA FARGE, OLIVER. "We Need Private Schools," *Atlantic Monthly*, 193:53-56 (Feb., 1954). Excerpt. *Time*, 63: 63-65 (Feb. 8, 1954).

D14   MEYER, AGNES E. "Public and Private Education," *National Education Association, Proceedings*, 1953. Pp.69-81.

     Address, echoing Conant, delivered at the NEA convention, Detroit, Mich., July 3, 1952. Reply. "Mrs. Meyer's Emotions," *America*, 87:394 (July 19, 1952).

D15   NATIONAL CATHOLIC EDUCATIONAL ASSOCIATION. "Resolutions" (Forty-Ninth Annual Meeting, Kansas City, Mo., Apr., 15-18, 1952), *National Catholic Educational Association Bulletin*, 49:39 (Aug., 1952). Same. *Catholic School Journal*, 52:169 (May, 1952).

D16   O'NEILL, JAMES MILTON. "Religion, Education, and American Democracy," *National Catholic Educational Association, Bulletin* (Proceedings issue), 49:45-49 (Aug., 1952) Same. *Vital Speeches*, 18:465-68 (May 15, 1952).

     Address delivered at the NCEA convention, Apr., 15, 1952.

D17   "Private School Controversy," *Saturday Review*, 35: 11-15, 39, 48 (May 3, 1952). James B. Conant, 11-14. R. J. Cushing, 14, 48. Allen V. Heely, 15, 39. Discussion. 35:26, 27 (June 7, 1952).

D18   SHEERIN, JOHN BASIL, C.S.P. "Conant and Catholic Schools," *Catholic World*, 175:161-65 (June, 1952).

D19   WHITE, LYNN, JR., "Democracy and Private Education," *Pacific Spectator*, 7:10-18 (Winter, 1953).

Note. The word "divisive" rings through this controversy. Dr. Conant claims not to have used it *(Education and Liberty,* p.140, footnote 23). It does not appear in the text which he released. The term was spoken by other leaders at the convention. It was printed without quotes in the *New York Times* report of the Conant address and it echoes through the statements expressed in support or rebuttal.

Additional material may be located through the *New York Times Index* for 1952, at pages 222, col.1 (under "Conant, (Dr.) James Bryant"), 330, col.3 (under "Education and schools, public vs. private"), and 976 (under "School Administrators, American Association of").

APPENDIX E

Introduction to Legal Literature

Note. Anyone seriously interested in Church-State relationships in education will have to consult statutes, court decisions, reviews of cases and other types of legal material.

Court decisions are entered with other material in this bibliography, but the standard form is retained for citations. One should get acquainted immediately with the *National Reporter System,* the *American Digest* and learn the use of key-number divisions and the value of a "word index" (or descriptive word index).

Introductory material in legal bibliography is suggested here to assist persons unaccustomed to work with law literature. Essential abbreviations and notes on the interpretation of citations are given in the pages preceding Unit I.

a) GENERAL HANDBOOKS:

BEARDSLEY, ARTHUR SYDNEY, and ORMAN, OSCAR C. *Legal Bibliography and the Use of Law Books.* Brooklyn, N.Y.: Foundation Press, 1947. 653pp.

FELD, BENJAMIN, and CREA, JOSEPH. *A Practical Guide to Legal Research.* New York: Marshall Law Book Co., 1950. 115pp.

> A concise introduction. A very helpful first guide. The other handbooks in this section offer more thorough treatment of the subject.

How to Find the Law. 5th ed. (William R. Roalfe, editor). St. Paul, Minn.: West Publishing Co., 1957. 207pp. (The 4th edition, 1949, was prepared by Carlton B. Putnam.)

PRICE, MILES O., and BITNER, HARRY. *Effective Legal Research; A Practical Manual of Law Books and their Use.* New York: Little, Brown, 1953. 633pp.

b) DEFINITIONS, ABBREVIATIONS:

BLACK, HENRY CAMPBELL. *Black's Law Dictionary*, 4th ed. Saint Paul, Minn.: West Publishing Co., 1951. 1882pp.

BOUVIER, JOHN. *Law Dictionary;* Baldwin's Century revision. Edited by William Edward Baldwin. Cleveland, Ohio: Banks Baldwin.

A number of other dictionaries are available.

c) SCHOOL LAW:

ALEXANDER, CARTER, and BURKE, ARVID J. "Legal Aspects of Education," in *How to Locate Educational Information and Data*. 4th ed. revised. New York: Bureau of Publications, Teachers College, Columbia University, 1958. Pp.304-316.

KEESECKER, WARD W. *Know Your School Law* (U.S. Office of Education, Bulletin, 1958, No.8). Washington, D.C.: U.S. Government Printing Office, 1958. 30pp.

Contains basic information (pp.3-10) and a bibliography (pp.11-27).

REMMLEIN, MADELINE KINTER. *School Law*. New York: McGraw Hill, 1950.

A basic text. Appendix B contains a guide to help locate the law of the various states.

REUTTER, E. EDMUND, JR. *Schools and the Law* (Legal Almanac Series No. 17). New York: Oceana Publications, 1960.

Replaces an earlier guide written by David Taylor Marke.

"School Pupils and the Law," *Law and Contemporary Problems*, 20:1-195 (Winter, 1955).

A very good digest of current legal relationships between the pupil and the school.

The Yearbook of School Law. Edited by Lee Orville Garber. Danville, Illinois: Interstate Printers and Publishers, Inc. 1950.

Revival of *The Yearbook of School Law,* published annually, 1933-1942 and numbered "First" to "Tenth."

d) STATE MATERIAL:

BEACH, FRED F., and WILL, ROBERT F. *The State and Nonpublic Schools* . . . (U.S. Office of Education, Misc. No.28, 1958). Washington, D.C.: U.S. Government Printing Office, 1958. 152pp.

A list of state sources is given on page 31.

COLUMBIA UNIVERSITY, LEGISLATIVE DRAFTING RE-SEARCH FUND. *Index Digest of State Constitutions.* New York: Oceana Publications, 1959.

Useful to explore the state constitutional basis for action.

HUSTON, WENDELL (compiler). *School Laws of the Forty-eight States.* Seattle, Wash.: W. Huston, Co., 1947-.

Note. Material on the legal aspects of Church-State relationships in education is listed with the various units of this bibliography.

List of Cases

Index

This Index includes

Authors, editors, compilers . . .
book titles
state material (with cases), by state
cases

REFERENCES ARE TO CONSECUTIVE ENTRY NUMBERS